In this wondrous book, Nathan Laufer gives us a stunningly fresh reading of the biblical holidays, illustrating how they celebrate the seven revelations of the Divine Presence during the first year of the marriage of God and Israel. A remarkable *tour de force*, *Rendezvous with God* weaves together thousands of biblical rituals with later rabbinic ordinances and popular holiday customs into a seamless whole, inseparably uniting Judaism's ethical and ritual dimensions. The book is so rich, it will provide understanding and pleasure to every kind of reader – from the wise, informed expert to the unlearned lay reader.

Rabbi Irving (Yitz) Greenberg
President Emeritus, CLAL

Nathan Laufer is the master teacher of Jewish holidays. *Rendezvous with God* is in actuality a rendezvous with all the biblical holidays by a teacher who is able to make complex issues clear and guide us to making our holidays what they are supposed to be – holy.

Rabbi Joseph Telushkin
Author of *Jewish Literacy, Rebbe*, and *Why the Jews?*

It is no small challenge to write yet another book about the Jewish holidays which says something new. But Nathan Laufer more than meets this challenge. His notion that the holidays represent different stages of the courtship between God and the Jewish people is a new prism – both fascinating and revelatory – through which to view the Jewish holiday cycle. Those who have been observing the holidays for many years, as well as those who are new to them, will emerge from *Rendezvous with God* inspired and challenged.

Rabbi Dr. Daniel Gordis
Koret Distinguished Fellow, Shalem College

Nathan Laufer brings the Jewish calendar year into a rich and meaning-saturated alignment. He demonstrates how the holiday cycle proclaims our origin story and its values, helping us relive and affirm it annually. We thank him for adding greater depth to our already sacred sense of time.

Dr. Erica Brown
Author of *Take Your Soul to Work*

Nathan Laufer has written a unique eye-opening and soul-revealing exploration into our festivals, immeasurably enhancing the quality of how we relate to our Jewish calendar and its holy commemorative days. *Rendezvous with God* demonstrates how the festivals express the Jewish romance with the Divine, stressing the marvelous interplay between sanctity of space and sanctity of time, the exquisite dance of the ethical and the ritual. A critical study for anyone who wishes to experience our tradition in an authentically profound and spiritually moving way.

Rabbi Shlomo Riskin
Chancellor, Ohr Torah Stone

An important book, a work of exceptional depth, spirit, and faith. Rabbi Nathan Laufer argues that our collective identity and purpose as a people are determined by the stories we tell about ourselves. As Jews, the carriers of our foundational stories are our holidays. Through innovative and precise exegeses, Laufer weaves a comprehensive new narrative for our core holidays, offering an inspiring vision for the *raison d'être* of Jewish life. An essential addition to every reading list.

Rabbi Dr. Donniel Hartman
President, Shalom Hartman Institute

Addressing the mind as well as the heart, this book offers new and startling interpretations of the textual and lived fabric of the Jewish holidays. It is written with such clarity and vigor that it will appeal to educators, religious leaders, and anyone interested in the rendezvous between texts, thought, and ritual.

Rabbi Professor Elie Holzer
Bar-Ilan University

Rendezvous with God is a cause for celebration in the field of Jewish education. The book succeeds – with impressive textual knowledge and profound educational wisdom – to build a spectacular bridge between the biblical canon, the sacred times and spaces of Jewish tradition, Jewish law, and contemporary Jewish values. All this Rabbi Laufer does in an enlightening, accessible, and superbly written style. An outstanding contribution to Jewish educational discourse in our day.

Dr. Avinoam Rosenak
The Hebrew University of Jerusalem

Rendezvous with God takes us on a new and original journey through the otherwise familiar Jewish calendar. Working from a broad biblical perspective and within the traditional framing of the Jewish holidays, Laufer illuminates well-known verses in a surprising new light. This book offers a novel and creative understanding of the holidays which will accompany the reader in his celebrations throughout the Jewish year.

Professor Jonathan Grossman
Bar-Ilan University

In this gracefully written and accessible volume, Rabbi Nathan Laufer astutely guides readers through the Jewish liturgical year. Exploring each holiday in turn, he weaves together classical wisdom with often arresting new insights. Whether you've been observing the holidays your whole life or you're discovering them for the first time, this book will make an inspiring and enlightening companion.

Rabbi Shai Held
Co-Founder and Dean, Mechon Hadar

Rendezvous with God

Revealing the Meaning
of the
Jewish Holidays
and Their
Mysterious Rituals

MAGGID

Rabbi Nathan Laufer

RENDEZVOUS
WITH
GOD

Revealing the Meaning
of the
Jewish Holidays
and Their
Mysterious Rituals

Maggid Books

Rendezvous with God
Revealing the Meaning of the
Jewish Holidays and Their Mysterious Rituals

First Edition, 2016

Maggid Books
An imprint of Koren Publishers Jerusalem Ltd.

POB 8531, New Milford, CT 06776-8531, USA
& POB 4044, Jerusalem 9104001, Israel
www.maggidbooks.com

The publication of this book was made possible
through the generous support of *Torah Education in Israel*.

ISBN 978-1-59264-455-1, *hardcover*

A CIP catalogue record for this title is
available from the British Library

Printed and bound in the United States

As for Me, this is My covenant … says the EverPresent God: "My spirit that is in you and My words that I have placed in your mouth will not depart from your mouth, or from the mouth of your children, or from the mouth of their descendants … from now and forever."

Isaiah 59:21

*To my
children, their spouses …
and all of their descendants*

Contents

Preface   *xi*

Introduction: *The Jewish People's
Founding Story*   *xix*

Passover: Leaving Egypt   1

"Not by Bread Alone": Counting the Omer, Celebrating Shavuot   45

Rosh HaShana: Remembering the Forgotten Day   77

Yom Kippur: "Return and Forgiveness"   113

Living With God: Sukkot, Shemini Atzeret, and Simḥat Torah   163

The Sacred Space-Time Continuum   203

Shabbat: The Purpose of Creating Heaven and Earth   225

The Hiddenness of God: Rabbinic and Modern Holidays   251

God, Torah, and the Holidays   263

Index   271

Preface

Children want to know from where they come. During the holidays, when our family gathers around the dining room table to celebrate, conversation sooner or later goes back to our past; sometimes our people's past, and sometimes our family's past. From time to time, the children will ask, and my wife and I will retell our little family's founding story: how we met (we were set up by her former boss while I was interviewing for a job); the tale of our first date together (in the midst of a passing snowstorm at the end of March); my first gift to her (a lithoprint of Psalm 23 to console her for the untimely loss of her father); the night of our engagement (after reading the Book of Esther in synagogue on the moonlit night of Purim); the day and place of our wedding (on my grandfather's yahrzeit in a community close to where our children grew up); our honeymoon (in Jerusalem and Netanya); the first home that we established together (a parsonage in Belleville, New Jersey, where I held a weekend pulpit); and the first meal that I cooked for her (she was very impressed!). Every detail is important, as it makes real for the children our origins as a loving, protective family. Within those stories are buried the deepest secrets of our collective being, the foundations for why we were initially attracted to each other, why we committed ourselves to each other, and why we chose to bring our children into the world and build a family together.

The human desire to know and understand the meaning of one's origins is a deep need not only of children but also of nations. Every nation has its founding story that is retold through its national holidays. In the United States, the holidays of Thanksgiving, Independence Day, Presidents' Day, and Veterans and Memorial Day are all days on which the American story is retold and commemorated. In the modern State of Israel, Yom HaShoa, Yom HaZikaron, Yom HaAtzma'ut, and Yom Yerushalayim are the days that retell the founding and history of the modern nation-state of Israel.[1]

The idea at the heart of this book is that for the Jewish people, the biblical holidays of Passover, Shavuot, Rosh HaShana, Yom Kippur, and Sukkot retell the founding stories of the relationship between God and the Jewish people in their honeymoon year together as a couple. Like the stories of our family's coming together, those stories contain within them the deepest secrets of our people's existence and our *raison d'être*, our collective purpose. These holidays are the central vehicle through which we make our people's narrative come alive and stay vibrant year after year.

---

1. Each nation's holidays commemorate and give expression to a formative event in the life of the nation. To take two examples from each nation: In the United States, Thanksgiving recalls the Pilgrims' valiant voyage across the Atlantic Ocean to achieve religious liberty, and reenacts the meal of thanksgiving for having arrived and survived the first year in the "New World." July Fourth celebrates the victory in the War of Independence against the British (the fireworks celebrate the "bombs bursting in air" that accompanied the victory in 1776 no less than in 1812), and the achievement of political freedom. In Israel, Yom HaShoa commemorates the Holocaust of six million Jews from 1933 to 1945, through memorial ceremonies that include the lighting of six torches for the six million Jews who perished. Yom HaAtzma'ut, which marks the achievement of Israeli sovereignty and political independence in 1948, is celebrated through the national pastime of outdoor barbecues, the awarding of the Israel Prize for outstanding national achievements, and a song and dance extravaganza, among other things. In short, each holiday is inextricably linked to a historical event with deep roots in the nation's memory, which is then reenacted and celebrated or commemorated.

The holidays, then, comprise not merely a series of fragmented, ritual acts we perform by rote at different times of the year – blowing the shofar, building a sukka, waving the palm branch and citron, leading the Passover Seder, or staying up to study Torah all night. All of these activities are enjoyable and significant, but not, as I will argue, ends in themselves. Nor are the many biblical and liturgical texts that we read and recite as a matter of tradition during the festivals – the *Akeda* on Rosh HaShana, the Temple service on Yom Kippur, the Hallel on Sukkot, and the Haggada on Passover. The significance of all these rituals, readings, and liturgies lies in the foundational stories they retell in dramatic fashion about our relationship with God, about who we are as a people, and about our purpose in life and history. Each individual holiday encourages us to relive a part of the story – taking us back to a particular foundational moment in our birth, growth, and maturing as a nation. Together, the holidays reenact our people's founding experience and reveal through ritual and liturgy our people's special mission. Finally, they infuse collective meaning and joy into our individual, everyday existence throughout the year.

How each of the holidays does so is what this book will explore.

ACKNOWLEDGMENTS

Although I have been privileged to fill a variety of leadership roles in my career, I think of myself primarily as an educator. One of my favorite texts, which has helped shape my educational approach generally and specifically in this book, is *Understanding by Design* by Grant Wiggins and Jay McTighe.[2] In the chapter entitled "The Six Facets of Understanding," they write: "To understand is to…bind together seemingly disparate facts into a coherent, comprehensive, and illuminating account. We can predict heretofore unsought or unexamined results and we can illuminate strange or unexamined experiences." In a later chapter, in a section entitled "Deep Understanding: Perceiving the Essence," they write:

---

2. Grant Wiggins and Jay McTighe, *Understanding by Design* (Alexandria, VA: Association for Supervision and Curriculum Development, 1998), 46, 80–81, 100. I am indebted to a wonderful Jewish educator, my colleague Steven Kraus, for introducing me to this book.

If we think … in terms of explanation … we … ask … : Is the explanation powerful? In other words, does it explain many heretofore unexplained facts? Does it predict heretofore unpredicted results? Does it enable us to see order where before there were only random or inexplicable phenomena? Good explanations are not just words and logic but insight into essentials. The best explanations involve inferences made from often limited evidence for fundamental principles or patterns. A good explanation … takes us "beyond the information given"[3] and toward ideas that define and structure other ideas, even a whole discipline.

Finally, quoting John Dewey,[4] they write: "No experience is educative that does not tend both to knowledge of more facts, entertaining of more ideas, and to a better, more orderly arrangement of them."

In this book, I have attempted to offer a comprehensive, coherent, and cohesive understanding of the biblical holidays, or to borrow Albert Einstein's term in relation to the fundamental forces of the physical universe, a "unified field theory" of the Torah. I am indebted to Wiggins and McTighe for articulating in writing what I have long only been able to intuit about my life's work which informed my educational objectives in writing this book.

In my personal biography, the genesis of this book began almost two decades ago. I had just turned forty and was acting as the High Holy Days rabbi of the Lake Shore Drive Synagogue in Chicago. A warm and welcoming, lay-led, Modern Orthodox synagogue throughout the year, Lake Shore Drive followed the custom of hiring a rabbi and cantor to lead their traditional High Holy Days services. From 1991 through 2004, acting upon the recommendation of my students and friends, Ray and Lori Lavin, whom I first met through the Wexner Heritage Foundation,[5]

---

3. Jerome Bruner, *Beyond the Information Given* (New York: W.W. Norton and Co., 1973).
4. John Dewey, *Experience and Education* (New York: Macmillan/Collier, 1938).
5. The Wexner Heritage Foundation educated lay leaders in the North American Jewish community in the history, thought, traditions, and contemporary challenges of the Jewish people. I served in a leadership role at the Foundation for nearly two decades. Today the Wexner Heritage program continues as one of the significant leadership initiatives of The Wexner Foundation.

the synagogue's lay leadership invited me to be the rabbi leading their High Holy Days services. It was in that role, writing a High Holy Days sermon, that I first noticed the lacunae in our current understanding of the biblical holidays and began to develop the comprehensive educational theory for teaching them which forms the core of this volume. Later, in my teaching capacity at the Wexner Heritage Foundation, my "day job" at the time, I had the opportunity to further refine and pilot this theory among several of the Foundation's leadership groups. I am grateful to the congregants and leadership of Lake Shore Drive, and especially to Les and Abigail Wexner, for granting me the opportunity to serve them, to try out my initial ideas in the sanctuary and seminar room among my congregants and students, and to develop the basic thesis that informs this work.

This book would not have come into being without the support of my former employer, The Tikvah Fund,[6] and the generosity of its chairman, Mr. Roger Hertog, and executive director, Mr. Eric Cohen. They supported and encouraged me to spend my sabbatical year working through the implications of my original thesis and setting it out in this volume. Their dedication to the Jewish world and to the development of Jewish ideas has been a source of inspiration to me and thousands of others who have participated in their programs and benefited from their publications. I am grateful for their close association over the past seven years, for their wide-ranging vision, and for their strong backing of this project.

My editor, Ms. Elisheva Urbas, with whom I worked closely on my previous two books, has been my alter ego throughout the writing process of this book as well. She helped me structure the book and align its chapters so that I was able to say what I wished to express. I am very grateful, as well, to my thoughtful and meticulous content editor, Shira Koppel, who challenged my ideas throughout while greatly improving the flow of prose in this book. I salute my publisher, Matthew Miller, his outstanding editor-in-chief, Gila Fine, and their talented staff at Maggid Books – Tomi Mager, Nechama Unterman, and Tali Simon – for their

---

6. The Tikvah Fund is a philanthropic foundation and ideas institution committed to supporting the intellectual, religious, and political leaders of the Jewish people and the Jewish state.

professionalism in overseeing the publication of this volume; they have been a pleasure to work with. I want to thank my friend Tova Naiman, who graciously illustrated the "Seder Clock" found in the Passover chapter of this volume, as well as her professional colleagues, Zahava Bogner and Rivka Farkas, for illustrating the "Hidden Face of God" found in the chapter on "Sacred Space."

As important as my professional colleagues have been, the legacy and support of my family are the ultimate reasons that I have been able to author this volume. Growing up, I was fortunate to be raised by parents – survivors of the Holocaust of European Jewry – who conveyed the richness of the Jewish holidays in our family practices. Every holiday had its mysterious rituals and its joyous songs. I loved practicing those rituals at home and in the little *shtiebel* in which we prayed; I reveled in singing the songs of my people with my parents around the family dining room table. Those memories of my youth will stay with me forever.

As the grandson of martyrs of the Holocaust, whose books and religious artifacts perished with them in the flames of Auschwitz, I always regretted not having anything substantial in writing from them that could address the questions about the meaning of God, Judaism, and Jewish peoplehood that often vexed me and that were the center of their respective lives. The three books that God has given me the privilege to author,[7] all based on the narrative of the Torah, are my best attempt to address the deepest meaning of our tradition, to complete, as it were, their unfinished lives and to leave a Jewish intellectual legacy for my children and their descendants.

My wife and life partner of thirty years, Sharon Laufer, has also been my biggest fan and supporter. She has given me a beautiful family and a base of emotional support that has enabled us to celebrate the holidays together with our children in the fullest, most joyful way. My debt of gratitude to her in creating a warm, welcoming Jewish home and in leading our Jewish lives together knows no bounds. *Ve'at alit al kulana.*

7. The two previous books are: *Leading the Passover Journey: The Seder's Meaning Revealed, The Haggadah's Story Retold* and *The Genesis of Leadership: What the Bible Teaches Us about Vision, Values and Leading Change.* Both books were published by Jewish Lights, Woodstock, Vermont, 2005, 2006.

My children, Becky, Michael, Leslie, and Matti Laufer, have brought incredible happiness and meaning into my life. It was through them, more than through anyone else, that I sensed God's EverPresent loving-kindness in the world. They taught me to see God's presence in the waving of the tree branches on a breezy day, in the beauty of the falling leaves of autumn and their reflowering in spring, and in the endless love of a parent to a child and a child to its parent. It is to each of them, their wonderful spouses, and their future descendants, that this book is lovingly dedicated.

Rabbi Nathan Laufer
Efrat, Gush Etzion, Israel
18 Adar II, 5776

Introduction

The Jewish People's Founding Story

T he story of the birth of the Jewish people as a free nation and of the first year of their relationship with God occupies much of the biblical books of Exodus and Leviticus. That first year was the foundational one for the Jewish people in biblical times and, as we shall see, for the Jewish experience of time ever since.

The narrative records seven revelations of God's presence to the entire people within that first year, from the moment that Jewish time began:[1]

---

1. In chapter 12 of Exodus, God told Moses to inform the Jewish people of their pending liberation from Egyptian slavery at long last. God also informed Moses that the Jewish calendar, "Jewish time," as it were, would begin then, on the first day of the Hebrew month of Nisan: "This month shall be for you the head of the months, the first month for you of the months of the year." As God promised, fifteen days later the Exodus took place and the people were liberated. Less than one year after the Exodus, God accepted the sacrificial offerings of the people in the new Mishkan and consumed the first "meal" that the people offered God in His new "home" (Lev. 9).

1. God's slaying of the Egyptian firstborns and the Jewish people's Exodus from Egypt (Ex. 12);
2. God's splitting of the Sea of Reeds to save the people and drown the Egyptian legions (Ex. 14, 15);
3. God's raining down the manna, literally "bread from heaven," when the people ran out of earthly food after thirty days in the desert (Ex. 16);
4. God's revelation of the Ten Commandments and the covenant at Mount Sinai (Ex. 19, 20, 24);
5. God's forgiving the Jewish people after they worshiped the Golden Calf and repented for their sins (Ex. 33);[2]
6. God's filling the Mishkan, the biblical Sanctuary, with the Divine Presence after the people completed its construction and furnishings (Ex. 40);
7. God's fire consuming the people's first sacrifices in the Mishkan, God's new home (Lev. 9).

These multiple revelations,[3] culminating in God's indwelling among the

---

2. See especially Ex. 33:7–10. All of the people saw the pillar of cloud, recognized it as a divine revelation, rose in its honor, and prostrated themselves from a distance.
3. When I say "multiple revelations," some people are puzzled. Most of us tend to think that God revealed Himself only once to the Jewish nation, in the theophany of the Ten Commandments at Mount Sinai. There are two reasons for this. The first is that in the Bible the theophany was the only one of God's revelations in which the people heard God's voice speaking to them. Through God's voice, the people heard the uttering of the Ten Commandments, which, like the rest of the Torah communicated to Moses alone, was given unique legal authority in traditional Jewish life. However, we err in conflating or reducing God's revelation to only God's voice. In the Bible, God demonstrated and communicated His intimate relationship to the Jewish people when He appeared and redeemed them at critical junctures, with or without words.

The second reason we tend to think that the theophany at Mount Sinai was the only revelation is because, for people who live in the twenty-first century, when God's presence seems almost entirely hidden, any revelation of God in history appears to be extraordinary. And it is. Even in the Bible, God's presence did not manifest itself regularly – certainly not in the presence of the entire Jewish body politic. Hence, our tendency is to want to minimize the number of times in our collective memory that we think God suddenly intervened in history and to limit it to Sinai. It is as if we say

people, were "peak experiences"[4] that redeemed the Jewish people in political, military, physical, and spiritual terms. Together, these experiences were nothing short of life-changing. They transformed the people from an inchoate rabble of former slaves to a proud nation with dignity and purpose. They also transformed the trajectory of history, from an unredeemed state where God was nowhere to be seen, to a redeemed state where God's saving presence became visible and palpable.

The books of Exodus and Leviticus also include the commandments to keep the Jewish holidays and an extensive description of the building of the Mishkan. As we will see, both the holidays and the Mishkan are meant to retell, reenact, and embody God's momentous multiple revelations.[5]

HOW THE HOLIDAYS TELL THE STORY

After the seventh and final revelation to the entire Jewish people in the Mishkan, God revealed to Moses a whole series of laws to keep the relationship between God and the people on track, and to further

---

to ourselves, "One exception to the world as we know it we can live with, but more than that begins to border on the unbelievable."

But comfortable or not, one revelation of God – at Mount Sinai – is not the story that the Bible conveys to its readers, and not what the Jewish people in the Bible desperately needed and personally witnessed. The Jews who left Egypt had been a nation in captivity for hundreds of years, much of it in oppressive slave labor. During that time, God's presence and comforting companionship were horrifically, painfully absent. To rectify the perception of God's absence, God felt it necessary to reveal His presence multiple times in the young nation's life and in their evolving relationship in order to rebuild their trust and place the relationship on a solid footing. In that first year of the Jewish people's freedom, God broke through the usual constraints of our historical experience, and the people witnessed seven extraordinary events which cumulatively added up to God's presence returning to history and to dwelling with the Jewish people. Exactly what God had dreamed of in creating the world, to live with the human beings that He created in "His image and likeness," came to fruition twenty-six generations later in the aftermath of the Exodus from Egypt.

4. I use this advisedly, as per Abraham Maslow's coinage of the term. Abraham Maslow, *Religions, Values, and Peak Experiences* (Columbus, Ohio: Ohio State University Press, 1964).

5. See the chart at the end of this introduction: "Rendezvous with God: A Unifying Theory of the Torah."

develop the relationship so that the Jewish people could live with God in the deepest sense, as a "couple." These holiness laws – encapsulated in the command "You should be holy because I your God am holy (Lev. 19:2)" – include, among other instructions, the laws of Judaism's "holy days," known traditionally as the Chapter of the Holidays.[6]

Each seasonal, biblical holiday commemorates a specific event in the biblical narrative in which God's presence became overtly manifest to the entire Jewish people in their first year as a free, collective community. The association of the biblical holidays with the events upon which they are based has always been understood in regard to the seven-day "bookend" biblical holidays – the pilgrimage festival of Passover, commemorating God's liberation of the Jewish people from Egypt (Ex. 12:14), and the pilgrimage festival of Sukkot, commemorating the protective "enclosures" in which God caused the Jewish people to dwell in the desert (Lev. 23:43). For both holidays, the Bible is explicit about which events they commemorate and celebrate. I will go further and endeavor to explain how the details of both these holidays emerge from, and help us reexperience, the particular events they are designed to evoke. I will demonstrate how the rituals, customs, and liturgy of the holidays are direct, conscious expressions of the events which they commemorate.

Regarding the other biblical holidays – Shavuot, which follows the Omer offering and attendant counting of fifty days, and the autumn holidays of Rosh HaShana, Yom Kippur, and Shemini Atzeret – none are explicitly linked by the Bible to events in the Jewish people's historical narrative. Different opinions in the rabbinic tradition have linked three of these holidays to biblical events – Shavuot to the Sinai revelation, Rosh HaShana to the creation of the world or of humanity, and Yom Kippur to God's forgiveness for the Golden Calf. While largely agreeing with, and explaining more deeply, the third, I will offer a different explanation for the first two. Finally, as the observance of the Omer and the holiday of Shemini Atzeret are not linked to specific events by either the Bible or mainstream rabbinic tradition, I will offer novel explanations for both.

---

6. "Holidays" is a conflation of the words "holy days." Leviticus 23 is called the "Chapter of the Holidays."

The order of the seven biblical holidays recorded in Leviticus 23 follows the precise order that the seven revelatory events occurred in the biblical narrative.[7] These seven events were the only ones in which God's presence appeared before the entire Jewish people in their first year of freedom. Like the Passover Seder, whose purposeful order tells in outline form the chronological story of the Book of Exodus,[8] the order of the cycle of biblical holidays over the course of the year tells the story of the key events in the Torah in chronological order from the twelfth chapter of the Book of Exodus through the ninth chapter of the Book of Leviticus. The order of these holidays is not incidental, as it represents the historical and religious process by which the Jewish people, in their first year of collective existence, became in biblical times, and annually strive to become, a sacred community living in relationship with God.

The Torah in Leviticus refers to the holidays as *"Mo'adei Hashem,"* usually translated as "God's festivals." However, this term might better be translated as "Days of Meeting" or "Days of Rendezvousing with God."[9] The encounter with God's presence, the extraordinary meeting of God and the people, is what made the event; it is also granted to the festival, in whole or in part, its characterization by the Torah as one of the *"Mikra'ei Kodesh,"* the "sacred days." In Judaism, God is the ultimate source of all things sacred, and the holidays are no exception to this rule.[10]

---

7. "In three places are the holidays recorded. **In Leviticus, because of their order;** in Numbers, because of their sacrifices; and in Deuteronomy, because of the leap year (to assure that Passover takes place in the 'spring month')," *Sifrei* to Deut. 16:1, Finkelstein edition [Hebrew], 185. Since the order, but not the content, in all three biblical books is the same, the *Sifrei*'s emphasis on the Leviticus text following the holidays' order suggests that they follow the order of the seven revelatory events, which they commemorate.

8. See *Leading the Passover Journey.*

9. With one exception relating to the plague of pestilence in Exodus 9:5, the prior use of the word *"moed"* in the Bible (seventy-three times as I count it) is in the context of the *Ohel Moed,* the Tent of Meeting in the Sanctuary, where Moses and the priesthood would encounter the Divine Presence. Others have translated the tent as the "Tent of Rendezvous" (see Everett Fox, in his biblical translation *The Five Books of Moses* [New York: Schocken Books, 1995], 413, citing Roland Devaux Fox on Exodus 27:21). Either definition is etymologically related to God's telling Moses that He would meet/rendezvous with him in the Tent of Meeting (Ex. 25:22).

10. My teacher, Rabbi Joseph B. Soloveitchik, in his *Shiurim LeZekher Abba Mori, z"l,* vol. 1 [Hebrew] (Mossad HaRav Kook, 2002), 170–171, made a similar claim in explaining

In each of the holidays, then, we reenact through liturgy, readings, and rituals the revelational event that the holiday commemorates: the Exodus from Egypt on the first day of Passover; the splitting of the sea on the seventh day of Passover; the falling of the manna in counting the Omer, culminating in the holiday of Shavuot; the acceptance of God's kingship at Mount Sinai on Rosh HaShana; God's forgiveness for the sin of the Golden Calf on Yom Kippur; and God's hovering presence and fiery passion on Sukkot and Shemini Atzeret. Cumulatively, each year, we relive the "honeymoon year" of our life as a nation in relationship with God.

Put in the terms of a typical young married couple, the seven rendezvous in the Bible constitute something akin to the courtship, engagement, wedding, honeymoon, forgiveness and reconciliation following marital discord, building/furnishing a new home, and sharing the first home-cooked meal. Those special, intimate moments of coming together that a couple recalls and relives provide the emotional energy to animate and invigorate the relationship throughout the marriage. So too, in the celebration of the holidays, the recollection and reliving of the people's moments of redemptive encounter with the Divine Presence have provided the emotional fuel to power the Jewish people's relationship with God for the many millennia since those events occurred. They instill in us a recurring gratitude for all that God did for our ancestors, and by extension for us, their spiritual descendants. In the midst of the

---

the reasons for the rabbinic choice of the Torah readings on the holidays:

> The holidays are sacred because lofty events occurred in them that are tied up with the revelation of God to "*Kenesset Yisrael*" [NL: the collective, eternal Jewish people] and His choosing us with love. In light of this reason, the sacredness of the holiday emanated from the miraculous and unique event that occurred then .... The holidays are called sacred because great and exalted things occurred on them such as the Exodus from Egypt, the Giving of the Torah and other similar events. The essence of the sacredness of the holidays is rooted in God's miracles and wonders that occurred on those days.

> Rabbi Soloveitchik goes on to say: "We are therefore obligated to read not only the Torah portions that deal with the laws of the festivals and the holiday obligations but also the biblical narratives concerning the great events that occurred on them and which serve as the source of their sacredness and of the very reason they are called 'sacred days.'"

uncertainties and vicissitudes of life and history, the holidays provide an anchor of stability and trust in the ultimate meaning and purposefulness of our existence.

By enacting and decoding the holiday rituals and liturgies we reawaken our original experience of rendezvousing with God in our shared consciousness. Through the reexperiencing of these encounters with God, year after year, we are touched, for brief intensive bursts, by the ineffable source of the universe; we hear the address of the divine voice at Mount Sinai, we glimpse again the mysterious veiled face of God that was hidden beneath the coverings of the Mishkan, and we feel God's palpable presence dwelling among us.

THE STRUCTURE OF THIS BOOK

This book will examine the seven instances of divine revelation – recorded in the books of Exodus and Leviticus – that the Jewish people experienced in their first year as a nation, and the ways those revelations are expressed in the holidays.

Chapters 1 through 5 will explore each of the five major biblical holidays. In each chapter, we will raise a series of questions about the holiday – questions that have troubled me for many years and for which I draw forth answers by returning to the narrative of the Jewish people's first year as a people. The most fundamental question that I will ask in each chapter is what dramatic event of divine revelation does the holiday commemorate and how do the rituals, liturgy, or biblical readings clue us in and give expression to that event. I will conclude each chapter by showing how the holiday's story has a carryover effect on the ethics, rituals, and liturgy of Judaism throughout the year.

Chapter 1 ("Leaving Egypt") will explore the holiday of Passover. There are actually two sacred days during Passover on which no work is permitted, the first and seventh days, which commemorate two separate, but related, revelational events in the biblical narrative: the Exodus from Egypt (Ex. 12) and the splitting of the sea (Ex. 14 and 15). The five days in between (Ḥol HaMoed Pesaḥ) correspond to the journey of the Jewish people from the borders of Egypt to the Sea of Reeds.

Chapter 2 ("Not by Bread Alone") will explore the meaning of the Omer and Shavuot. Although we may not think of the Omer as being integrally connected to a holiday, the Torah in Leviticus 23 apparently thinks otherwise, giving extensive treatment to the rituals of the Omer and connecting it, using several literary devices, to the sacred day of Shavuot.[11] Contrary to our current conventional understanding of Shavuot, I will argue that in the Bible, both the Omer and Shavuot correspond and give grateful expression to God's revelation of the manna in the wilderness, a story told in Exodus 16.

Chapter 3 ("Remembering the Forgotten Day") will investigate the holiday of Rosh HaShana. I will argue that this holiday gives expression, not primarily to the story of creation as is commonly thought, but first and foremost to the Jewish people's acceptance of the kingship, covenant, and coronation of God at Mount Sinai, embodied in the revelation of the Ten Commandments (Ex. 19 and 20).

Chapter 4 ("Return and Forgiveness") will explore the sacred day of Yom Kippur. I will show how most of the enigmatic rites and rituals of Yom Kippur give expression to the revelation of the Divine Presence as the Jewish people repented and God forgave them for the sin of the Golden Calf (Ex. 32–34).

Chapter 5 ("Living with God") examines Sukkot/Shemini Atzeret. Like Passover, this festival includes two sacred days – one on

---

11. There are four literary devices used in the biblical text to link the two sections together:

   (i) Unlike all the other sacred days, there is no separate introduction to the sacred day of Shavuot other than the introduction to bringing the Omer, which precedes it.

   (ii) The offering of the Two Breads is introduced as being a "new grain offering" (Lev. 23:16) to distinguish it from the previous grain offering of the Omer which preceded it by only forty-nine days.

   (iii) The separation between the Omer portion and the Two Breads portion of Shavuot in the written Torah scroll is done via a "*parasha setuma*," a closed notation, which indicates that the two are meant to be read in conjunction with one another. (Note also that the sections about Rosh HaShana and Yom Kippur are also separated by only a closed notation, meaning that they are meant to be read in connection to one another. See the chapter on Rosh HaShana below.)

   (iv) The root word – K-TZ-R (cutting) – is used precisely seven times in the two sections, making it what Buber and Cassuto identify as a "*leitwort*," a "key word" that is meant to signal a common theme, running from the beginning of the first section to the conclusion of the second section. This frames the Omer and Shavuot into one large whole.

the first and one on the eighth day. The two sacred days correspond and give expression to two separately narrated but related events: the revelations of the Divine Presence at the completion of the Sanctuary (Ex. 40) and on the day that the Sanctuary was inaugurated (Lev. 9). The seven days prior to the Eighth Day of Assembly parallel the seven days of preparation for the priests before they began their service in the Sanctuary, which we, "God's kingdom of priests," reenact through the rituals of Sukkot.

Chapter 6 ("The Sacred Space-Time Continuum"[12]) will explore how the furnishings and architecture of the Mishkan, to which the Bible devotes so much attention in the books of Exodus, Leviticus, and Numbers, embodied the same seven events of divine revelation as commemorated by the *Mo'adim*, the seven biblical sacred days. The sacred space of the Bible thus reinforce the sacred times of the holidays in retelling the story of the Jewish people's first year, constituting a unified theory of the Torah.[13]

Chapter 7 ("The Purpose of Creating Heaven and Earth") explains the traditional rituals and customs of Shabbat, the first biblical sacred day commanded in the chapter on the holidays in Leviticus 23. Shabbat brings together both the expression of sacred time commemorated by the biblical holidays[14] and sacred space embodied by the furnishings and the priestly service in the Mishkan.

---

12. "Space-time" is a mathematical model which combined space and time into a single, interwoven idea called a "continuum." Like the "unified field theory" noted in the preface, the "space-time continuum" is a term made famous by Albert Einstein as part of his theory of general relativity. The joining of space and time helped cosmologists understand how the physical universe works. I am using it here, modified by the term "sacred," to suggest that in the Bible, sacred space and sacred time were interwoven. Together, they help us to understand and reenact our "spiritual universe," our rendezvous with God.

13. See the chart concluding this chapter, "Rendezvous with God: A Unifying Theory," p. xxxii.

14. More than that, it is the very source of the idea that time can be made sacred. The Jewish people imitate God who made the Shabbat sacred by declaring when the new moon would occur, thereby determining and sanctifying the days of the festivals. It is plausible that Shabbat is the first sacred day mentioned in Leviticus 23 because the

Chapter 8 ("The Hiddenness of God") addresses the celebration of the rabbinic festivals of Ḥanukka and Purim and the modern commemorations of Yom HaShoa, Yom HaZikaron, Yom HaAtzma'ut, and Yom Yerushalayim. In contrast to the biblical holidays, in which God's presence was revealed to the entire Jewish people in the full light of day, these later commemorative days, in which God was hidden or even absent, represented a challenge to the rabbinic leaders of the Jewish people. The chapter will explain how the rabbinic sages and one modern rabbi have interpreted these commemorative days in light of the biblical holidays.

Chapter 9 ("God, Torah, and the Holidays") will explain the take-home value of this understanding of the holidays as the yearly reliving of our rendezvous with God.

HOW THE HOLIDAYS AFFECT THE YEAR

The holidays are not just celebrated annually and then forgotten for a full year. Rather, they penetrate the way we think, behave, and pray throughout the year.[15] They celebrate formidable events which have inspired a series of norms that guides the Jewish people, not only on the holidays, but all year long. These norms are of two kinds: ethical norms, in relation to other human beings created in God's image, and ritual/liturgical norms, in relationship to God's Self.

The biblical tradition established that the ethical cannot be separated from the ritual. One could not be part of a holy people if one blatantly disregarded the moral expectations of the Jewish tradition. How one treated other people, the images of God encountered in daily life, was as much a proof of one's piety as how one related to God and observed the ritual commands.[16] This is why the Ten

---

sacredness of the festivals is derivative of the sacredness of Shabbat and modeled in great part on its observance.

15. In Nahmanides' gloss on the first positive command (i.e., the duty to believe in God) in Maimonides' *Book of Commandments*, he concludes, "The belief in the existence of God which was made known to us through the signs, wonders, and revelations of the Divine Presence before our very eyes, is the main point and the root from which the commandments were born."

16. In this regard, see *Leading the Passover Journey*, 74.

Commandments list God's ritual commands on one tablet and God's ethical commands on the other in a single, continuous narrative. This is also why chapter 19 in Leviticus (known by biblical scholars as the "Holiness Code") interweaves ritual and ethical commands in a seamless tapestry, as if to say: One cannot pull out the ethical threads from the ritual threads without unraveling the entire fabric of what constitutes the holy in Judaism.

But the ritual is no less important. My colleague, Professor Michael Chernick,[17] in a private conversation, once framed the importance of ritual this way: "Ritual is the ethics we owe God for having created us and for having done what He did for our people." The powerful symbolic rituals in which the Jewish people have engaged for literally thousands of years are tokens of appreciation to God for the gift of our peoplehood and tradition. As part of that tradition, the rabbis also devised liturgy to be recited throughout the year, which reminds us of the revelational events most intensely celebrated by the holidays.

Passover is a prime example of how the ethical, the ritual, and the liturgical penetrate Jewish life all year long. Judaism's ethical duty every day of the year is to show empathy toward the stranger and the impoverished. This imperative is the moral consequence of Passover, of our powerful annual experience of our estrangement and impoverishment in Egypt, and God's redemption through the miracles of the Exodus.

Similarly, the daily ritual command to bind our arms to God through the wearing of phylacteries and the weekly command to observe Shabbat are expressions of our reexperiencing of God's liberation "with a strong hand" from slavery in Egypt.[18] In addition, the daily Jewish liturgy includes prayers such as the Song of the Sea and the third paragraph of the *Shema*, which are meant to reinforce the centrality of the Exodus in the daily consciousness of the Jewish people.

---

17. Professor of Talmud, Hebrew Union College, New York, and long-time instructor in the Wexner Heritage Foundation, which I led for many years.

18. Ex. 23:9 and 13:9. For fuller elaboration, see chapter 1, "Leaving Egypt."

This reexperiencing of the foundational events of our people through the biblical holidays, and their impact on how we understand ourselves and act out our values during the rest of the year, is the greater religious purpose of their celebration, one to which we will devote attention in our discussion of each individual holy day.

A NOTE ON TRANSLATIONS

The Jewish tradition refers to the Jewish people's rendezvous with God's presence as "*giluyei Shekhina*," literally, "revelations of the Divine Presence." The seven biblical revelations presuppose that God is always present in the world, but only very rarely allows that presence to become manifest to human perception, and even more rarely to become fully manifest before the entire nation.

God's ever-present existence is embodied in the name by which the Jewish people come to know God in the Bible, "*yud-heh-vav-heh*." Although pronounced by traditional Jews as "*Adonai*," which translates as "my Lord," it is actually a conflation of three words – *haya, hoveh, yiheyeh* – meaning God was, is, and will be. Parallel to the word "*HaMakom*" – meaning literally "the place," but usually translated in reference to God as the "Omnipresent" – "*yud-heh-vav-heh*" means that God is ever-present, that is, present in past, present, and future (see Ex. 3:13–15). What both appellations share is they are meant to convey reassurance and comfort. God was, is, and will be present even when, on the surface of human experience, that does not seem to be the case.

God therefore identifies Himself as "*yud-heh-vav-heh*" in promising to fulfill His vow to the patriarchs to redeem the Jewish people after hundreds of years of slavery in Egypt (Ex. 6:2–8). God's presence and uniqueness in the world is also one of the lessons that He is intent on teaching Pharaoh and the Egyptians through the events of the Exodus (E.g., Ex. 8:18, 9:14). As we will see in the course of this book, the Exodus is the foundational event upon which all of the Jewish holidays, and indeed upon which the very covenant with the Jewish people, is based. I will thus translate "*yud-heh-vav-heh*" as the "EverPresent" or, more frequently, as the "EverPresent God."

Although God is neither male nor female, literary convention refers to God in the male gender ("He" said, "His" will). Despite my misgivings with this practice, and trying to be gender-neutral whenever possible, I have nevertheless followed literary convention in this book.

The Bible is the story of the relationship between the Ever-Present God and the descendants of Abraham, Isaac, and Jacob/Israel – "Benei Yisrael." In this volume, I have preferred the term "Jewish people" over the literal translation "Children of Israel" or "the Israelites," sometimes used as an alternative. This is because of my understanding that all of the Jewish holidays are attempting to bridge the millennia between our ancestors' stories and our own. During each holiday, we put ourselves, as it were, in our ancestors' shoes and reenact, reexperience, and retell what our ancestors did three thousand years ago. To enable us to fully identify with our biblical ancestors, I have chosen to name them as Jews today think of themselves, as members of the Jewish people.

Finally, while I have relied primarily on the old[19] and new[20] translations of the Bible by the Jewish Publication Society of America, I have resorted to other translations – including my own – when they better fit the context of the chapter. Any errors in translation that result are, of course, entirely my own.

---

19. *The Holy Scriptures According to the Masoretic Text* (Philadelphia: The Jewish Publication Society of America, 1917).

20. *Tanakh: A New Translation of the Holy Scriptures According to the Traditional Hebrew Text* (Philadelphia: The Jewish Publication Society of America, 1985).

Rendezvous with God:
A Unifying Theory

Mikra Sacred Story: Revelations of God	*Moed* Sacred Time: Holidays	*Mishkan* Sacred Space: Furnishings
Exodus from Egypt (Ex. 12)	Passover – first day	Copper Sacrificial Altar, sacrifices
Splitting of the sea (Ex. 14–15)	Passover – seventh day	Pitcher and Basin, singing of Levites
Falling of manna (Ex. 16)	Omer, Shavuot	Table with twelve display breads, jug of manna
Sinai revelation (Ex. 19–20)	Rosh HaShana	Ark, cherubs, Ten Commandments, Torah scroll (Holy of Holies)
Forgiveness for Golden Calf (Ex. 32–34)	Yom Kippur	Golden Altar of Incense, incense offering
Tabernacle construction and consecration (Ex. 35–40, Lev. 8)	Sukkot	Menora and olive oil, eternal candle, walls and curtains, Clouds of Glory
Inauguration of the Altar (Lev. 9)	Shemini Atzeret	Altar's eternal flame, priestly service

Chapter One

Passover: Leaving Egypt

Each biblical holiday commemorates a specific event in which the collective Jewish people encountered God's saving presence. The Passover Haggada,[1] in recalling these moments of "great awe" (Deut. 26:8), references an additional verse that explicitly describes God's revelation to the nation:

> "Great awe" alludes to the revelation of the Divine Presence, as it is written (Deut. 4:34): "Has God ever attempted to take unto Himself a nation from the midst of another nation by trials, miraculous signs, and wonders, by war and with a mighty hand and outstretched arm and by great awe, just as you saw the Lord your God do for you in Egypt, before your eyes?"

The events surrounding the redemption of the Exodus were witnessed firsthand by the entire Jewish people.[2] To mark God's miraculous

---

1. In *Maggid*, the fifth item in the Passover Seder.
2. In the Haggada, Rabban Gamliel, in insisting that the eating of matza and the reason for eating it must be included in the Passover Seder, also makes this point: "Why do we eat matza? Because the dough of our ancestors did not have time to become

appearance, a sacred day was established in the Jewish calendar, as it was for each event in the first year of the Jewish people's history in which God's presence was revealed. These days in which the people experienced God's presence were appropriately designated in Leviticus 23 as *"mo'adim"* or "days of meeting," that is, days of meeting between God and His people. The rituals and liturgy established for those sacred days were designed for future generations of Jews to remember, reexperience, dramatically reenact, and verbally retell those events that were experienced by the Jewish people's founding generation – the generation of the Exodus. The purpose of all of these rituals was to empower us once again to meet God in our own lives or, as the Haggada tells us, to enable us to see ourselves as if we personally were redeemed from Egypt.

PASSOVER IN THE BIBLE

Passover is the first seasonal holiday listed in Leviticus 23, the chapter devoted to the biblical holidays:

> These are God's festivals, sacred holidays, that you shall celebrate at their appropriate times. In the afternoon of the fourteenth day of the first month, you shall offer a Passover sacrifice to God. And on the fifteenth day of this month it is a festival of matzot to God, for seven days you shall eat matzot. The first day is a sacred holiday to you … and the seventh day is a sacred holiday. (Lev. 23:4–8)

Passover is mentioned first because, from the Bible's perspective, the Jewish calendar does **not** begin when we might imagine – in the autumn month of Tishrei, when Rosh HaShana occurs. In fact, it begins in the springtime month of Nisan, when Passover falls: "This month [i.e., Nisan – the month of Passover] shall be the starting month for you, the first month for you in the months of the year" (Ex. 12:2). In Nisan, the Jews left Egypt, were freed from the burden of slavery as well as from the pagan calendar, and became masters of their own time and

---

fermented before the King of kings, The Holy One, Blessed Be He, **revealed Himself to them and redeemed them."**

2

fate. Therefore, the first **seasonal** holiday of the Jewish people, marking the Jewish people's birth as a nation, is Passover – not Rosh HaShana.

The Exodus from Egypt was such a formative and foundational experience of meeting God that **all** of the biblical holidays, even those that seem on the surface to have little to do with the Exodus (such as Rosh HaShana and Yom Kippur), are actually "in commemoration of the Exodus from Egypt." They commemorate events that came after the Exodus and were predicated upon it. The narrative of the Exodus in the Passover Haggada not only tells the story of leaving Egypt, but retells, in abbreviated fashion, almost all of the major revelatory events that occurred in the Book of Exodus. The Exodus from Egypt is thus the orienting event for the biblical events that follow, as well as for all the holidays in the Bible.

Understanding Passover's central role in commemorating this first great moment of divine revelation will help us see how all the Passover traditions work together to shape our experience of the holiday – and also echo in the ethics and rituals observed yearlong, far beyond the week of Passover.

OBSERVING PASSOVER, RETELLING THE STORY

Why do we celebrate Passover the way that we do? How does the observance of the holiday help us reexperience that meeting with the Divine? On Passover, asking fundamental questions is a core part of the holiday experience. The most outstanding example is the recitation of *Ma Nishtana*, the Four Questions, prior to the *Maggid* portion of the Seder. So essential are questions to the Passover experience that these Four Questions are asked aloud even by a person who conducts the Seder alone, with no interlocutors to address them to (Pesaḥim 116a). Many Passover questions are generated by the celebration itself, which begs us to examine the specific aspects of the holiday whose logic, on the surface, is unclear. For instance:

- Why are the three primary commandments associated with Passover – the removal of all *ḥametz*, the eating of matza, and the retelling of the story of the Exodus on the evening of Passover – so important to the Passover experience?

- Why, when we retell the story, do we use as our sacred text the Passover Haggada, a secondary source composed by the rabbinic sages of the early Common Era – rather than the biblical Book of Exodus? Would it not have made more sense at the Seder to read from our primary source, the Bible itself?
- What is the significance of each item in the sequence of fifteen dramatic and unique Passover rituals that define the Seder? Is the total number of rituals, in some way, meaningful?

Let us begin with our preparations for the holiday to understand why *ḥametz* and matza are so pivotal to reexperiencing the Exodus.

ḤAMETZ AND MATZA ON PASSOVER

As Jewish homemakers know, there is a biblical command to get rid of all of one's leavened products (*ḥametz*) prior to the onset of Passover. Indeed, the elimination of *ḥametz* in traditional households is perhaps the main and most onerous task in preparation for the holiday. The Bible instructs the Jewish people to eat flat, unleavened bread (matza) on Passover, instead of leavened bread, the staple that nourishes much of humanity until today.[3] The Passover Haggada offers two, seemingly contradictory, reasons for why we eat matza on Passover. The first reason, found immediately following *Yaḥatz*, is that matza is the bread of impoverishment (*"laḥma anya"* from the word *"ani,"* a poor person) that our ancestors ate in Egypt. Later on, toward the end of *Maggid*, Rabban Gamliel, basing himself on a verse in the Book of Exodus, offers a different reason for eating matza:

> Because the King of kings, The Holy One, Blessed Be He, revealed Himself and redeemed the Jewish people as it is written, "And they baked unleavened flatbread from the dough which they had brought out of Egypt, because it had no time to rise, since they were driven out of Egypt and could not delay; and they made no other provisions of food to carry with them (Ex. 12:39)."

---

3. For a more thorough investigation of why we eliminate *ḥametz* prior to Passover and instead eat matza, see *Leading the Passover Journey*, 1–6, 40–41.

The disparity between the first reason, in which matza (what the Bible itself later calls *"leḥem oni"*) is associated with the impoverishment of the Jewish people in Egypt (Deut. 16:3), and the second reason, which understands matza as the bread of freedom (what the rabbinic tradition later calls *"leḥem deḥeruta"*), has to do with the moment in the Seder when each reason is provided. The "impoverishment" reason is offered immediately following *Yaḥatz* when, in the story traced by the Seder, the Jewish people are still enslaved in Egypt, after Pharaoh's decree of infanticide. The "freedom" reason is offered toward the end of *Maggid*, when, in the Haggada's verbal retelling of the story, the Jews are on their way out of Egypt. The same physical substance, matza, takes on two completely different meanings depending on when and how one relates to it in the course of telling the story – within the chains of bondage, or the exhilaration of freedom.

If matza, in the earlier iteration, while the Jews were still in Egypt, was "poor man's bread," then what was "rich man's bread"? None other than *ḥametz*. *Ḥametz* was rich man's bread in two ways. First, the ingredients, which included fermenting yeast, enriched it (unlike matza, which was made only of flour and water). Second, the time that it took for the dough to rise was a luxury that only the Jewish people's wealthy Egyptian masters could afford.[4] The Jews, under the constant prodding of their taskmasters, were left with no time to breathe (Ex. 6:9), and could not afford the cost or the time of the yeast. The Jewish slaves had to make do with the tasteless, flat, pseudo-bread called matza.

It is precisely because *ḥametz* was associated with the Egyptians, who attained their wealth and their luxurious lifestyle by expropriating our ancestors' slave labor, that the Bible prohibits not only **eating** *ḥametz* but also deriving any benefit from it during – or even following – the holiday. *Ḥametz* on Passover is taboo for the Jewish people because

---

4. It is common knowledge that fermented bread was invented in ancient Egypt and was itself a form of currency. See, for instance, Jimmy Dunn in "Prices, Wages and Payments in Ancient Egypt": http://www.touregypt.net/featurestories/prices.htm.

the richness with which it is associated is what is called in tort law "the product of unclean hands." In this case, it was the result of the ancient Egyptians' abuse of our ancestors' slave labor. This is why the tradition has us search for *ḥametz* before Passover and dispose of it – in fact, burn it – on the morning prior to the beginning of the holiday.[5] With the *ḥametz* destroyed, and matza spread out on the festival table, the Jewish people are then bidden to retell the Passover story at the evening Seder.

THE PASSOVER SEDER

The Passover Seder reenacts the Jewish journey in the Book of Exodus, from its opening verses in chapter 1 until its closing verses in chapter 40. Rather than the Bible, which was authored centuries before the Common Era, the liturgical text that guides us through the Seder is the Passover Haggada, authored by the rabbis of the Common Era, since it is considerably shorter and more compact, packing greater punch with fewer words. Moses himself modeled the creative and more succinct retelling of the Passover story in the Book of Deuteronomy. There, speaking to the next generation of Jews, who had not themselves experienced the Exodus, he offers several powerful restatements of the Passover tale, which we incorporate into the *Maggid* section of the Haggada.[6]

Notwithstanding the creative retelling by the rabbis of the content of the Passover story, the rabbinic sages followed the Bible in using the three primary human senses to shape the form of their retelling – the visual, the verbal/audial, and the kinesthetic/active senses. For the generation that left Egypt, the visual telling of the Jewish story took the form of the Mishkan, that was placed in the center of the Jewish encampment in the desert and reminded the people of their

---

5. The only other commandment aside from *ḥametz* on Passover that has a similar set of laws governing it is idolatry. *Ḥametz* on Passover is like idolatry all year long.

6. Including the Haggada's opening line in response to the Four Questions, "We were slaves to Pharaoh in Egypt" (Deut. 6:20), and the centerpiece of *Maggid*, the exegesis of the pilgrims' restating of the Passover journey (Deut. 26:5–8).

formative experiences;[7] the verbal/audial telling took place through the narrative in Exodus and Leviticus; and the active/dramatic telling occurred through the biblical holidays commanded to the Jewish people in chapter 23 of Leviticus. The Haggada too retells the biblical story using all three of the primary human senses, with the Seder plate constituting the visual, *Maggid*, the verbal/audial, and the fifteen dramatic action items at the Seder, the kinesthetic.

The Bible, then, and the Haggada in the times of the rabbinic sages, used all three mediums to tell and retell the story because different people rely on and are motivated by different modes of perception. For some, "seeing is believing." For others, what one hears and repeats is what one remembers. For yet others, only by doing and acting out something is the underlying idea internalized. Both the Bible and the rabbis used all three mediums to assure that the message of the biblical story was effectively communicated.

THE SEDER PLATE – VISUAL RETELLING

As soon as one approaches the table on Passover, before one has even sat down, one is struck by the visual pageantry on the table, a pageantry that is meant to visually retell the Passover story. In the center of the table, aside from the three matzot that are usually covered, lies the Seder plate. The Seder plate is so called not merely because it is used to conduct the Passover Seder, but because, like the Seder itself, it too has an order, or "*seder*." The order to the plate's arrangement is crucial because it faithfully recreates, in visual form, the story that the plate retells.

There are myriad customs as to the arrangement of the Seder plate.[8] None of these is arbitrary. Rather, each custom represents a different visual interpretation of the crucial elements of the Seder and their role in telling the story of the Exodus. Since I understand the entire Seder to be a chronological representation of the Jewish people's journey

---

7. See the chapter on "The Sacred Space-Time Continuum" later in this volume.
8. See Gavriel Zinner, *Nitei Gavriel – Hilkhot Pesach, Ḥelek Beit* (New York: Moriah Press, 1989), 322–323, 658–667, which presents eighteen different Seder plate arrangements.

in the Book of Exodus, the arrangement of the Seder plate that I have developed mirrors this chronological progression.

The Seder plate is arranged in a circle, using the organizing principle of an analog clock telling time (see image on following page).

At one o'clock is the *karpas*, a vegetable, preferably green, like parsley, which symbolizes the prolific growth of the Jewish people in their early years in Egypt (corresponding to Ex. 1:7). At three o'clock is the *ḥaroset*, which simulates mortar and symbolizes Pharaoh's stratagem to put the Jewish people through difficult physical work in order to stem their rate of growth (Ex. 1:11). At the five o'clock station is the *maror*, symbolizing the next step in Pharaoh's nefarious scheme – embittering and oppressing the Jewish people, not merely through hard work, but through harsh, oppressive bondage (Ex. 1:13, 14). At the seven o'clock station is the *ḥazeret* – a solid chunk of ungrated horseradish. Unlike the grated horseradish, this knobby, disfigured chunk is impossible to swallow. The *ḥazeret* embodies Pharaoh's ugly decree of infanticide to cast every newborn Jewish male into the Nile River, a royal order which the Jewish people could not withstand (Ex. 1:22).[9]

At the nine o'clock station is the *zero'a* – the roasted shank bone that symbolizes the Paschal sacrifice that the Jewish people courageously ate on the night of the Exodus (Ex. 12:3–11). The word *zero'a* also presages the *"zero'a netuya"* – God's outstretched arm that split the sea seven days after the Exodus.[10] At the eleven o'clock station is the *beitza* – a roasted egg, symbolizing the festival sacrifice that was brought in the Temple on Passover, and evoking the construction of the Mishkan, the precursor to the Temple, which concludes the Book of Exodus (Ex. 40:34–38). In the center of the plate, our family has the custom of placing a small bowl of salt water in which to dip the *karpas*, the vegetable eaten as the third item in the Seder, and then later to dip a hard-boiled egg before the multi-course meal known as *"Shulḥan Orekh"* (the eleventh item in the Seder).

---

9. Unlike Pharaoh's previous attempts to suppress their rate of growth, which the people somehow managed to overcome, the biblical text does not tell us that they continued to proliferate after the infanticide decree – cf. Ex. 1:22 to Ex. 1:12, 17, and 20.
10. See Ex. 14:16, 21, 26, 27.

The Seder Plate Clock

Like the matza, which symbolizes the bread of suffering and impoverishment in the early part of the Seder ("This is the bread of affliction that our ancestors ate in the land of Egypt") and later symbolizes the bread of redemption when the Jewish people leave Egypt, the salt water too has a double meaning. At the beginning of the Passover saga – signified by two o'clock – it symbolizes the sweat of Jewish slaves toiling under the hot Egyptian sun; toward the latter part of the Passover saga – signified by ten o'clock – it symbolizes the liberating waters of the splitting sea, where the Jewish people were saved. The hands of the clock signal the two opposite sides of the story; the right hand points toward the side of developing suffering, while the left hand points toward developing redemption. What separates the two is the passage of time on the proverbial clock.

Altogether, there are seven items on the Seder plate, symbolizing the seven days of Passover which the Seder meal inaugurates.[11]

Thus, the Seder plate that we see in front of us as we take our seats at the table already narrates the story of the Book of Exodus in chronological order, just as the *Maggid* section of the Haggada and the entire Seder will each tell the story of the Passover journey in its own unique, but overlapping way.

THE SEDER'S KINESTHETIC RETELLING

In total, there are fifteen activities in the Passover Seder whose names are chanted or sung, in an almost universal custom, as a type of "Table of Contents" to the proceedings of the evening. A newcomer at a Passover Seder would justifiably wonder why the participants are singing the Table of Contents, instead of delving straight into the evening's program itself. In fact, the fifteen Seder activities and our preliminary chanting of their names are related to several other "fifteens" connected to Passover:

- The holiday of Passover falls on the fifteenth day of the Jewish month of Nisan.
- The song "*Dayenu*," found toward the end of the *Maggid* section of the Seder, also mentions fifteen events for which the participants praise God.
- In the Torah scroll, the central column of the Song of the Sea (sung by the Jewish people after the splitting of the Sea of Reeds) contains fifteen lines that form a sort of ascending ladder (Ex. 15:1–19).

All these fifteens,[12] and the interlacing of songs with most of them, are related to yet another fifteen, the name of God associated with the

---

11. As we will see later in the book, the number seven is the symbol of the covenantal bond between God and the Jewish people and the organizing numeral of all the biblical holidays.

12. And several more fifteens as well, not directly related to Passover, but linked to encountering God's presence:
    - fifteen Psalms (120–134) that begin with the words, "A Song of Ascents" that were sung by the Levites on the steps leading up to the Temple in Jerusalem;

Exodus and found in the Song of the Sea. The name "*Yah*," the most primal of God's names, comprises the two Hebrew letters *yud* and *heh*, which in *gematria* – Hebrew numerology in which each letter has a numerical equivalent – equal fifteen.

All of the fifteens connected to Passover lead to the experience of, or an encounter with, the Divine Presence. It is not at all surprising that these fifteens are associated with song, because the propensity of the soul when having an experience with the Divine is to break out in song.

But beyond giving song-filled expression to being touched by God, the chanting of the Seder's program also helps to remind the Seder participants of the order of the activities in their proper chronological sequence. After all, the entire purpose of the Seder in the Haggada is to take the Seder participants on a fifteen-step voyage that recreates God's saving presence in the Book of Exodus and makes it their own.

Maggid, the fifth in the sequence of Seder activities, does a masterful job of verbally encapsulating the whole of the Exodus narrative, from the enslavement of the Jewish people until their redemption. Why then, we might ask, do we need the other fourteen activities in the Seder? Because just as the Seder plate is organized to retell the story of the Jewish people's founding event visually, and the *Maggid* will retell the story verbally, so too the other fourteen steps of the Seder are equally important and powerful instruments to retell the Exodus story kinesthetically, through symbolic actions.

Each of the fifteen activities in the Seder has a unique and dramatic role in retelling the story of the Exodus journey:

1. *Kadesh*
Recitation of the holiday Kiddush over the first of the four cups of wine

The blessing over wine marks the day as sacred. Unlike the other Jewish holidays, in which a blessing is recited over only one cup of wine, on

---

- fifteen words chanted in the priestly blessing;
- fifteen words of praise in the "*Yishtabah*" prayer that is recited daily and concludes the "Verses of Praise" section of the morning prayers.

Passover night we recite blessings over four cups of wine. Why four? The rabbis linked the four cups to the four terms of redemption, which God instructs Moses to convey to the Jewish people:

> Therefore say to the Jewish people: "I am the EverPresent God. **I will bring you out** from under the burdens of the Egyptians, and **I will save you** from their servitude, and **I will redeem you** with an outstretched arm and with great judgments, and **I will take you** to be My people and I will be your God, and you shall know that I am the EverPresent, your God, who brought you out from under the burdens of the Egyptians (Ex. 6:6–7)."

Despite the numerical parallelism between the four cups and the four promises of redemption, the rabbinic insight begs the question of what these cups of wine have to do with the process of redemption. The answer lies in the fact that the four cups of wine serve to subdivide the Haggada text and the Passover story of redemption into four parts. Each cup of wine takes the participants to a different moment in the journey of redemption, to a different rendezvous of God with the people. The four cups serve as "stage directions" in performing the Passover saga on the night of the Exodus. Each of these four cups of wine, by intermittently loosening up our state of consciousness, enables us to enter the "time machine" at each point and imagine the four different moments in the Passover journey.[13] Thus, the Seder participants can imagine and reexperience the different points of redemption that the Jewish people experienced in the story of the Exodus; they are transported in their minds to the key moments in the biblical narrative in which God's saving presence made itself manifest to the Jewish people. As God rendezvoused with our ancestors, we rendezvous with God.

---

13. Within the recitation of the Kiddush, the word for time, "*zeman*," is found three times: "the time of our freedom.... He who sanctifies the Jewish people and the times [of meeting]...who has brought us to **this time**." In my interpretation, the latter words transport us to the time that the Jewish people entered Egypt, the place where we ultimately encountered God's saving presence.

The first cup, corresponding to the first term of redemption in Exodus 6, "I will bring you out from under the burdens of Egypt," takes the participants of the Seder from the beginning of the Passover story when Jacob and his descendants arrive in Egypt (verse 1 of Exodus), through their period of enslavement, and through the first nine of the ten plagues that God brings upon the Egyptians (Ex. 1–11). The plagues, which the Egyptians experienced and the Jewish people witnessed, lightened the burdens of the Jewish slaves as they progressively freed them from their oppressive conditions. For example, their "work in the fields" (Ex. 1:13–14)[14] could no longer be foisted upon them by their Egyptian overseers because the fields were destroyed, first by the plague of hail and then by the plague of locusts, which consumed whatever vegetation had remained standing (see Ex. 10:15).

The second cup of wine, corresponding to the second verse of redemption, "I will save you from your servitude," brings the participants to the night of the Exodus, when God brought the tenth plague and freed the Jewish people from ever serving the Egyptians again.

The third cup, corresponding to the verse, "I will redeem you with an outstretched arm and with great judgments," carries the participants to the point in time, seven days after the exit of the Jewish people from Egypt, when they stood at the shores of the Sea of Reeds. There the people witnessed the legions of their enemy, who were on a mission of vengeance to massacre or reenslave them, drown before their very eyes, while they emerged unscathed on the other side. Moses, God's servant, acting as God's "outstretched arm," was instructed to stretch out his arm over the sea. With his staff – God's scepter – in hand, he was first to split the sea and lead the Jewish people through the dry seabed; he was then to recongeal it to drown the Egyptian army in punishment, bringing "great judgments" on the Egyptians for their many sins, including the drowning of the newborn Jewish males.[15]

---

14. Thousands of years before the enslavement of African-Americans in North America, the Jewish people were the slave laborers who worked the fields under the searing Egyptian sun.

15. This is apparently how Yitro understood the drowning of the Egyptians in Ex. 18:11: "Because the very thing that they intended to do came upon them."

Finally, the fourth cup of wine, corresponding to the fourth expression of redemption, "I will take you to be My people and I will be your God," brings the Seder participants, six weeks or so after the splitting of the sea, to the foot of Mount Sinai, where God took the Jewish people in a covenantal act to be His people and where God's presence came to rest in the Mishkan that the people built.

2. URḥatz
The ritual laving of hands without reciting the usual blessing

Just as the wine of *Kadesh* prepares the Seder participants' minds to reexperience the events of the Exodus and God's saving presence manifested there, the ritual washing of the hands symbolically prepares their bodies to do the same.[16] In the Bible, whenever there was an expectation of encountering the Divine Presence, the people had to wash their bodies in anticipation. Therefore, in Exodus 19, Moses instructed the people to immerse themselves in a pool of water to prepare for the revelation of God's presence at Mount Sinai.[17] Similarly, the priests, before they could enter the holy section of the Sanctuary close to where God's presence dwelled, had to wash their hands and feet (Ex. 30:17–21). So too, do the participants of the Seder, who have now through the *Kadesh* journeyed in their minds' imagination back to Egypt, wash their hands without a blessing in anticipation of the revelations of the Divine Presence to the Jewish people that will occur in the course of the Seder.

We do not recite a blessing, which would require *kavana* – the mind's focused concentration – because in *URḥatz* it is our bodies, not our minds, that we are preparing for redemption. By designating a separate item in the Seder to symbolize the preparation of our bodies, we convey the fact that the Exodus was first and foremost a liberation of

---

16. Of the fifteen steps in the Seder, only *URḥatz* begins with the Hebrew letter *vav*, meaning "and." This indicates that *Kadesh* and *URḥatz* are linked to one another, both serving to prepare the Seder participants – mind and body – for undertaking the Passover journey through the Book of Exodus.

17. This is what is meant by the people "sanctifying" themselves and washing their clothes in Ex. 19:10, 14.

the Jewish body-politic from the physical/political bondage of Egypt. Our spiritual liberation came later in the story. Regardless, together *Kadesh* and *URḥatz* serve as the introduction to the story, which begins with *Karpas*.

3. *Karpas*
The eating of a vegetable dipped in salt water or *ḥaroset* and reciting the appropriate blessing for "creating the fruit of the earth"

When the Jewish people first came down to Egypt they experienced it as if it were the long-lost Garden of Eden. Back in the Garden, God had blessed human beings with the words, "Be fruitful, multiply, and fill the earth" (Gen. 1:28). In Egypt, as related in the Bible, the Jews "were fruitful, and swarmed, and multiplied and became very, very strong and the land was filled with them" (Ex. 1:7) in fulfillment of God's primordial blessings. Their very prodigious growth alarmed Pharaoh and gave him the pretext to launch a policy of oppression against them lest they continue to grow and join his enemies in overthrowing the regime (Ex. 1:10). The oppression took the form of slave labor in construction and fieldwork under the burning Egyptian sun (Ex. 1:13–14).

To symbolize the fertility and growth of the Jewish people in Egypt, we take a vegetable that grows in the earth, preferably green in color to symbolize its vitality. Ashkenazi Jews then dip it into salt water, representing the sweat-drenched bodies of our ancestors. Sephardi Jews dip the vegetable in *ḥaroset*, symbolizing the construction mortar in which the bodies of the Jewish people were caked while building Pharaoh's garrison cities (Ex. 1:11).

We know from the Haggada that *karpas* is intended to represent the Jewish people's growth and fertility. The author/editor chooses to explain the word "*varav*," "and [they became] many," in *Maggid* with a verse from Ezekiel: "Many, like the plants in the field, I have made you" (Ezek. 16:7). Therefore, we take a vegetable from the field, which symbolizes fertility and growth, and dip it in salt water or *ḥaroset*, which symbolizes the slavery which the very growth of the Jewish nation precipitated.[18] In this same vein, some medieval rabbinic sages deconstructed the word *"karpas"* into two constituent words – *"samekh perakh"* – meaning sixty (the numerical value given to the Hebrew letter *samekh*) and oppressive. According to the Midrash, the *samekh* symbolizes the robust growth of the Jewish people from seventy to 600,000 males in only a few hundred years, by virtue of miraculous births of sextuplets. "Oppressive" because, as the Bible tells us in two consecutive verses (Ex. 1:13–14), the slave labor was oppressive. Thus, *Karpas* mirrors the first fourteen verses of the Book of Exodus and sets the context for the story that follows.

4. *Yaḥatz*
Breaking the middle of the three matzot, wrapping and hiding the larger broken segment for the *afikoman*

In the biblical story, Pharaoh's tactic of slave labor fails to stem the prodigious growth of the Jewish people. Increasingly frustrated and desperate, Pharaoh tries to persuade the Jewish midwives to strangle the boys when they are born; to his great consternation, the midwives do not cooperate and the people continue their unabated growth. Ultimately, he commands all of his people simply to throw all of the male Jewish babies into the Nile. Unlike his previous efforts, this brutal decree appears to break the spirit and stem the growth of the people.[19]

In one, apparently exceptional, instance, a Levite man marries the daughter of Levi and they have an infant son. The birth mother hides the baby for three months and then, nestling him in a straw basket that she weaves and waterproofs especially for the purpose, places her child adrift on the Nile, while the infant's older sister looks after him. The daughter of Pharaoh discovers him crying and is persuaded by his sister to hire the infant's biological mother as wet-nurse, thus returning the infant to his parents for the early years of his upbringing. After being

---

18. If it seems repulsive to consume something symbolically drenched in sweat or caked in mud, that is as it should be, for the enslavement of people against their will is indeed repulsive.

19. See footnote 9, p. 8 above.

weaned, he is brought to Pharaoh's daughter who adopts him and names him Moses (Ex. 2:1–10).

At the Passover Seder, we reenact the story of Moses' birth and rescue with *Yaḥatz*. First, we break the middle matza. Why do we do this? In biblical times, the Jewish people comprised three castes: Israelites, Levites, and priests. The three matzot, each representing one of the castes, collectively represent the Jewish people. The breaking of the middle matza in half, first and fundamentally represents the breaking of the collective spirit of the Jewish people by Pharaoh's decree of infanticide. The middle matza, representing the tribe of Levi, is broken because the Bible goes out of its way to inform us that both parents of Moses came from that tribe.

We take the larger broken fragment of matza, representing Moses, the son of his Levite parents and the most important actor in the biblical drama. Then we wrap it and hide it as Moses was enwrapped as an infant and hidden. The smaller segment of matza, representing Miriam and Aaron, Moses' siblings, from whom he was separated, is returned in between the two remaining complete matzot – as they remained in Egypt among their enslaved brethren. Just as Moses' sister looked on with concern to see what would happen to him floating on the Nile, the children sitting at the Seder carefully observe where the matza is hidden so that they can "steal it back." They then negotiate for its return to the parent who hid it in the first place, just as Miriam did for her mother.

How do we know that this is the correct interpretation of *Yaḥatz*? Because the point later on in the Seder, when the hidden matza is taken out and eaten, is called *"Tzafun"* – literally, "the hidden one." The root word TZ-F-N, denoting hiding, is precisely the word used (twice) when Moses' mother hid him as an infant, an unusual usage to denote hiding that is found nowhere else explicitly in the five books of the Torah (Ex. 2:2–3).

Moses' birth and subsequent maturing into a caring and courageous young man (Ex. 2:11–22) set the stage for the next point in the biblical drama and the Passover Seder: God's remembering His promise to Abraham to rescue his descendants from captivity and to punish their oppressors – both of which will take place in the course of the Seder's fifth activity, *Maggid*.

5. *Maggid*
The Haggada's retelling of the Exodus

The word "*Maggid*," literally "telling," corresponds to the word "Haggada," the book in which the Seder is embedded. This fifth step in the Seder plays a central role in verbally retelling the story of the Exodus and fulfilling the command of, "And you should tell your child on that day" (Ex. 13:8).

The section of *Maggid* seems, at first glance, anything but ordered and structured. The text moves around from the biblical tale of the Exodus to rabbinic stories and interpretations of those biblical stories in what appears to be a helter-skelter, hodge-podge manner. Upon more careful inspection though, it turns out that *Maggid* is highly structured and, in its retelling, advances the biblical story just as we might expect it to. The constituent parts of *Maggid* follow the precise order of the biblical verse from which we learn the duty to tell the story of the Exodus in the first place: "And you should tell your child on that day saying: 'Because of this [or: this is because of what], the EverPresent God did for me when I left Egypt'" (Ex. 13:8).[20]

The *Maggid* section is arranged in six subsections following the precise order of this verse. The six constituent parts are: Telling, to your child, on that day, saying "Because of this," did for me, when I left Egypt.

The "telling" section begins with the paragraph, "We were slaves in Egypt," continues with the tale of the five sages in Benei Berak, and concludes with the final words of R. Elazar b. Azaria's paragraph ("all the days of your life to include the Messianic era"). This section informs us

---

20. I first came across the deciphering of the general order of *Maggid* in a brilliant introductory essay by Rav Naftali Maskil LeAison (1829–97) to the English translation of the Malbim Haggada (New York: Targum Press, Feldheim Publishers, 1993), V–XXVI. Although my analysis, like his, follows the order of Exodus 13:8, it parses the verse differently in two instances: separating the words "and you should tell" from "to your child," since the Haggada treats each as a distinct topic, and combining the words "saying" with "because of this" since that entire subsection of *Maggid* deals with the causes of the enslavement and redemption. For an insightful, more recent treatment of this verse to explain *Maggid*, see Menachem Leibtag, "Understanding *Maggid*" (Yeshivat Gush Etzion, Tanakh Study Center Archives, http://www.tanach.org/special/magidq.txt).

what we are supposed to tell, why we tell it, who does the telling, and what is the optimal length for telling the Exodus story.

The section "to your child" follows, telling us that all members of the Jewish people and of future generations are to be engaged with the story of the Exodus, from the wise, to the wicked, to the simple, and even to the one who has not yet learned enough to question. This section begins with the words, "Blessed is the Omnipresent, blessed is He," and continues with the four children, concluding with the paragraph of "the child who does not know how to ask."

The section corresponding to the words "on that day" informs us precisely what day and what time of the day we are to tell the Exodus story, and is encapsulated in the paragraph which begins: "Perhaps from the first day of the month."[21]

The section explaining the words "saying, 'Because of this'" represents the longest subsection, by far, of *Maggid* as it has to explain how and why the Jewish people were both enslaved and redeemed ("Because of this..."). This section begins with the paragraph, "In the beginning our ancestors were idol worshipers," and extends for several pages, all the way through Rabban Gamliel's prescription of why we eat *maror* at the Seder.

The words "did for me" in the biblical verse are given expression in the paragraph, "In every generation a person should see him/herself as if he/she were taken out of Egypt."

Finally, the section of "when I left Egypt" is encapsulated in the first two paragraphs of the traditional Hallel, beginning with "*Halleluya*," "Praised be God," and concluding with the paragraph, "When Israel left Egypt."

The *Maggid* section, then, which seemed to be disorganized on the surface, turns out to be highly organized. The underlying order is a brilliant metaphor for the Jewish people's experience in

---

21. Notice how the verse, "You should tell your child on that day" (Ex. 13:8) is used by the Haggada as a proof text in this paragraph in response to the wicked child as well as to the child who does not know how to ask. Toward the end of *Maggid* the Haggada will again use this verse as the proof text for the paragraph beginning, "In every generation." The editor of *Maggid* clearly had this verse in mind in structuring the retelling of the Exodus narrative.

Egypt and throughout history: While historical events often seem haphazard and incomprehensible, they are actually purposeful and meaningful. Behind the curtain of Jewish history stands structured divine intention recognized only from a distance and with the benefit of hindsight.[22]

In addition, there are two dramatic moments in *Maggid* that correspond to the key moments which unfold in the biblical tale: first, when we raise our cups in a toast, praising God for His promise of redemption to our ancestor Abraham at the Covenant between the Pieces,[23] and second, when we dip our fingers into our wine for each of the ten plagues. These two actions correspond to the two pivotal moments in the Exodus story. The first is God's memory of His covenantal promise and decision to act – after Moses' growth and exile from Egypt – at the end of chapter 2 in the Book of Exodus.[24] The second is the execution of the plagues, the tenth of which ultimately persuades Pharaoh to release the Jewish people from Egypt (Ex. 7–12).

The Seder participants recite *Maggid*, the redemption narrative, which leads up to the reenactment of the final meal in Egypt. At that point in the Seder, the participants drink the second cup of wine commemorating God's second promise to the Jewish people to "save them from the servitude of Egypt." Indeed, as the people in Egypt sat down to eat what was, perhaps, one of the most filling meals of their entire sojourn in Egypt, their servitude to the Egyptians came to a long-awaited end.

---

22. "And when My Presence passes, I will place you in the cleft of the rock, and will cover you until I pass. You will see Me from behind, but you will not see My face" (Ex. 33:22–23).

23. Gen. 15:13–14: "You should know that your descendants will be strangers in a foreign land where they will be enslaved and oppressed for four hundred years. However, the nation that enslaves them I will judge and afterward they [Abraham's descendants] will leave with great wealth."

24. Ex. 2:24–25: "God heard the cries of the Children of Israel and God remembered his covenant with Abraham, Isaac, and Jacob; and God saw the Children of Israel and God knew."

6. Raḥtza
The ritual laving of hands before eating "bread," followed
by the recitation of the appropriate blessing

In the biblical story, the Jews were commanded to plan for their departure from Egypt by setting aside a lamb and preparing one last, barbecue dinner on their final night in Egypt (Ex. 12:3–11). During the Passover Seder, the participants now reenact this last meal. But first, in preparation for the meal, they wash their hands, this time with a blessing, in order to eat the matzot that God commanded the Jews to eat on that final night in Egypt.

7/8. Motzi Matza
Eating a portion of matza, reciting beforehand the usual
blessing over bread and the special blessing over matza

The Bible records that the Jewish people were commanded to eat, as their final meal in Egypt, the Paschal sacrifice with matzot and bitter herbs (Ex. 12:8). Since matzot are mentioned first, the participants begin by reciting two blessings over them. The first is for bread – because while matza does not look like a loaf of bread, it was the only bread that our ancestors could afford in Egypt and had time to prepare as they left Egypt[25] – and the second blessing is "over the eating of matza," which was specifically commanded by God to be eaten that evening. Having recited both blessings, they eat a substantial portion of this unleavened bread.

9/10. Maror/Korekh
Eating a portion of bitter herbs (romaine lettuce and/or ground
horseradish) dipped in ḥaroset, after reciting the special blessing

Following the eating of the matzot, the participants eat the bitter herbs mentioned in the biblical command. Since the command was in the plural (bitter herbs), they are consumed in two forms: first, dipped in ḥaroset – as the bitterness of Egypt was associated with the servitude

---

25. See the section on ḥametz and matza, above.

signified by the *ḥaroset*/mortar[26] – and then in sandwich form with matza (the "Hillel Sandwich"), since the verse implies the herbs were to be eaten with the matzot.[27]

11. *Shulḥan Orekh*
Partaking of a festive meal, including at least two cooked dishes

In the biblical story, the Jewish people were instructed to eat the roasted lamb that they had designated as the Passover sacrifice. This was the first, and paradigmatic sacrifice, for all future sacrifices in the biblical Sanctuary and Temple.[28] In later Temple times, Jews also ate parts of the festival offering, a second sacrifice that they brought to the Temple, at the Seder meal. Since we have had neither animal sacrifices nor the Temple in Jerusalem for close to two thousand years, by tradition, the participants take part in a sumptuous feast that is to contain at least two cooked foods, one for each of the sacrifices that was eaten.[29] This accounts for some people's custom to eat a hard-boiled egg at this point in the meal, a cooked food, representing the festival sacrifice, in addition to whatever is served as the regular main course, standing in for the Paschal sacrifice.

12. *Tzafun*
Eating the matza of the *afikoman*, previously hidden away during *Yaḥatz*

In the biblical story, it was only on the night of Passover that Moses was able to fulfill the mission for which he was commissioned by God at the burning bush: "Now go, and I will send you to Pharaoh and take out My people, the Jewish people, from Egypt" (Ex. 3:10). Thus, at this

---

26. Ex. 1:14: "And they embittered their lives with mortar and brick."
27. Ex. 12:8: "Eat the meat during the night roasted over fire. Eat it with matza and bitter herbs."
28. In *Sefer Korbanot* (Book of Sacrifices) in Maimonides' compendium of Jewish Law, the *Mishneh Torah*, the Laws of the Passover Sacrifice are the first that are codified. See also the chapter later in this book on "Sacred Space" and particularly the interpretation of the meaning of the Sacrificial Altar in the outer courtyard of the biblical Sanctuary.
29. According to Rav Yosef's interpretation of the Mishna, found in Pesaḥim 114b.

point in the Seder, the *afikoman*, the matza that was wrapped up and hidden during *Yaḥatz* (the fourth step in the Seder), is now unwrapped and consumed by the Seder participants, representatives of the beneficiaries of Moses' mission as he was about to lead them out of Egypt.[30]

13. *Barekh*
Reciting the traditional Grace After Meals

In the biblical story, Pharaoh comes running to Moses after the plague of the firstborns, urging him to lead his people out. Then, almost as an afterthought, Pharaoh adds, "And you (plural) should bless me too" (Ex. 12:32). The biblical narrative implies that the Jews were blessing, singing the praises, not of Pharaoh of course, but of their God, who had brought the tenth plague and finally liberated them from Egyptian bondage. Thus, the Seder participants reenact their blessing by reciting the Grace After Meals in which God is praised in the first and second paragraphs "for the sumptuous meal we have just eaten ... and for taking us out of the land of Egypt, the house of bondage."

After reciting the Grace, the blessing over the third cup of wine is recited, setting the stage for the next key chapter of redemption in the Book of Exodus: God's promise to "redeem the people with an outstretched arm and with great judgments," that is, with the splitting of the sea (Ex. 6:6).

14. *Hallel*
Reciting psalms of praise

In the biblical story, after he released the Jewish people from captivity, Pharaoh had second thoughts about his decision and decided to pursue them with his cavalry and chariots, drawing near to them as they were encamped at the Sea of Reeds. The people were terrified at the approach of Pharaoh's army. Moses, in turn, prayed to God for the

---

30. As the Haggada states emphatically in the chapter after the recitation of the Four Questions: Had The Holy One, Blessed Be He, not taken our ancestors out of Egypt, then we, and our children, and all of our descendants would still be enslaved to Pharaoh in Egypt.

people's deliverance. The prayer of "Pour Out Your Wrath," which is recited immediately following the third cup of wine, is meant to reflect Moses' prayer at the shore of the sea.[31] God then instructed Moses to stretch out his arm with his staff in hand (symbolizing God's royal scepter), and split the sea so that the people could escape Pharaoh by fleeing on dry land to the other side. When Pharaoh's legions followed, God instructed Moses to stretch out his arm again to bring back the waters, thus drowning the Egyptian army. In response to these miraculous events witnessed by the entire nation, the people, led by Moses, broke out in a song of praise that is called the "Song of the Sea" (Ex. 15).

To reenact that song of praise at the Passover Seder, the participants also break out in singing psalms of praise known as the Hallel. Apparently understanding that the role of the Hallel is to be a stand-in for the Song of the Sea, the Talmud states that the first Hallel was sung by the people after the splitting of the sea (Pesaḥim 117a). The Haggada then adds other songs of praise, instantiations of Hallel (Ps. 136 and the *Nishmat* prayer, usually recited on the Sabbath and holidays during the morning service), each of which gives prominence to the deliverance from the Egyptians at the Sea of Reeds. At the conclusion of these prayers of praise, the blessing over the fourth cup of wine is recited, setting the stage for God's fulfillment of the fourth promise of redemption: "And I will take them to be My people and I will be their God" (Ex. 6:7).

15. *Nirtza*
Concluding the Seder with a prayer that God accept our reenactment of the Exodus and redeem the Jewish people once again

The word "*Nirtza*," the final step in the fifteen-part Seder, means "acceptance." In the biblical story, already at the burning bush, when Moses was first commissioned to lead the people out of Egypt, God told him to bring the people to the very mountain on which God revealed Himself to Moses: "And this will be the sign that I sent you: When you take the people out of Egypt you [collectively] will worship Me on this mountain"

---

31. See *Leading the Passover Journey*, 138–141, to understand how the wording of this prayer reflects Moses' prayer at the sea.

(Ex. 3:12). This was to be the moment when God formally accepted the people as His nation, and the people accepted upon themselves the kingship of God. And so it was. God offered the people the covenant (Ex. 19:3–6), the people accepted (Ex. 19:7, 8; 24:7), and they were supposed to live happily ever after as "husband and wife" in covenantal bliss.

Except that forty days later, the people, believing that Moses, God's emissary, had abandoned them, created and worshiped the Golden Calf, a stunning betrayal of their loyalty to God and their covenantal commitment (Ex. 32:7, 8). As happened with Noah and his family, God was prepared to start human history all over again, this time beginning with Moses' progeny, but Moses would have none of it (Ex. 32:9, 10, 31, 32). He argued with God until God relented and forgave the people, after they displayed true remorse (Ex. 33:6–10).

To test their sincerity, God commanded the people to build a home in which His presence could dwell in their very midst. The people were overjoyed at being given a second chance, and with great enthusiasm built the Mishkan to house God's presence. In the last five verses of the Book of Exodus, God's presence indeed revealed itself and filled the Mishkan that the people built. At this moment, there was *Nirtza* – God's acceptance of the people, imperfect though they were, and the people's true acceptance of God, despite their earlier indiscretions. This was the moment of spiritual redemption for the people because, conscious of their deficiencies, they were nevertheless made to feel worthy by God's presence coming to dwell among them. Hence, the Seder ends with *Nirtza*, reenacting that redemptive moment when God's presence came to dwell among the Jewish people and to accompany them on all their future journeys (Ex. 40:34–38; see Appendix 2 for an outline of the Seder's fifteen steps of redemption).

WHERE IS MOSES IN THE HAGGADA?

Moses plays a central role throughout the biblical story that the Passover Seder and the Haggada reenact. It is therefore rather strange that in the Haggada's narrative of the story, Moses' name appears only once,[32] and

---

32. In the Ashkenazic Haggada; in the Sephardic version Moses' name does not appear even that one time.

that it is only in an obscure, secondary role, as a proof text for another point that the Haggada is making.[33] Why is Moses virtually invisible in the Haggada?

To understand why Moses is hidden in the Haggada's retelling of the Exodus story, why he is *tzafun*, we have to turn to two events in the Book of Exodus. First, when the people, after leaving Egypt, journey in the desert and run out of food, they come running to Moses and Aaron to complain. Strikingly, the people ask them accusingly why **they** took the people out of Egypt if they were fated to perish thirty days later of starvation in the desert. Moses parries their complaints by assuring them that God would provide food for them and rebukes them, insisting that their complaints be directed against God (Ex. 16:3, 7, 8), "for who are we that you lodge your complaints against us" (Ex. 16:7).

Apparently, Moses understood that there was some confusion among the people about who actually took them out of Egypt. Later on, in the events that led up to the Golden Calf, the people said to Aaron, "Make us a god that will lead us, for this man, Moses, who took us out of Egypt, we do not know what has become of him" (Ex. 32:1). Apparently, here too, in even starker form, the people seem to believe that Moses is the divine being who took them out of Egypt.

For this reason, the participants of the Seder, who imagine themselves on the night of Passover as having been themselves liberated from Egypt,[34] leave Moses out of the story. His role in the Exodus is minimized so that God's role is maximized in the retelling. This is also why Elijah makes an unexpected appearance in the story prior to the prayer "Pour Out Your Wrath" (the placeholder for Moses' prayer to God at the sea). Elijah is invoked to represent Moses in disguise. Elijah was the angry prophet of God who, like Moses, had a revelation at Mount Horeb/Sinai and who faced down the idolaters of his generation (I Kings 18–19). Just as Moses had to wear a mask after he came down from Mount

---

33. In the proof text cited by R. Yose HaGelili in the *Maggid* section for how many plagues occurred at the sea, citing the verse: "And they believed in God **and in His servant Moses**" (Ex. 14:31).

34. As the Haggada says toward the end of *Maggid*: "In every generation, each person is to see himself as if he left Egypt."

Sinai with the second set of tablets containing the Ten Commandments, so that the people would not be blinded by his radiant presence (Ex. 34:29–35), in the Haggada he must also be "masked," hidden, disguised as Elijah, so that his radiant visage does not blind the Seder participants to God's presence.

The point and purpose of Passover, the first of the year's biblical holidays, and its reliving of the biblical events that it commemorates, is to firmly anchor the people's relationship with God. It is to remember God's redemption of the Jewish people when no human being, not even as great a "miracle worker" as Moses,[35] could or would rescue them. As the author of the Haggada states at the beginning of *Maggid*: "If The Holy One, Blessed Be He, had not taken us out of Egypt, then we, and our children, and our children's children would still be enslaved to Pharaoh in Egypt." Moses is made virtually invisible to instill in us today an attitude of gratitude to God for His redemption. We rendezvous with God, as God rendezvoused with our ancestors. That attitude of indebtedness finds expression in our people's loyalty to God and God's Torah whose story and reenactment have sustained our people for thousands of years. We are only Jews today because of those saving events of three millennia ago and because of the Torah's story of those events, which has been passed down to us from generation to generation.

AND WHERE IS THE LAND OF ISRAEL?

In the biblical narrative, the promise made to Abraham was not merely that God would redeem his descendants from captivity and punish their oppressors, but that God would return Abraham's descendants to the Land of Israel (Gen. 15:13–21). Indeed, consistent with that promise and God's memory of it, there was a fifth promise of redemption that God made to Moses, found in the Book of Exodus immediately following the first four promises of redemption mentioned previously: "**And I will bring you** to the land which I swore to Abraham, Isaac, and Jacob that I would give it – and I will give it to them as an inheritance in perpetuity – I, the EverPresent God" (Ex. 6:8).

---

35. See the epitaph to Moses in Deut. 34:11–12.

Despite this fifth biblical promise, in the retelling of the story of Passover in the Haggada and as part of the Seder, this promise is left out.[36] The author of the Haggada, living after the destruction of the Second Temple and the exile of most of the Jewish people from the Land of Israel, could not include this promise, which was unfulfilled for them and for roughly nineteen centuries of Jews afterward. There was only a hint to the fifth promise in the Cup of Elijah that sat at the center of the Seder table. That cup – named after the prophet who not only resembled Moses but who, according to the later prophet Malachi, was also to herald the future redemption of the Jewish people and their return to their ancestral land (Mal. 3:23–24) – was traditionally not drunk at the Seder because its promise had not been fulfilled for so many centuries of Jewish life.

Perhaps now that nearly half of the world's Jews have returned over the past century to reinhabit their ancestral homeland, this cup may – perhaps should – be drunk at the Seder.[37] The most appropriate time to do so might be at the very end of the Seder before singing "Next Year in Jerusalem," in recognition and gratitude for God's fulfilling the promise to Abraham in our parents', and in our, generation. Coming, as it does, after the participants have already drunk four cups of wine and may be edging toward intoxication, the fifth cup of Elijah could be shared among all the Seder participants. This "taste of redemption" would convey the reality that although a substantial portion of the Jewish people has returned to the Promised Land, a substantial portion has not, nor is the biblical dream of a rebuilt Temple in Jerusalem yet a reality. So the redemption which we have been privileged to witness and experience is not complete.

---

36. It is also left out of the core of *Maggid*, the paragraph of "*Arami oved avi*" – the pilgrim's declaration recited as he brings the first fruits to Jerusalem, upon which the Haggada weaves an elaborate midrash (as per the instructions of Mishna Pesaḥim 10:4). In the Haggada, the pilgrims' formulation is truncated and does not include the verse, "And He brought me to this place, and He gave us this land, a land flowing with milk and honey" (Deut. 26:9).

37. Maimonides rules that a fifth cup may be drunk; however, he suggests doing so prior to reciting Psalm 136, "the Great Hallel" (*Mishneh Torah*, Laws of Ḥametz and Matza 8:10).

This sharing of the cup of Elijah would also point to a cautionary tale from the prologue to the story of the Exodus: a lack of fraternal solidarity, between Joseph and his brothers, is what led to the enslavement of the Jewish people in the first place. Therefore, only by sharing this cup of redemption in communal solidarity will the Land of Israel under Jewish sovereignty remain an "inheritance in perpetuity" as God promised.[38]

THE TIMELESS ETHICAL VALUES OF THE EXODUS

In addition to recalling and reliving the Exodus on Passover night, ethical norms emerged from the narrative through which the Jewish people imitated God's redemptive actions in the Exodus year-round. And this model of *imitatio Dei* developed in the Jewish tradition for all the Jewish holidays so that the people's relationship to God as human beings created in God's image, or of spouse to spouse ("I will take them to be My people and I will be their God" [Ex 6:7]), would be plain for all to see.

These dynamics resemble those of intimate human relationships. As two people come together to become a "we" instead of two separate "I's," they share their most intimate selves with each other and begin to act more and more like a single unit. After many years of a successful marriage, people sometimes begin to resemble each other physically, unconsciously mimicking each other's language, facial expressions, and even gait. More importantly, in their dealings with both their own children and with the outside world, they unite in a common front on issues of principle and deep-seated values. So too, the "marital" relationship between God and the Jewish people shaped the ethics of the latter to closely resemble the ethical actions of the divine partner.

The Jewish tradition legislated a slew of ethical values and actions that emulated God's redemptive acts when He took the Jewish people out of slavery, estrangement, and impoverishment. The first such value is the mitzva of *pidyon shevuyim*, the ransoming/freeing of endangered Jews from slavery or captivity, about which Maimonides

---

38. "And I will give it to them as an inheritance in perpetuity, I the EverPresent God" (Ex. 6:8). See also the brief discussion of the modern holiday of Yom Yerushalayim (Jerusalem Day) in chapter 8 of this volume entitled, "The Hiddenness of God."

says, "There is no greater commandment."³⁹ The Book of Leviticus mandates that Jews should redeem their relatives who have been forced to sell themselves into slavery to a non-Jew, connecting that command to God's actions at the Exodus: "For it is to Me that the Jewish people are servants, they are My servants whom I freed from the Land of Egypt, I am the Lord your God" (Lev. 25:55).⁴⁰ Leviticus, in effect, has God saying: As I redeemed you when you were held in captivity as slaves in Egypt, you should redeem each other when you are enslaved or held captive.⁴¹

Second, in Exodus, God instructs Moses to command the Jewish people to request from the Egyptians gold, silver, and fine clothes before they leave Egypt (a token payback, presumably, for the hundreds of years of free slave labor that accrued to the Egyptians). Hence, they leave Egypt with the spoils that God had promised Abraham hundreds of years earlier in the Covenant between the Pieces when God first informed him of his descendants' enslavement and liberation.⁴² Just as the Jewish people were freed from slavery in Egypt, endowed with some of their former masters' wealth, the Torah mandated both that Jewish servants be freed from their Jewish masters after six years and that, upon their release, they be endowed with a material dowry upon

39. Maimonides, *Mishneh Torah*, Laws of Gifts to the Poor 8:10.
40. Although the primary obligation still falls on the relatives, Maimonides later extends the obligation to all Jews (not only relatives) to free a fellow Jew who has sold himself into slavery to a non-Jew. Maimonides, *Mishneh Torah*, Laws of Slaves 2:7.
41. This reinforces the point that God made in the first of the Ten Commandments. In the opening speech God identifies Himself to the Jewish people, not as the Creator of the world, but as the one "who has freed them from the Land of Egypt from the house of bondage." God's very identity by which He makes Himself known to the Jewish people is as the one who freed them from captivity and slavery. In *imitatio Dei*, the Jewish people are therefore commanded to do the same. See also Shabbat 133b; *Sifrei* on Deut. 10:12; Maimonides, *Mishneh Torah*, Laws of Ethics 1:6 and *Guide for the Perplexed* I:54.
42. Gen. 15:13–14. This promise was itself a reward for Abraham's refusing to sully his rescue of Lot from captivity by accepting the booty of his military victory. God therefore promises that Abraham's descendants will benefit from the wealth that Abraham refused to take for himself. In both of these cases, Abraham's actions in Genesis can be seen as the precursor to God's actions in Exodus, which the Jewish people are commanded to emulate in subsequent books of the Torah.

which to rebuild their lives.[43] In addition, Jewish masters are enjoined by the Torah to treat their Jewish servants as hired laborers and not to work them "oppressively" – the very word used to describe the slave labor of the Jews in Egypt.[44] The Exodus taught the Jewish people to be the opposite of their Egyptian oppressors.

Third, in addition to being held as slaves in Egyptian captivity, the Jews in Egypt experienced the suffering and travail of being strangers in a foreign country. Therefore, the Torah commands the Jewish people to be constantly vigilant and solicitous of the legal rights and the economic and emotional needs of the stranger and other vulnerable populations such as orphans and widows.[45] In fact, more ethical commandments are explicitly connected by the biblical text to the experience of slavery and the subsequent Exodus from Egypt than to any other biblical event, including the oft-quoted revelation at Sinai. Time after time, the Bible commands us to remember the events of the Exodus that expressed God's compassion for the Jewish people, and to behave compassionately and morally as a result.

It should be noted that the command to "remember" the past in order to identify and empathize with those downtrodden in the present is not, as might be thought, directed to the individual to recall an event that he or she personally experienced. Rather it is directed at the individual and the nation as a whole, to recall the event experienced collectively by their Jewish ancestors, and motivated by that vicarious memory to act empathetically and ethically. In other words, most uses of the term "remember" in the Bible refer to remembering our ancestors' story about which we were told, and creatively reimagining those events as our own memories. "Creative imagination" sparked by the biblical narrative is at the heart of the Jewish religious enterprise.[46]

---

43. Ex. 21:2; Deut. 15:15.
44. Cf. Lev. 25:39–43 to Ex. 1:13–14.
45. See, for instance, Lev. 19:33–36; Deut. 10:19; 24:17–22.
46. This is why the main text of the section of *Maggid*, which was recited each year by the pilgrim bringing his first fruits to the Jerusalem Temple, starts from the imaginative first person singular – "My father was a fugitive from Aram" (making the patriarch Abraham or Jacob in effect his own father) – moves to the first person plural – "and God took us out of Egypt ... and brought us to this land" (making the Exodus and the

It could not be otherwise for a religion that posits an invisible God, whose presence became manifest to the Jewish people millennia ago and has not since been publicly, overtly witnessed. By retelling the saga of our ancestors' experiences and journeys from generation to generation, these events and God's redemptive presence in these events come alive. Imagined and remembered in this creative fashion, they become real – so real, that as the Haggada says in *Maggid*, "In every generation, each person is to see himself as if he left Egypt." It is this memory that is the basis for the people's identity, ethical values, and religious ritual.

REMEMBERING THE EXODUS YEAR-ROUND: RITUALS AND LITURGY

The redemptive events in the Bible for which we celebrate the biblical holidays are so pivotal and foundational in the Jewish story that they shape not only our ethics but also our rituals year-round. There are three major rituals in Jewish life that emerge from the Exodus and overflow to the rest of the Jewish year: the life-cycle ceremony of *pidyon haben* (the redemption of the firstborn son), the daily donning of *tefillin* (phylacteries), and the weekly celebration of Shabbat.

Since God saved the firstborn males of the Jewish people when He slew the Egyptian firstborns on the night of the Exodus, all firstborn males – human and animal – are considered to belong to God (Ex. 13:1, 11–15). As God redeemed them, we "redeem" our firstborn male children from God, by giving God's representative, the priest, a symbolic monetary sum of five silver coins. This symbolic life-cycle event is representative of all other firsts in the natural world that the Torah mandates we offer God, from the first grains (Lev. 23:10, 17), to the first bit of dough that we knead when we bake bread (Num. 15:17–21), to the first fruits of the land that we bring from the holiday of Shavuot through

---

original settlement of the land something of which he was a part as a member of the collective Jewish people), and then back to the real first person singular: And now I have brought these first fruits of the land that God has given to me." By internalizing the story of the Jewish people's past into his own identity, the pilgrim internalized the lessons of previous generations and made them his own, year in and year out.

the holiday of Sukkot (Deut. 26:1–11). By offering these "firsts" to God, we acknowledge that all of our fecundity and growth are ultimately the result of God's loving-kindness and beneficence.

While the redemption of the firstborn is a once-in-a-lifetime opportunity, the wearing of phylacteries, *tefillin*, is a daily one. The biblical command to wind the *tefillin* around one's arms and hands and place them upon the top of one's forehead is traditionally directed to Jewish males on weekdays. The rituals of redeeming the firstborn and of wearing phylacteries are commanded together, immediately following the account of the slaying of the Egyptian firstborn males and the Exodus from Egypt. Both are explicitly linked to God's redeeming the Jewish people from Egypt "with a strong hand" (Ex. 13:9, 10, 16). God took the people out of Egypt with a strong hand and therefore Jews bind the *tefillin* on the muscle of their arms and around their hand. In so doing, they symbolically bind their own energies and direct their hearts and minds to God.[47]

There is a knot on both the hand and head *tefillin* symbolizing that the Jewish people are inextricably knotted together with God in covenant. This covenantal relationship is reinforced by the number of times – seven – that the arm *tefillin* are wound around the forearm. The number seven symbolizes the Jewish covenant with God (reflected, for example, in the observance of the Sabbath on the seventh day of each week – Ex. 31:16–17). The arm *tefillin* are also wound tightly around the hand forming and imprinting on one's skin the letters *shin, dalet*, and *yud* – to form the word "*Shaddai*," one of God's names.[48] This specific name of God is mentioned in the story of the Exodus as the name by which God revealed Himself to the patriarchs of the Jewish people.[49] The

---

47. The black box of the *tefillin* wrapped around the arm, containing the four places in the Torah that the commandment of *tefillin* is iterated, is placed facing the heart. The placement symbolizes the keeping of the covenant with all of one's heart (Deut. 6:4–9). The second box of *tefillin*, worn on the head, is placed in between and above the eyes.
48. Often translated as "Almighty." This name of God is usually correlated in the Bible with God's blessings of fecundity and fruitfulness – one of the two blessings, along with the land, that God bestowed upon the patriarchs, and that fueled the prolific growth of the twelve tribes to become a veritable nation in Egypt.
49. Ex. 6:3; Gen. 17:1, 28:3, 35:11.

imprint of God's name on the hand each morning may be why the Torah calls the hand *tefillin* an *"ot"* (Deut. 6:8, 11:18), which literally means a "letter" but has come to mean more loosely, a "sign" of the people's distinct relationship with God.

In addition to tightly binding one's arms and strength to God Almighty in covenant, there is, if you will, royal symbolism to donning the head *tefillin*. The head *tefillin*, secured by a leather strap, is reminiscent of the crown worn by the Pharaoh of the Exodus, Rameses II, as evidenced by the extraordinary remains found at the Temple of Abu Simbel.[50] The difference, of course, is that instead of having a golden serpent at its apex, which in Egyptian lore was the symbol of the Pharaohs,[51] the "crown" of the head *tefillin* is a box containing four biblical chapters and adorned by the two *shin* letters on the outside – a three-stemmed *shin* on one side and a four-stemmed *shin* on the other.[52]

The head *tefillin*/crown symbolizes the royal status of the Jewish people as God's covenanted people: "a **kingdom of priests** and a holy people" (Ex. 19:6). Like the High Priest in the biblical Sanctuary, who wore a headband around his forehead the entire time that he ministered, imprinted in gold with the words "Holy to God" (Ex. 28:36), all Jewish males traditionally wear a headband during morning prayers with the first letter of God's name *Shaddai* embossed on both the left and right sides. This is why the head *tefillin* are referred to in the rabbinic tradition as embodying the verse: "For the peoples of the earth will see that God's name is placed upon you and they will be in awe of you" (Deut. 28:10).[53]

Despite their royal symbolism, which might lead wearers to a sense of self-aggrandizement, one might view the *tefillin* in quite the

---

50. See the photo of the twin statues of Rameses II in *The Archaeological Haggada* (Adama Books, 1992), 25.

51. See Ezek. 29:3, in which Pharaoh is referred to as the "the large serpent."

52. Aside from the seven stems, whose number again symbolizes the Jewish covenant with God, the two *shin* letters are reminiscent of the male and female cherubs with their wings spread that sat above the Holy Ark, of which the *tefillin* are supposed to remind us, I believe, in miniature. The two *shin* letters are so designed that the three-stemmed *shin* and the four-stemmed *shin* could embrace and intertwine as could the male and female cherubs, symbolizing God and the Jewish people, above the Ark in the Holy of Holies (see Yoma 54a).

53. Berakhot 6a on the verse from Deut. 28:10.

opposite way, as a compensatory mechanism, which God graciously gave the Jewish people to build up their self-esteem. Hundreds of years as slaves under the brutal oppression of Pharaoh left the Jewish people with a deeply embedded negative self-image. The recurring anxiety and frequent whining of the generation that left Egypt give ample testimony to their fragile self-concept. Crowning them through the wearing of *tefillin* was designed to help redress that downtrodden sense of self and make all Jews feel as if they came from a proud lineage and were now part of the royal household of the King of kings.

Although thousands of years have passed since the Exodus from Egypt, the persecutions of the Jewish people in every generation[54] and the absence of God's overt and palpable presence through most of Jewish history have made it continuously challenging for the Jewish people to remain steadfast in their identity and in their positive sense of themselves as God's beloved people. The *tefillin* today, no less than three thousand years ago, still serve their original function of binding each individual Jew to God and giving each person a positive self-concept of being cherished by God.

The third major ritual associated with the Exodus that overflows into the whole year is the weekly observance and celebration of Shabbat, which also recalls our enslavement and redemption from Egypt. Like the *tefillin* and the mark of circumcision,[55] Shabbat in the Bible is called an "*ot*," a symbol of the covenant between God and the Jewish people. In the second iteration of the Ten Commandments, the Jews are bidden to give their servants rest on Shabbat because of their "memory" of having been slaves in Egypt and then freed by God from bondage (Deut. 5:14–15). As we will see in chapter 7, Shabbat picks up this idea of remembering our redemption from slavery and makes it one of the two pillars on which we base that day of rest and relationship, every week of the year.

---

54. The Haggada tells us in *Maggid*, as we raise the toast to God: "In every generation, there are those who have risen up against us to annihilate us. But The Holy One, Blessed Be He, has saved us from their hands."

55. Although the circumcision ceremony and commandment goes back to Abraham (Gen. 17:9–14), the Torah attaches it to the story of the Exodus by making it a prerequisite for eating the Paschal sacrifice (Ex. 12:43–50).

Liturgically, we therefore recall the Exodus in the recitation of Kiddush on Friday nights as part of our observance of Shabbat. As the Torah commands,[56] the Exodus is also remembered every single day through the recitation of the closest thing Judaism has to a creed – the *Shema* – recited daily both in the mornings and evenings.[57] We recall the Exodus in the closing verse of the third and final section of the *Shema*, making it the final thought with which we leave its recitation, thereby highlighting its importance.[58]

"Front-loading" the memory of the Exodus through the Kiddush recited weekly at the beginning of the first Shabbat meal and "back-loading" it as the concluding verse of the *Shema* recited twice daily is the way we assign the Exodus its special place in Jewish memory and liturgy.

THE SEVENTH PASSOVER DAY:
REMEMBERING THE SPLITTING OF THE SEA

Although the splitting of the sea was recalled at the Seder on the first night of Passover, the Torah gave the event its own sacred day of commemoration. Here's why. After the Jews left Egypt, they journeyed into the desert and the ancient Egyptians pursued them. The Egyptian intent was either to reenslave them or to annihilate them. Seven days later, as recorded in chapters 14 and 15 of Exodus, as the Egyptian army was about to overtake the defenseless Jewish masses, God split the Sea of Reeds, saved the Jewish people, and drowned the Egyptian legions before their very eyes. In so doing, God's redemptive presence again became patently manifest to the entire Jewish people. In other words, the second revelation of the Divine Presence before the people took place at the sea:

---

56. "In order that you shall remember the day that you left Egypt all the days of your life" (Deut. 16:3).

57. Maimonides, *Mishneh Torah*, Laws of Reciting the *Shema* 1:1.

58. Ibid., 1:3. The relevant passage recited is: "I am the EverPresent, your God, who took you out of the land of Egypt to be your God, I am the EverPresent, your God" (Num. 15:41). The question of whether this section of the *Shema* should be recited at night is the subject of the discussion in the Haggada near the beginning of *Maggid* between R. Elazar b. Azaria and the rabbinic sages.

Thus the EverPresent God saved Israel that day from the hand of the Egyptians; and Israel saw the Egyptians dead upon the seashore. And Israel saw the great hand that the EverPresent God wrought against Egypt and the people were awed by the EverPresent God and believed in the EverPresent God and in His servant Moses. (Ex. 14:30–31)

On that day, in an emotional response to their deliverance, Moses and the Jewish people sang the Song of the Sea. Although the Bible does not specify that the splitting of the sea took place on the seventh day following the Exodus, it brilliantly suggests it with the parallel language and plot line to the story of Israel/Jacob, the Jewish people's patriarchal ancestor and archetype, fleeing from servitude to Laban and being rescued by God. There (Gen. 31), the Bible tells us that Laban overtook Jacob and his camp on the **seventh** day following his flight. The Jewish tradition therefore concludes that the Egyptians overtook the Israelites – compelling God to save them by splitting the sea – on the seventh day after the Jews left Egypt.

That miraculous, redemptive event at the sea, witnessed by all the people, is why the seventh day of Passover is a sacred holiday and why, liturgically, the Song of the Sea is included in the liturgy for the day as part of the Torah portion read in synagogue. It is also part of the reason why, throughout Passover, during the morning prayers, we sing parts of Hallel, which were first sung, according to the rabbis, after the splitting of the sea.[59] Recollecting and celebrating the rescue at the sea on the seventh day of Passover fulfills Moses' charge to the Jewish people in the Book of Deuteronomy:

> You shall surely remember what the EverPresent, your God, did to Pharaoh and all the Egyptians: the wondrous acts that you saw with your own eyes, the signs and the miracles, the mighty hand, and the outstretched arm by which the EverPresent, your God, liberated you. Thus will the EverPresent God do to all the peoples you now fear. (Deut. 7:18–19)

---

59. Pesaḥim 117a. See also the Hallel section of the Seder, above.

As pointed out earlier, the "mighty hand and outstretched arm" is a reference to the miracles at the sea.[60] If the purpose of the Exodus from Egypt was to free the Jewish people from slavery, the purpose for the splitting of the sea was to free them from fear and anxiety, both of the Egyptian armies and the Canaanite armies, whom they anticipated soon facing.[61] Thus, the revelation of God's presence to the Jewish people at the sea was certainly worthy of being remembered and retold for future generations on its own special day, the seventh day of Passover.

To mark the conclusion of this final day of Passover, the custom of holding a *seuda shel Mashiaḥ*, a festive meal anticipating the arrival of the Messiah, which originated in hasidic circles in the nineteenth century, has gained wider currency in recent years among both traditional and non-traditional Jews. The basis for the custom is that the redemption of the Jewish people from Egypt and at the Sea of Reeds, for which we celebrate Passover, presages the final redemption of the Jewish people in the Messianic Age. This festive concluding meal of Passover which bookends the Seder meal of the holiday's opening night, is often celebrated communally and incorporates many of the Seder's elements, including singing songs, telling stories of redemption, eating matza, and drinking (four cups of!) wine. It has become a meaningful way for the community to bid farewell to this foundational holiday, which celebrates the memory of, and hope for, redemption.

INTERNALIZING GOD'S REVELATION AT THE SEA

The miraculous events at the sea found ethical expression in the Torah's mandate that the Jewish people imitate God – who rescued them from being reenslaved by their former Egyptian taskmasters – by offering safe sanctuary to runaway slaves in both their individual homes and in their communities (Deut. 23:16–17). This law ran against the nearly universal rule in the ancient Near East under which escaped slaves had to be returned to their masters, usually under penalty of death, and bounty

---

60. See above, my explanation for the third cup, and *Leading the Passover Journey*, 136–137, for why God's outstretched arm refers to the splitting of the sea.
61. Therefore, part of the song is devoted to the fear instilled in the Canaanites because of the miracles of the sea. Ex. 15:14–17.

hunters were rewarded for these slaves' return.[62] Again, we see here the power of *imitatio Dei* in the Bible: God came to the defense of fleeing slaves and expected the same of the people created in God's image, who carried God's name into the world. Indeed today, the Jewish state provides asylum to individual refugees who flee to Israel out of genuine danger to life and limb, while Diaspora Jewry, through their financial contributions, helps support the costs of resettlement for these refugees within Israel or in another safe country.

The events at the sea were so powerful that they also dramatically impacted Jewish liturgy for all time. The Song of the Sea and the verses describing the events leading up to it are recited not only on the seventh day of Passover but every single day in the morning prayers as part of the Verses of Song (*Pesukei DeZimra*) which precede the call to prayer (*Barekhu*). The belief in a God who is capable of rescue and redemption, and to whom we offer our silent devotional prayer each day, is rooted in the retelling of the rescue at the sea. That retelling is therefore also alluded to daily in both the morning and evening blessings of the *Shema* which precede the *Amida* (*Shemoneh Esreh*) and conclude with "Blessed are You God, the Redeemer of Israel."[63] Belief in God's redemptive power as evidenced by the events at the sea is a *sine qua non* for praying for God's deliverance and redemption today.

Finally, existentially, commemorating the seventh duty of Passover as sacred because of the Jewish people's rescue at the sea embodies the challenge for Jews and for all human beings to live "free from fear." Human beings who are constantly anxious about their ability to survive are, in a sense, enslaved. To be truly free of that pervasive anxiety that is part and parcel of the human condition, one needs some sort of deep, internal assurance that one's basic survival needs will be met – that in

---

62. See Laws of Hammurabi §§16–20; Hittite Laws §§22–24; and Marc Brettler and Adele Berlin, eds., *The Jewish Study Bible* (Oxford University Press, 2004), 419. See also the impassioned argument of Rabbi Shai Held in his online commentary on *Parashat Ki Tetzeh* (2014), "Why Runaway Slaves Are Like God": http://myemail.constantcontact.com/Parashat-Ki-Teitzei---Rabbi-Shai-Held.html?soid=1 101789466973&aid=eBLt85D6x5M.

63. For this reason, in Jewish tradition there may not be an interruption between the recitation of this blessing and the commencement of the *Amida*.

some way God, who our tradition teaches us is EverPresent, will provide. By rescuing our ancestors from the mighty legions of Egypt, God provided testimony to that truth.

After several weeks in the desert, however, a new challenge emerged: running out of food and potential starvation. Would the people continue to trust in God's ability to provide for an entire nation in the midst of a barren wilderness? This led to the next revelation of God's presence to the people in the story of the manna, the focus of chapter 2.

Appendix

The Seder: Fifteen Steps to Redemption

- First cup: Journeying back to ancient Egypt

  1. *Kadesh*
  Preparing the mind to enter sacred time (Ex. 1:1)

  2. *URḥatz*
  Preparing the body to enter sacred space (Ex. 1:1)

  3. *Karpas*
  Initial, prolific growth (Ex. 1:7)
  Salt water – sweat of slave labor (Ex. 1:11–14)

  4. *Yaḥatz*
  Breaking the spirit of the Jewish people (Ex. 1:22)
  Hiding the matza – baby Moses (Ex. 2: 1–10)

5. *Maggid*
The verbal, ordered telling: Beginning in shame, ending in praise
(Ex. 13:8)
 – Remembering the covenant (why we were redeemed)
 – Recalling the plagues (how we were redeemed)

• Second Cup: Journeying to the last night

6. *Raḥtza*
Preparing body and mind for the sacred meal
"On matzot and *marors* you shall eat it" (Ex. 12: 8)

7. *Motzi*
Blessing God for the staff of life

8. *Matza*
From bread of poverty to bread of redemption

9. *Maror*
Recalling the bitterness of Egyptian slavery

10. *Korekh*
"On" matzot and *marors* shall it be eaten

11. *Shulḥan Orekh*
Substituting for the Paschal sacrifice (egg – holiday sacrifice)

12. *Tzafun*
Moses called to lead the Jews out of Egypt (Ex. 12:31)

13. *Barekh*
Blessing God for exiting Egypt (Ex. 12:32 – "And bless me too")

- Third Cup: Journeying to the seashore
  - *Shefokh Ḥamatkha* ("Pour Out Your Wrath")
  - Moses' prayer at the sea (Ex. 14:13–14)
  - Elijah – Moses in disguise (Ex. 14:31 – I Kings 18:36)

  14. *Hallel*
  The Song of the Sea (Ex. 15)

- Fourth Cup: Journeying to Mount Sinai

  15. *Nirtza*
  Mutual acceptance of God and the people (Ex. 19, 40)

- Fifth Cup: Journeying to Jerusalem

Chapter Two

"Not by Bread Alone": Counting the Omer, Celebrating Shavuot[1]

*And God spoke the following to Moses: "Speak to the
Children of Israel and say to them, 'When you come to
the land which I am giving to you, and you cut the harvest,
then you shall bring an Omer of the first cuttings to the
priest…. And you shall count for yourselves seven complete
weeks* (Shabbatot) *beginning from the day following the
day of rest* (Shabbat), *the day that you brought the waved
Omer, until the day after the seventh week* (Shabbat
HaShevi'it), *you shall count fifty days. Then you shall
bring a new offering to God. From your habitations you
shall bring two waved breads, two tenths of an ephah of
fine flour baked with leaven, a first fruit gift to God.'"*

· (Lev. 23:9–17)

---

1. An earlier and much abbreviated version of this chapter appeared on pp. 18–21 in the
    Spring 1999 issue of the *Jewish Spectator*, vol. 63, #4.

In Jewish tradition, it is customary to count, for seven consecutive weeks, the days that have passed from Passover – the holiday commemorating the Exodus from Egypt – until the holiday of Shavuot. The Torah offers no explicit rationale for this counting, as it does for the holidays of Passover and Sukkot. When I was younger, this period was confused in my mind, as it apparently is for many other young people, with the overlapping period that is colloquially referred to as "the *Sefira*" (lit., "the Counting"). The *Sefira* period of bereavement is marked by abstention from joy and a prohibition on haircuts, parties, and instrumental music. This somber period was instituted by the Jewish sages as a sign of national mourning for the twelve thousand pairs of students of R. Akiva, who died during this period in the second century CE because "they did not extend honor to one another" (Menaḥot 62b). At the time, I thought that the seven-week count must have something to do with the grieving over these students' early demise. Yet I soon realized that despite being called the *Sefira*, this period of customary mourning had nothing to do with *Sefirat HaOmer*, the biblical commandment of counting the Omer, which preceded the demise of R. Akiva's students by some fourteen centuries.[2]

THE MYSTERY OF THE OMER

When I got a bit older, I began searching for the rationale behind the earlier biblical commandment. The most satisfying explanation that I found for the count, which begins with bringing the Omer sacrifice on the second day of Passover and culminates in the sacred day of Shavuot, was offered by the twelfth-century Jewish philosopher and codifier of Jewish law, Maimonides. In his *Guide for the Perplexed*, Maimonides writes that in counting the Omer, the Jewish people are counting the days in eager anticipation of God's revelation at Mount Sinai on the holiday of Shavuot.[3] Like young lovers who count every day as they look forward with nervous excitement

---

2. However, see the end of footnote 4, p. 47 below.
3. Maimonides, *Guide for the Perplexed* III:43. The *Sefer HaḤinukh* adopts this explanation as well; see mitzva 306.

to their upcoming wedding day, the Jewish people count the days leading up to Shavuot, their wedding day with God under the canopy of Mount Sinai.[4] This interpretation has largely been accepted by traditional Jews as conventional wisdom.

Although romantic and seductive, Maimonides' explanation, which links the counting of the Omer and the holiday of Shavuot to the revelation of God's presence at Mount Sinai, is not without its drawbacks. First and foremost is that, in the five places in the Torah in which the holiday of Shavuot is mentioned, not once is it linked with the epiphany at Sinai and the giving of the Torah.[5] Nor is the revelation at Mount Sinai, in both places where it is dramatically described in the biblical text, linked to the holiday of Shavuot.[6] This despite the

---

4. Since Maimonides links the mitzva of counting the Omer to receiving the Torah, he writes in his code of law, the *Mishneh Torah*, Laws of Regular and Supplemental Sacrifices 7:22, that the mitzva to count the Omer is a *mitzva deoraita*, a biblically based commandment that still obligates Jews. Most other legal scholars, including the great French biblical commentator Rashi, link the counting of the Omer, as is clearly implied in the biblical text of Leviticus, to the Closeness offering of the Omer of (barley) bread on the second day of Passover and the offering of the two wheat breads on Shavuot that were brought when the Temple stood. For these scholars, since the Temple is no longer standing and those offerings cannot be brought, the counting between the two offerings is only a *mitzva derabbanan*, a rabbinic precept, "*zekher lemikdash*," so that we not forget the traditions of the Temple. It is further worth noting, albeit homiletically, that according to the latter position, there is cause for feeling despondent during this period of counting because of the absence of the Temple and the ability to fulfill these biblical commandments as the Torah instructed. According to Rabbi Yechiel Epstein in his twentieth-century code of law, the *Arukh HaShulḥan* (*Oraḥ Ḥayim* 489:5, citing the Rashba), this is why we do not say the blessing of *SheHeḥeyanu* on the first night of counting the Omer, to praise God for keeping us alive, sustaining us, and allowing us to reach this day, because there is an absence of joy due to the loss of the Temple and its offerings.

In a similar vein, one might argue that the dishonoring by R. Akiva's students of each other led to the failure of the Bar Kokhba revolt in 135 CE, because the students could not work together harmoniously to achieve victory. That failure, in turn, spelled the death knell of the movement to regain sovereignty, rebuild the Temple, and bring the biblically mandated Omer offerings. This too might help explain why the period of counting the Omer was transformed from being a period of gratitude and joy into a period of mourning and sadness.

5. Ex. 23, 34; Lev. 23; Num. 28; and Deut. 16.
6. Ex. 19, 20 and Deut. 4, 5.

fact that, in the second iteration, Moses warns the Jewish people not to forget the day that they stood before God at Horeb, a synonym for Mount Sinai (Deut. 4:10). Would it not have been appropriate to link the holiday of Shavuot to that momentous day, in the same manner as the Torah linked the holiday of Passover to the Exodus (Ex. 12:24–27, 13:3–8) and the holiday of Sukkot to the Jews living in sukkot (booths) while wandering in the desert (Lev. 23:42–43)?

Aside from this fundamental question, four additional questions jump out in considering the persuasiveness of Maimonides' explanation. First, why does the Jewish tradition mandate the counting up from the Exodus instead of counting down to Sinai? Were Maimonides correct, the counting should be reversed: "Forty-nine days remaining… three days remaining, two days remaining, one day remaining." In the current form of counting up, it is the Exodus from Egypt rather than the revelation of the Torah that is the starting and focal point of the count.

Second, according to the Mishna in Tractate Megilla (Megilla 30b), the main Torah reading for Shavuot, which focuses on the counting of the Omer, concludes with the words, "Remember that you were a slave in the land of Egypt, and [therefore] guard and do these laws" (Deut. 16:12).[7] This reading identifies the slavery experience in Egypt as the root of the commandment to count the Omer, rather than the revelation experience at Sinai.

Third, the explanation of counting toward Sinai fails to explain why an Omer offering of barley from the new harvest was brought in the Mishkan to inaugurate the count. Nor does it explain why two omers of wheat bread were brought in the Mishkan on the fiftieth day, what we call the holiday of Shavuot, as a "first fruits gift," to conclude the count. What do gifts of barley and wheat breads from the new harvests have to do with God's revelation of the Ten Commandments at Mount Sinai?[8]

---

7. In the Diaspora, this has become the traditional Torah reading for the second day of Shavuot. In Israel, where only one day of Shavuot is celebrated, this reading has been eclipsed by the revelation of the Ten Commandments (Ex. 19 and 20).

8. Homiletically, Rabbi Epstein in his *Arukh HaShulḥan* says that the barley offering is symbolic of animal food which is where the Jews start off when they leave Egypt, while the two wheat breads, human food, symbolize what the Jews become as a result of receiving the Torah – fully human. However, this homiletic explanation

Fourth, according to rabbinic tradition, if we accept Maimonides' explanation for why we count forty-nine days, we are actually off by one day. According to that tradition, the Exodus took place on a Thursday and the revelation at Sinai took place on a Shabbat.[9] This means that the revelation actually took place fifty-one days after the Exodus, not fifty. This led biblical exegetes like Don Isaac Abrabanel and Samson Raphael Hirsch in their respective commentaries to Leviticus 23:9–22 to disassociate the holiday of Shavuot from the day of the Sinai revelation.[10]

In addition to these four questions, which place Maimonides' identification of Shavuot with the revelation at Mount Sinai in a problematic light, careful scrutiny of the biblical and rabbinic traditions reveals many other anomalies regarding the Omer, the counting of the Omer, and the celebration of Shavuot, which call out for further explanation.

The Omer is brought on the second day of Passover. It seems odd that the ritual of the bringing of the Omer and the onset of the count is interposed into the holiday of Passover rather than initiated at its start. It would be analogous to the Bible requiring the eating of matza beginning on the second day of Passover and the taking of the Four Species on

---

inadvertently demeans the offering of the barley crop which God bestowed upon the Jewish people, for which they are to thank God by offering their first yield, and which allows them to begin to eat of all the new grains during the year. The Midrash Rabba on Lev. 28:6 forewarns treating the Omer of barley with contempt or relative disdain by categorically stating: "One should never treat the mitzva of the bringing of the Omer lightly."

9. In the Babylonian Talmud (Shabbat 86b–87b), there is a disagreement between the rabbis and R. Yossi as to what day precisely the revelation took place. Rabbi Abraham Gombiner, the *Magen Avraham*, a seventeenth-century Polish commentator on the *Shulḥan Arukh*, the code of Jewish law authored by Rabbi Joseph Karo, states categorically in agreement with Rabbi Yossi's opinion in the Talmud (*Oraḥ Ḥayim* 494) that the revelation took place on the seventh day of Sivan, and not on Shavuot, which commences on the sixth day of Sivan.

10. See also Baruch Halevi Epstein (the son of Rabbi Yechiel Epstein cited above) in his commentary on the prayer book entitled *Barukh SheAmar*, who points out that this is why we say in the *Amida* that Shavuot is "**Zeman matan Toratenu**" rather than "**Yom matan Toratenu**" – the "period" rather than the "day" of the giving of the Torah – since we are off by one day; see also Rabbi Mosheh Lichtenstein: "The upshot of all of these calendar calculations is that Shavuot is essentially independent of *Matan Torah* and its essence must be sought elsewhere," http://vbm-torah.org/shavuot/shv6oml.htm.

the second day of Sukkot. Also oddly, while stating the requirement, the biblical text fails to spell out what grain should be used for the offering of the Omer (spelt? oats? barley?) and in what condition it should be brought (as a sheaf of raw grain? baked into a bread?).[11] One ponders further why the Bible prohibits the eating of the new grain harvest until the Omer is brought (Ex. 23:14) and what the Bible meant to signify by having the Omer and the Two Breads waved by the priest outward and then inward, up and then down (Menaḥot 61a, 62a).

Regarding the counting of the Omer, there seems to be unusual biblical emphasis on the Shabbat.[12] Perhaps related to this is the prevailing rabbinic tradition that one needs to count the passing of weeks as well as the passing of days, a redundancy whose purpose is unclear.[13] Nor is it obvious why the tradition insists that every single Jew should count the Omer[14] and it is not sufficient for the Jewish community as a unit to count the forty-nine days. After all, only one Omer grain offering was brought in Temple times by the priest on behalf of the entire Jewish nation on the second day of Passover. One would thus think that the nation of Israel or its representative in Temple times, the High Court in Jerusalem, would alone be commanded to count.[15] In fact, the tradition seems quite strict about this requirement on each individual, as the dominant rabbinic position states that if one missed counting for a day, one can no longer continue the count with a blessing.[16]

---

11. In contrast, the Torah does specify that the Two Breads offering brought in Temple times on Shavuot should be made of fine flour (wheat) and brought as two baked breads.
12. The Torah tells us that the count should proceed for precisely "seven Shabbats" beginning with the "day after Shabbat" (by which the tradition really means "the day after the first day of Passover," in itself a strange use of language that calls out for an explanation), and extending until the seventh "Shabbat."
13. Maimonides, *Sefer Avoda*, Laws of Regular and Supplemental Sacrifices 7:22.
14. Ibid., 7:24.
15. In fact, for the counting of the forty-nine years toward the Jubilee, the fiftieth year, the command to count was incumbent only on the High Court in Jerusalem – not on each and every individual Jewish person (Maimonides, *Sefer Zera'im* [Book of Seeds], Laws of the Sabbatical Year and Jubilee 10:1).
16. Rabbi Joseph Karo, *Shulḥan Arukh, Oraḥ Ḥayim*, Laws of Passover, 489:8. There is no "make up" from one day to the next, and each day is self-contained. In contrast,

Finally, after concluding the three **ritual** commandments – of the Omer offering, the counting of the Omer, and the offering of the Two Breads on Shavuot – the Torah suddenly digresses into the **ethical** laws of leaving the fallen gleanings and corners of the field unharvested so that the stranger and impoverished members of society can gather them. This digression, which brings the biblical section on the Omer and Shavuot to a close, causes nearly all biblical commentators to speculate why these ethical laws toward one's fellow Jews are inserted here as the denouement of the preceding ritual laws toward God.[17]

UNLOCKING THE MYSTERY: THE TRAUMATIC EXPERIENCE OF THE JEWISH PEOPLE IN EGYPT

To identify the revelatory event in the Bible that is the basis for the traditions surrounding the Omer and the celebration of Shavuot, we must return to the Jewish people's foundational story, the story of the slavery experience in Egypt.[18]

Three elements marked the bondage of the Jewish people in Egypt. The first was the rigor of the work and the bitterness it seared into their souls: "And they embittered their lives with hard labor, with mortar and bricks and with all types of field work; all of the work which they forced them to do was rigorous" (Ex. 1:14). This backbreaking, heavy construction work in the mud and mortar of Egypt was the first element that epitomized our people's slavery experience in Egypt.[19]

---

in Temple times, if one missed bringing the Passover offering, one still had the opportunity to do so thirty days later.

17. The question is further exacerbated by the fact that these laws were already stated almost verbatim just four chapters earlier in Lev. 19:9–10.

18. The centrality of Passover to understanding the Omer and Shavuot traditions is implied both by the text in Deut. 16:12 – "You should remember that you were enslaved in Egypt and you should therefore guard and perform these laws" – and by the onset of the count during the Passover holiday.

19. As we saw in the previous chapter, the memory of this brutal, embittering work is why *ḥaroset* and *maror* are eaten at the Passover Seder. See also *Leading the Passover Journey*, 11–12, 31–33. This brutal slave labor is precisely what the Bible emphatically outlawed thrice when it set strict parameters for sanctioned servitude toward one's fellow Jews (Lev. 25:43, 46, 53).

The second characteristic of this enslavement is that with all their backbreaking work, the Jews had nothing to show for it but the barest necessities of subsistence – a bit of flour and water that enabled them to make matza, poor man's bread. The Passover Haggada states: "This is the bread of poverty that our ancestors ate in the land of Egypt." The matza upon which this passage is recited is the smaller, broken half of the middle matza, symbolizing not merely the poor quality but the meager, insufficient quantity of the foodstuff available for the poor Jewish slaves in Egypt.[20]

The third aspect that marked the Jewish people's slavery was that the work never ended. There was no day of rest, no Sabbath, no holidays off from work, and certainly no Sabbatical years, just endless, grueling work every day, all day, seven days a week, fifty-two weeks a year until one's dying day. When Moses approached Pharaoh to request, not political freedom, but merely a three-day religious festival for the Jewish slaves, Pharaoh attributed the request to the surfeit of free time that the Jewish "slackers" had on their hands. In response, Pharaoh increased the workload of his already exhausted slave laborers.[21]

In the biblical narrative, after God "remembered His covenant with Abraham, Isaac, and Jacob" (Ex. 2:24) and decided to take the Jewish people out of slavery in Egypt, God faced perhaps an even more difficult challenge, namely, how to take the trauma of Egyptian slavery out of the hearts and souls of the Jewish people. God had to figure out a way to heal their suffering psyches before He could hope to transform them into a holy people at Mount Sinai.

How did God meet this challenge? First, God brought the ten plagues in Egypt, which demonstrated that the Jewish people had a

---

20. As we saw in the previous chapter, Jews today identify with their ancestors and remember the hunger that they experienced as slaves by eating the same broken matza at their Passover Seder. See also *Leading the Passover Journey*, 1–4, 40–42.
21. Ex. 5:4–9. In the Bible, the prohibition of work on the Sabbath and holidays (Lev. 23), the various laws pertaining to the abstinence from agricultural work during the Sabbatical and Jubilee years (Lev. 25), as well as the six-year limitation on Hebrew indentured servitude (Ex. 21:2) were ways in which the Torah, in effect, later outlawed this type of unceasing, endless slavery.

champion for their cause.[22] Second, at the sea, God's saving power caused the Egyptian army to drown before the Jewish people's very eyes.[23] When the Jewish people encountered God's saving power and saw the Egyptian army decimated before them, their fears of being recaptured by Pharaoh's troops and taken back into slavery, or worse, massacred on the seashore were, once and for all, eradicated. This liberating revelatory event, as we saw in the previous chapter, is commemorated on the seventh day of Passover.

After the plagues and nightmares, however, there remained a people conditioned to slavery, a people used to endless toil and to a dry, flat, tasteless life, a people who were still perpetually anxious and insecure, who did not trust the world and who, after the passage of only three, thirst-filled days in the desert, no longer trusted God, the source and foundation of the world (Ex. 15:22–24). "Healing" the Jewish people from their traumatic experiences in Egypt thus became an urgent divine concern. As the Torah explicitly states shortly after the splitting of the sea and just prior to the story of the manna: "If you surely listen to the voice of the EverPresent your God ... I will spare you from every malady which I set upon Egypt, for I am the EverPresent God your healer" (Ex. 15:26).

HEALING THE JEWISH PEOPLE FROM THE TRAUMA OF SLAVERY: THE GIFT OF THE MANNA

How did God continue the healing of this people? As the Jewish people traveled deeper into the desert, they ran out of food. As recounted in

---

22. By the tenth plague, the Jewish people's confidence was built up enough that each Jewish family summoned the courage to slaughter a lamb, an Egyptian idol, and smear its blood on their doorposts and lintels, in the face, as it were, of their Egyptian overlords and taskmasters.

23. During the ten plagues, the Jewish people were sequestered in the Egyptian district of Goshen. There, they certainly witnessed the **results** of the plagues (see Deut. 4:34) and heard the anguished cries of the Egyptian households when their firstborns perished in the tenth plague (Ex. 12:30), but they did not see the **actual** plagues as they were striking the Egyptians in real time. That is why the Torah, in describing the events of splitting the sea, utilized a threefold expression of seeing to emphasize the uniqueness of that experience: "And the Jewish people **saw** the Egyptian [army] dead on the seashore; and the Jewish people **saw** the 'great hand' which God had used against the Egyptians; and the people **saw** (lit., were awed by) God, and they trusted God and Moses His servant" (Ex. 14:30–31).

Exodus 16, on the fifteenth day of Iyar, the second month in the Jewish calendar (thirty days after they left Egypt), they challenged Moses and Aaron: "If only you had let us perish at God's hand in the land of Egypt ... rather than take us to this desert to cause this whole mass of people to perish of famine" (Ex. 16:3). In response to these cries of anguish, God made a "house call" to the Jewish people. God revealed His presence before the entire nation and promised to further heal them by raining down upon them "bread from the heavens," which the people later called "manna":

> And Moses and Aaron said to all the Jewish community, "In the evening you shall know it was the EverPresent God who took you out of the land of Egypt and in the morning you will see the presence of God ...." Then Moses said to Aaron, "Say to the entire community of the Jewish people, 'Approach God for He has heard your complaints.'" And as Aaron was speaking to the entire community of the Jewish people, they turned toward the desert, and behold, the presence of God appeared in a cloud. The EverPresent God spoke to Moses: "I have heard the complaints of the Jewish people. Speak to them and say, '... In the morning you shall have your fill of bread and you shall know that I am the EverPresent, your God.'" (Ex. 16:6–12)

From the narrative, we see that the people not only come forward, at Aaron's request, to meet God, but God's presence comes forward as it did on the night of the Exodus and during the splitting of the sea to rendezvous with the people and address their needs. This revelation of God's presence, heralding the arrival of the manna to all the Jewish people, is the reason we count the Omer and celebrate Shavuot.

The gift of the manna was expressed in three miracles, three manifestations of the Divine Presence, corresponding to the three traumatic elements of Egyptian slavery.

First, the manna was a gift of bread that came directly from the heavens. In Pharaoh's universe of harsh slave labor, the Jewish people had to search for and gather straw, which they then had to mix with mortar, to make the bricks, to build the buildings, to erect Pharaoh's garrison cities, to be able to eat a meager meal (Ex. 5:6–19 and 1:11–14). In contrast, in God's universe, the Jewish people needed only to step outside their tents and gather up the fresh, door-to-door delivery of their daily bread.[24] The desert floor, quite literally, was God's table, and the layer of dew served as the tablecloth upon which God served the people/guests their heavenly meal, as described in the Book of Exodus:

> In the morning, a layer of dew fell around the camp. When the dew lifted, there over the surface of the desert lay a fine and flaky substance, as fine as frost on the ground. When the Jewish people saw it, they said to one another, "What is it?" ("*Man hu?*") – for they did not know what it was. And Moses said to them, "This is the bread which the EverPresent God has given you to eat." (Ex. 16:13–15)

Second, the enriched bread, or *leḥem ashira*, that was the manna, was quite a contrast to the *leḥem oni* (Deut. 16:3), the poor man's bread of matza, which was the Jewish people's food staple in Egypt. The Torah describes it as having the appearance and texture of white coriander seed with a taste described variously as wafers dipped in honey (Ex. 16:31) or rich crème (Num. 11:8). The description of this thick, luscious bread is meant to remind the people, and the biblical reader, of the land toward which the people were journeying: "*eretz zavat ḥalav udvash*" – a land dripping with milk and honey. Furthermore, unlike the scant quantity of available food in Egypt, there was enough manna to fully satiate each and every person (Ex. 16:8, 12). Miraculously, no matter how much manna a person gathered, he or she always ended up with exactly the same amount: "*omer lagulgolet, mispar nafshotekhem*," "exactly one **omer** for each person, according to the **count** of the people" (Ex. 16:15–18). No more food shortages, no more broken fragments of matza with which to try to fill their empty stomachs.[25]

---

24. Ex. 16:13–18. Also compare the language of quotas/rations, *dvar yom beyomo*, in Ex. 5:13, 19 and 16:4. These are the only two places in the Torah that this language appears.
25. In Yoma 75a, R. Abbuha, who understood the healing and nurturing purpose of the manna, comments on the term in Num. 11 that describes the taste of the manna as

Today, the manna may be symbolically remembered through the custom to eat dairy foods, and specifically cheesecake, on Shavuot; in fact, the latter seems to be an unconscious reenactment of the eating of the manna. Just as the Jewish people are commanded to eat matza during Passover to commemorate what their ancestors ate during the Exodus, so too do they customarily eat cheesecake to commemorate the sweet, rich, white, and creamy food that the Jewish people began to eat thirty days after departing Egypt, as they approached the foothills of Sinai, where they stood to receive the Ten Commandments.[26]

Third, the manna obviated the need to work on the Sabbath. Although one omer of manna fell on the first five days of the week, two omers of heavenly bread, *lehem mishneh*, miraculously fell on the day prior to the Sabbath, providing enough food for both days.[27] The Torah describes this novelty:

> On the sixth day they gathered double the amount of bread (*lehem mishneh*), two omers for each; and when all the heads of the community came and told Moses, he said to them, "This is what the EverPresent God said: 'Tomorrow is a day of rest, a sacred Sabbath for the EverPresent God. Bake what you want to bake and cook what you want to cook, and all that is left put aside to be kept until morning.'" (Ex. 16:22–23)

Unlike the manna that fell on Sunday through Thursday, which would spoil if it was left over for a second day, the two omers of manna that fell on Friday wondrously did not spoil the next day (Ex. 16:19–25). This double gift, this double portion of bread for

---

"*leshad hashamen*," "rich crème," that it should be read not as *leshad*, crème or cake, but as *shad* – breast: "As the infant finds many tastes in his mother's breast milk so also did Israel find many tastes in the manna."

26. This may explain why R. Elazar, in Pesahim 68b, insists that an integral part of the holiday of Shavuot entails feasting to celebrate the holiday.

27. Because of these two bread portions, the Jewish tradition designates the two breads (*hallot*) eaten by Jews on the Shabbat as "*lehem mishneh*" in commemoration of the double portion of manna.

the Sabbath, taught the Jewish people to trust the world and to trust the Creator and Sustainer of that world.[28] No more seven-day workweeks, fifty-two weeks per year, as in Egypt; now, one day a week, each and every week, the Jewish people in the desert would rest from work on the Sabbath in identification with their Creator and Redeemer.[29]

REMEMBERING AND RECIPROCATING THE GIFT OF THE MANNA: THE OMER

God wanted the memory of the miraculous manifestation of the Divine Presence through the daily gift of the manna to be safeguarded not only

28. This is why in the holy section of the Mishkan, the display breads on the table were arranged in six pairs of two breads each for a total of twelve breads. These signified God's feeding of the twelve tribes of Israel during their desert wanderings, and were arranged in pairs to remind the people of the double portion of manna that fell on Fridays. Like the manna, of which a double portion fell on Friday in order to provide for the Shabbat, the display breads were also baked in pairs on Fridays, the day that the double manna fell, in preparation for being placed on the Mishkan's table on Shabbat. Each display bread was also made from two omers of fine flour (Lev. 24:5), symbolizing the amount of manna that fell for each person on each Friday (see Maimonides, *Mishneh Torah*, Laws of Regular and Supplementary Offerings 5:7, 10). Maimonides, in Book III:45 of *Guide for the Perplexed* writes: "As to the table and the bread that was always upon it, I do not know the reason for this and I have not found up to now something to which I might ascribe this practice." Our explanation provides such a reason.

While the display breads were prepared and replaced in the Mishkan on a weekly basis, the High Priest also brought a meal offering that was entirely burnt on the Sacrificial Altar every single day (*minḥat tamid*). This offering consisted of twelve wafers, baked and then fried in olive oil, half of which were brought with a dash of frankincense in the morning and half in the evening (Lev. 6:12–16; Maimonides, *Sefer Avoda*, Laws of the Sacrificial Process 13:2–4). The twelve wafers totaled one omer (one-tenth of an ephah) – a clear correlation and reciprocation for the omer of manna that tasted like wafers dipped in honey and which fell daily in the desert. Thus, in Mishkan/Temple times the manna was commemorated daily through this offering of the High Priest, weekly through the display breads on the Show Table, and annually through the Omer and Two Breads offerings. This triple commemoration throughout the year mirrored the threefold command to safeguard the manna as a keepsake for all generations (Ex. 16:32–35).

29. See Pesaḥim 117b, *Tosafot*, s.v. *"Lemaan Tizkor"*; see also Maimonides, *Guide for the Perplexed* II:31 and III:43.

for the generation of the desert but for all generations. At God's behest, Moses instructed Aaron to put an omer of manna in a jug, to be later placed next to the Ark of Testimony that was to contain the Ten Commandments. Three times the Torah describes this jug containing the omer of manna as a "*mishmeret ledorotekhem*," a way of safeguarding the memory of this remarkable, healing gift for future generations (Ex. 16:32–34).

This plan for preserving the manna and its memory was designed to salve the long-term trauma in the Jewish collective psyche induced by Pharaoh's regimen of cruel slavery. It was meant to instill the memory of divine love and healing shown by God to His people not only for the forty years that they wandered in the desert, but for all time. Like the Ark of Testimony before which it was to be placed, the jug would testify to God's beneficent sustenance of His people:

> Moses said, "This is what the EverPresent God has commanded: 'Let one omer of [manna] be safeguarded throughout the generations, in order that they may see the bread that I fed you in the desert when I took you out of the land of Egypt.'" And Moses said to Aaron, "Take a jug, put one omer of manna in it and place it before the EverPresent God, to be safeguarded throughout the generations." And Aaron placed it before the Ark of Testimony as a keepsake, as the EverPresent God had commanded Moses. (Ex. 16:32–35)

But despite this physical evidence, God knew that an earthenware jug of manna was indeed a fragile vessel within which to preserve memory for all generations. Therefore, God instituted a "backup system" to remember the threefold miracle of the manna: the threefold rituals of the Omer offering, the counting of the Omer, and the first fruits offering of the two wheat breads.[30]

---

30. It is important to note the philological support for interpreting the bringing and counting of the Omer as related to the omer of manna. The word "omer" appears for the first time in the Bible in Exodus 16 when it is used multiple times in describing the manna. The word does not appear again until Leviticus 23, where the bringing of the Omer is commanded and where it again appears multiple times. It is interesting that the only other book in the Bible in which the word "omer" appears more than once is the Book of Ruth (see below, "Emulating the Gift of the Manna: Biblical

The Omer offering was an omer of barley from the new harvest that was brought as a gift into the Temple on the second day of Passover and demonstratively waved toward the heavens by the priest. This gift was the acknowledgment by later generations of the Jewish people that their food, which they grew and gathered in the Land of Israel, was no less heaven-sent than the manna bread which fell directly from heaven for the generation that left Egypt. Moses, in the Book of Deuteronomy, makes this very point to the next generation of Israelites. He reminds those about to enter the Promised Land that God brought the manna to make them aware that "human beings do not live by bread alone but rather by virtue of God's promise (lit., word)"(Deut. 8:3). Moses may be alluding here to God's promise in Exodus 16 to satiate the people with bread every single day that they wandered in the desert – a promise that God fully kept. Using the manna as a springboard, Moses also pointed forward in time to God's promise to bring the people to a fertile land flowing with milk and honey that would fully provide for their sustenance (Deut. 8:7–10).

The Omer offering of barley as well as the double Omer offering of wheat were brought as gifts from these two new grain harvests to pay God back in kind. Just as **God gave** the Jewish people who left Egypt their first, fresh bread after they ran out of matza in the desert, so too did later generations of **Jews give** God their first, fresh bread from the grains which they grew in their richly fertile land. This is why no new grain (*ḥadash*) could be eaten prior to bringing the Omer offering (Lev. 23:14). As the generation of the desert had no bread to eat prior to God's gift of the manna, so too did later generations refrain from eating

---

Ethics and the Book of Ruth"). It is also worth noting that the episode of the manna in Exodus 16 concludes by giving us a piece of information that ties it directly to the beginning of the section regarding the Omer in Leviticus 23. The text tells us: "And the Jewish people ate the manna for forty years, until they arrived in the land of their habitation; they ate the manna until they came to the edge of the land of Canaan." The commandment of the Omer in Leviticus picks up on this language by commencing, "When you come to the land that I am giving you." The commandments surrounding the Omer are made explicitly dependent on the arrival in the land (see below: "The Omer Calendar").

bread of their new grain crops until they had symbolically returned God's gift through the Omer and first fruits offerings.[31]

The biblical law to dedicate the first yield of one's grain crops to God mirrors the biblical command given immediately after the Exodus to dedicate the firstborn of one's children and livestock to God (Ex. 13:2, 11ff.). There, because God spared the Jewish firstborns in Egypt, the Jewish people reciprocated God's kindness by dedicating their firstborns to God. Here, because God spared their ancestors from starvation in the desert, the Jewish people offered God their first barley and wheat crops each year before eating from the land's new yield.

The offering of the Omer of barley, as well as the offering of the Two Breads of baked wheat, were waved by the priest out and then in, up and then down, to show that the people had to go **out** to gather **in** the manna, and to demonstrate that the food brought **up** from the ground of the Land of Israel was as much a gift of the Divine as was the manna that rained **down** each morning from the heavens.[32]

In the Jewish legal tradition, there is further congruence between the commands to bring the Omer and Two Breads found in Leviticus and the manna saga found in Exodus. First, the Torah in Leviticus does not specify that the Omer should be brought from the first cuttings of the barley crop. The Torah simply states: "When you come to the land which I am giving to you, and you cut the harvest, then you shall bring an Omer of the first cuttings to the priest" (Lev. 23:10). Like the manna in Exodus which the Jewish people had difficulty identifying (asking "*Man hu?*" "What is this?" and thus introducing the name "manna") until Moses told them expressly, "This is the bread that God has given you to eat" (Ex. 16:15), there is mystery in the Torah surrounding the "identity" of the Omer offering and the manner in which it is to be prepared.[33]

---

31. The blessing for bread thanks God for "bringing forth bread from the ground." This is also why today Jews utter a blessing thanking God before eating any food. According to Berakhot 35a, to do otherwise would be a form of ingratitude or, even worse, theft from the Divine.

32. See also the commentary of the *Sefat Emet* on Shavuot in his *derashot* on Numbers, where he too compares and contrasts the "*leḥem min haaretz*," the Two Breads waved by the priests, with the "*leḥem min hashamayim*" of the manna.

33. Ground and prepared with olive oil, as were other grain offerings in the Temple.

The Torah leaves it to the Oral Tradition (according to Maimonides, a tradition taught by Moses as a verbal, rather than written, Sinaitic tradition) to tell us that the Omer offering was in fact a barley offering, to be prepared like other sacrificial offerings.[34] Thus, the command to bring the Omer prompts the reader of Leviticus to ask metaphorically *"Man hu?"* – "What type of offering is this?" – just as the Jewish people asked when they first received the manna. In both cases, it is Moses who explains what the bread is.

Second, after the Jewish people who left Egypt learned from Moses what the manna was, when Friday arrived in the desert they were puzzled anew about why they had received a double portion. The Torah explains that the double portion was provided on Friday so that they could prepare some of it before Shabbat: "Bake whatever you want to bake, and cook whatever you want to cook" (Ex. 16:22–23). Therefore, the Torah specifies clearly that the Two Breads offering on Shavuot, which symbolizes the people's gratitude for the double portion of manna that God provided the Jewish people in the desert for Shabbat,[35] should be kneaded and **baked** beforehand into breads before they are offered. And unlike the Omer of barley bread which was cut and prepared even on Shabbat,[36] the offering of the Two Breads, which was meant to thank God for the double gift of manna that freed them from work on Shabbat, was not allowed to be prepared in violation of the Sabbath.[37]

THE OMER CALENDAR

When was the Omer offering brought? The Torah in Leviticus states:

> **When you come to the land** that I am giving to you and you cut the harvest, **then you shall bring an omer** of the first cuttings…. And [the priest] will wave the Omer before God to

---

34. See Menaḥot 68b which bases itself on the analogy of the crops of spring in Ex. 9:31; see also Maimonides, *Mishneh Torah*, Laws of Regular and Supplementary Sacrifices 7:12.
35. Ex. 16:22 – "*leḥem mishneh, shenei haomer.*"
36. Menaḥot 72b; Y. Rosh HaShana 1:8; Megilla 2:7. See also Maimonides, ibid. 7:6, 11.
37. Menaḥot 95b; Maimonides, ibid. 8:8.

win acceptance for you, on the day following the day of rest (*mimaḥarat HaShabbat*). (Lev. 23:10)

We know from the fifth chapter of the Book of Joshua that the manna ceased to fall and that the Jewish people began to eat the produce of the Land of Israel on the second day of Passover. The words regarding the bringing of the Omer in Leviticus, "When you come to the land," were not meant only metaphorically but literally. The people were commanded to bring the Omer and begin the count each and every year precisely on the anniversary of the day that the Jewish people, led by Joshua, "came to the land," cut their first harvest, and began to eat from the produce of the land – that is, the second day of Passover.[38]

The Torah instructed the Jewish people to bring the Omer when they entered and cut the harvest of the Land of Israel because so long as the manna fell and fed them in their desert wanderings, there was no danger of them forgetting it, or the divine source of their food. However, as soon as the manna ceased to fall and the Jewish people entered the Land of Israel, cut the harvest by themselves, and began to eat from the natural produce of the land, they were prone to forget not only the manna but also its source, and the source of their new, land-based sustenance. In fact, in Deuteronomy, Moses forewarned the people regarding the danger of forgetfulness once they settled into the land:

> Be very careful! Lest the people forget the EverPresent, your God … lest they eat and become satisfied … and the people become haughty and forget the EverPresent, your God, who took you out of the land of Egypt, the house of bondage. Who led you through the great and awesome desert and fed you manna in the desert … lest you say to

---

38. Josh. 5:11 – note the language "*mimaḥarat HaPesaḥ*," the day following Passover, which closely parallels the language of Lev. 23:15, "*mimaḥarat HaShabbat*." This adds credence to the Pharisaic sages' claim in Menaḥot 65b, in contrast to the Sadducee scholars (the *Tzedukim* and *Baitusim*), that the term *mimaḥarat HaShabbat* likewise refers to the day following Passover, and not the day following the Sabbath. See Maimonides, *Mishneh Torah*, Laws of Regular and Supplemental Sacrifices 7:11, where he also links the two.

yourselves: "My strength and the power of my efforts [alone] produced my success." Therefore remember that it is the EverPresent,
your God, who gives you the strength to be successful. (Deut. 8:11–17)

Accordingly, the people were instructed to bring the Omer offering and to commence the count of the Omer each and every year
on the anniversary of the day that the manna ceased and the Jewish
people began to eat of the land's produce. This taught them that just
as God nurtured the Jewish people with the manna every day that
they were in the desert, so too it is God – and not merely their own
efforts – who feeds them and sustains them every day that they are
in their land.[39]

The Omer is counted day by day, as God "counted" and appor-
tioned one omer of manna for each and every Jewish person each day
(Ex. 16:16). Rather than have the counting done collectively (i.e., symbolically, by the court) as was done in establishing the Sabbatical and
Jubilee years, every single, individual person was instructed to count the
Omer.[40] This obligation of each individual person to count the Omer
mirrored God's provision for each individual of the amount of food
necessary to sustain them and satiate their appetites.

The connection between God's provision of the manna and our
personal obligation to count the Omer is alluded to in the following
midrash:[41]

R. Benaya said: The Holy One, Blessed Be He, said to Israel, "My
children, when I gave you the Omer, I would give each and every one
of you an omer of food, as it says: 'An omer for each person, according to the count of the number of souls to take into their tents.' Now
that you give Me an Omer, you only give Me an offering of one omer
from all of you, and moreover it is only from barley and not from

---

39. This is precisely why this chapter of Joshua is read as the *haftara* of the first day of
    Passover – to remind us of the reason why we begin the count that evening.
40. "*USefartem – shetehei sefira lekhol eḥad ve'eḥad*" (Menaḥot 65b).
41. *Pesikta DeRav Kahana* (Mandelbaum edition, *piska* 8 – the mitzva of the Omer,
    paragraph beginning, "R. Avin said, come." See also *Pesikta Rabbati*, Ish Shalom
    edition, *piska* 18, on the Omer, words beginning, "What is the advantage to man").

wheat." Therefore Moses cautions the Israelites that "you" [plural] should count.[42]

Tradition enjoins that one may not miss a day of the count and make it up the next day,[43] just as in the biblical narrative the Jewish people were not permitted to leave over part of their omer of manna from one day to the next (Ex. 16:19–20).

In addition to the Omer being counted by the passing of each day, the Omer is also counted by the passing of the weeks. This parallels how God kept count, as it were, of the passing of the week so as to provide a double amount of manna each Friday in anticipation of the people's Shabbat respite. In turn, the people in the desert learned to keep count of the passing of each week in order to know when they were permitted to gather two omers in preparation for the Sabbath.[44] This was the way that God educated the Jewish people to rest on and observe the Sabbath.[45]

Finally, two omers of leavened, "enriched" wheat bread were brought in the Mishkan as a first fruits offering on the holiday of Shavuot

---

42. Implying, as in Menaḥot 65b above, that each person individually should count.
43. With a blessing; however if one missed a day of the count, one can continue the count on the remaining days without a blessing. See Rabbi Israel Meir Kagan, *Mishna Berura*, Laws of Passover, 489:8.
44. After completing this chapter of the book, I was pleased to find that the essential insight of the Omer commemorating the manna, as well as several of the details – including the reason for the offering of the Omer on the sixteenth of Nisan, as well as the counting of both the weeks and days – to have been presaged in the second volume of a two-volume Hebrew work, *Be'er Yosef Al HaTorah* (Jerusalem: Mekhon Beit Horaah Publishing, 1972), 48–55. This work was authored by Rabbi Yosef Zvi Salant (1885–1981), a pious scholar and teacher in Jerusalem of the *Musar* ethical movement. The volumes received the approbation of Rabbi Shlomo Zalman Auerbach (1910–1995), one of the most outstanding and beloved Torah scholars in Jerusalem during the late twentieth century. I am indebted to Edo Pollack for calling my attention to Rabbi Salant's insights during his 2015 Shabbat HaGadol *derasha* in our neighborhood synagogue. Rabbi Salant's hermeneutics lend support to the core thesis of this chapter and my own, independently developed, understandings of the biblical text, which I first published in the Spring 1999 edition of *The Jewish Spectator*.
45. Ex. 16:23–29. Even though, according to rabbinic tradition, Moses first taught the Jewish people about Shabbat at Marah (Sanhedrin 56b commenting on Ex. 15:25), nevertheless the people only learned to internalize the observance of Shabbat through the story of the manna.

to symbolize the two omers of manna, God's enriched bread, that fell each Friday in the desert in preparation for Shabbat (Ex. 16:22). Just as Shabbat is the seventh day that caps the completion of each week, so too is Shavuot the day that caps the completion of seven complete weeks (Lev. 23:15). Philologically, the centrality of the Shabbat component of Shavuot is emphasized in Leviticus 23 by the fourfold repetition of the word "Shabbat," which parallels the fourfold repetition of the word "Shabbat" in the manna narrative of Exodus 16.[46] It is further worth noting that the Hebrew word "*Shavuot*" contains within it the letters of both the word "*Shabbat*" and "*sheva*" (seven), and represents a shortened form, therefore, of *sheva Shabbatot*, or seven weeks, the length of time necessary to complete the count of the Omer.

This begs the question of why the biblical text places so much emphasis on Shabbat within the context of the story of the manna. Perhaps because the concept of the seven-day week, with the seventh day a day of rest, was revolutionary in the ancient world. Unlike the day, month, or year, each of which has a parallel in the natural universe, the seven-day week with the first six days being designated as days of work and the seventh as a day of rest, was largely a biblical construct. Egypt, the land in which the Jews lived for two centuries, had a ten-day week with no day of rest.[47] The Jewish people learned about this revolutionary seven-day construct in practical terms through the rhythm of the falling and gathering of the manna, one month after they left Egypt.

Therefore, the Torah commanded that forty years later, when the Jewish people would come to the land, at the completion of seven seven-day weeks, on the holiday of "weeks," "Shavuot," they should bring two baked breads as an offering in the Mishkan to

---

46. First, Exodus: "And (Moses) said to them, 'This is what God has spoken – a **Shabbaton**, a holy **Shabbat** to God tomorrow...' And Moses said: 'Eat it today, because today is **Shabbat** for God.... Six days shall you gather but on the seventh day, **Shabbat**, there will not be manna to gather" (Ex.16:23–26). Now, Leviticus: "From the day after **Shabbat** the priest shall wave it ... and you shall count for yourselves seven complete **Shabbatot** beginning from the day following the **Shabbat**, the day that you brought the waved Omer, until the day after the seventh **Shabbat**, you shall count fifty days" (Lev. 23:11, 15–16).

47. http://www.polysyllabic.com/?q=calhistory/earlier/egyptian.

commemorate the gift of the two omers of manna bread that enabled them to rest at the end of each week while they wandered in the desert. By bringing the two wheat breads on Shavuot, they were able to offer a symbolic token of gratitude to God for providing them with enough food so that they could cease work one day each week and celebrate the Sabbath.[48]

To sum up our thesis until now: The Omer sacrifice, the counting of the Omer, and the gift of the Two Breads that was brought on Shavuot to the Temple were rituals that helped the Jewish people recall and reciprocate the threefold miracle of the manna. The provision of the heaven-sent manna bread to the Jewish people journeying through the desert was remembered through the bringing of the Omer offering in the Temple; the allocation and accounting of precisely one omer of manna for each person each day was – and is – remembered by the counting of the Omer by each person, each day; and the provision of a double omer of manna bread to enable the people in the desert to cease work on Shabbat was remembered by the bringing of a double omer of baked bread after the completion of seven full Shabbats/weeks of counting. The threefold observance of these rituals and their remembrance was an expression of what the Jewish tradition calls *hakarat hatov* – acknowledging and thanking God for the overflowing goodness which restored our ancestors' human dignity, their *tzelem Elokim*, "divine image," after they left Egypt.[49]

EMULATING THE GIFT OF THE MANNA:
BIBLICAL ETHICS AND THE BOOK OF RUTH

The restoring of our ancestors' divine image helps us understand why the Torah concludes the ritual laws of the Omer in Leviticus with the ethical admonition to leave the gleanings and the corners of the field

---

48. Another way of explaining why the count is for fifty days is that the manna fell for exactly thirty-nine years and eleven months: 39+11 = 50.

49. Saadia Gaon, in the second section of the third chapter of his classic tenth-century philosophic work, *The Book of Doctrines and Beliefs*, predicates all of Jewish law on this principle of "*hakarat hatov*"; see Alexander Altmann, ed., *Three Jewish Philosophers* (Atheneum, 1974), 93–95. Rabbi Baḥya ibn Pekuda, in his important eleventh-century ethical work, *Duties of the Heart* (*Ḥovot HaLevavot*), makes a similar argument.

for the poor and the stranger. It also explains why we read the Book of
Ruth on Shavuot.

We said that the jug containing the omer of manna, as well as the
laws surrounding the Omer, safeguarded the memory of God's loving
nurturance and healing of the Jewish people when they emerged from
the poverty and alienation of Egyptian slavery. This safeguarding of
memory, however, was needed not only to **acknowledge and reciprocate** God's kindness through symbolic, ritual laws but to **emulate** God's
kindness through demonstrative, ethical laws.

In Egypt, the Jewish people embodied God's forecast to Abraham, their founding father, at the Covenant between the Pieces that,
"Your descendants will be **strangers** in a foreign country which will
enslave and **impoverish them**" (Gen. 15:13). God brought the manna
to restore the dignity of the collective Jewish people after the Exodus.
The Jewish people, in turn, were instructed to safeguard that lesson by
emulating God's kindness and charity to **poverty-stricken strangers**
in their midst.[50]

The biblical commandments not to harvest the corners and
fallen gleanings of the field created an ethical obligation on the landowner. They also bestowed an opportunity and a responsibility upon
the estranged and the poor to gather their food in dignity. The rich did
not simply "give charity" to the poor by leaving the gleanings and corners of the field for them. Rather, through the laws of leaving the corners
and the fallen gleanings for the poor and the stranger, the landowners
motivated and empowered the poor to work for their food by gathering
the grain with which they could bake their own bread.[51] By participating in the process of acquiring their own food, the honor and dignity of

---

50. See also Maimonides, *Guide for the Perplexed* III:54, where he ends his philosophical
    magnum opus by quoting Jer. 9:22, 23 and interpreting it to mean that human perfec-
    tion is not achieved by merely knowing God intellectually but by assimilating that
    knowledge into one's character and emulating God's virtues in compassionate and
    righteous behavior toward other people – i.e., *imitatio Dei*.
51. The importance of participating in the earning of one's bread is amplified and ex-
    panded in the kabbalistic concept known as "bread of shame" to include all benefits
    derived from this world.

the stranger and the poor as productive workers and as images of God was maintained and enhanced.

The emulation of God by restoring the dignity of the marginalized members of society is why the section of the Omer offering in Leviticus concludes with the words, "For the poor and the stranger you shall leave them, I am the EverPresent, your God" (Lev. 23:22). These words charge the biblical landowner, "Care for the poor and the stranger just as I, God, cared for you in the desert after you were impoverished and estranged in Egypt."

This may also explain why the Shavuot reading from Deuteronomy includes the injunction to "rejoice before God, you, and your son, and your daughter, and your servant, your maid, and the Levite, and the stranger, and the orphan, and the widow, who are in your midst," and concludes with the words, "Remember that you were slaves in the land of Egypt, and therefore guard and do these laws" (Deut. 16:11–12). With our new understanding of the Omer offerings and the counting of the Omer, we can parse the verse as follows: "*vezakharta*"– remember that you too were foreigners and slaves in Egypt; "*veshamarta*"– guard the ritual of counting the Omer to recall and thank God for having restored your dignity in the desert through the manna; "*ve'asita*"– act and emulate God by behaving ethically and empathetically toward the vulnerable and oppressed in your own land.

These three elements of memory,[52] observance,[53] and ethical action in *imitatio Dei*[54] are first encountered in the Shabbat, the first holy day listed in Leviticus 23 and arguably the paradigm of all sacred time in the Bible. The Jewish people were commanded to emulate God who freed the enslaved from their labors in Egypt, by freeing their workers from work on Shabbat (Deut. 5:15). Here too the Jewish people

---

52. "*Zakhor et yom HaShabbat lekadesho*," "Remember the Sabbath Day to make it sacred" (Ex. 20:8).
53. "*Shamor et yom HaShabbat*," "Observe the Sabbath Day" (Deut. 5:12).
54. The ethical dimension of Shabbat, in terms of freeing your family, servants, and even animals from work because you were slaves in Egypt, is found in the second iteration of the fourth commandment in Deut. 5:12–15. The Sabbath commandment there concludes, "Therefore your EverPresent God commanded you to **do** (*laasot*) the Shabbat."

were commanded to emulate God, who gave them the opportunity to gather their own food in dignity in the desert, by enabling the poor and estranged to gather their food in dignity in the Land of Israel.

The elements of narrative-based memory, ritual observance, and ethical emulation – the trilogy of *vezakharta, veshamarta*, and *ve'asita* – found in Deuteronomy (Deut. 16:12), were and are the inextricable building blocks of the biblical holiday cycle and of much of Judaism.

Together, memory, observance, and emulation of the Divine constitute the "*ḥut hameshulash*" (Eccl. 4:12), the intertwined triple helix of our people's spiritual DNA that gives life-sustaining meaning to the Jewish people.

Against this backdrop, we now possess a deeper understanding of why the Book of Ruth is read on Shavuot and how the narrative reminds us of the story and ethical lessons of the manna. First, like the story of the manna, the story of the Book of Ruth revolves around the shortage and then the provision of bread. In the first chapter, the family departs from and returns to Bet Leḥem, literally, "house of bread." The lack of bread during a famine precipitates a crisis, which causes the family to leave the Land of Israel. The famine's end and the return of bread then becomes the reason for Naomi and Ruth to journey back to the land and begin the process of their personal and familial redemption (Ruth 1:6). Once in the land, the entire story revolves around Ruth, who gathers grain during the barley and wheat harvest season – a seven-week time segment that coincides with the period from Passover to Shavuot in the Jewish calendar year.

Second, Ruth's personal story embodies the Jewish people's story that led up to the manna and to the ethical commands which emerged from and commemorated that story. Like the Jewish people who left Egypt, Ruth herself was both desperately poor and a stranger to the native Jewish people in the Land of Israel. She represented as an individual what the Jewish people represented as a historic community in Egypt. Like the Jewish people in the desert, Ruth was able to gather her food in dignity thanks to the graciousness and hospitality of her protector Boaz, who internalized God's commandment regarding the treatment of the stranger and the poor person in the Land of Israel, and emulated God's sustenance of the people in the desert.

It is no accident that Boaz evoked God's name even in prosaic greetings to his workers.[55] Boaz acted as God's surrogate, embodying God's image and essence and emulating God's empathetic kindness and charitable graciousness.[56] He did this by first inviting Ruth to sit at his table and physically nourishing her with "**bread dipped in a condiment**" (Ruth 2:14);[57] second, by ensuring that she be treated with solicitousness and dignity by his employees (Ruth 2:15, 16); and then by taking Ruth to be his wife (Ruth 4:13). These actions paralleled God's feeding the Jewish people with heavenly bread placed on a tablecloth of dew sitting on the desert floor; providing bread that tasted like "**wafers dipped in honey**"; restoring the people's status as images of God by enabling them to gather their daily bread in dignity; and shortly thereafter, by taking the Jewish people to be His "bride" at Mount Sinai (see Ex. 6:7 and 19:4). Both stories also end with the permanent settling of the Promised Land: Boaz enabled Naomi and Ruth to return and settle permanently in their family's ancestral parcel in the Land of Israel (Ruth 4), thus emulating God, who enabled the Jewish people to return and settle permanently in the land promised to their ancestors.

We have now put into place the final pieces of the Omer puzzle in the Torah. The counting of the Omer, the Omer sacrifice, and the gift of the first fruits were devices to remember the threefold miracle of the manna. These observances, in turn, had three purposes: to remember the miracle of the manna; to acknowledge in gratitude and ritually

---

55. "And behold, Boaz came from Bethlehem and he said to the harvesters, 'God be with you!' and they answered him, 'May God bless you!'.... And Boaz said to Ruth ... 'May God reward your work and may your reward be complete from God, the God of Israel, under whose wings you have come to seek protection'.... And he said: 'You are blessed of God, my daughter'" (Ruth 2:4, 8, 12; 3:10). Note Boaz's reference to Ruth's seeking refuge under God's protective wings, an allusion to Ex. 19:4, which is read on the holiday of Shavuot: "I have carried you on eagles' wings and brought you to Me." See also Deut. 32:11.

56. See Sota 14a: "R. Simlai taught: The Torah begins with an act of kindness and ends with an act of kindness. It begins with God clothing the naked – 'The EverPresent God made for Adam and his wife garments of skin and clothed them' – and it ends with Him caring for the dead – 'And He [God] buried [Moses] in the Valley.'"

57. By inviting her to dine among his employees, Boaz also fulfilled the commandment of *hakhnasat orḥim*, welcoming guests.

reciprocate God's loving-kindness to the Jewish people in the desert when they were exceedingly vulnerable; and to act as an ethical model for future generations to emulate God's loving-kindness, as Boaz later did, in their God-given, fertile land.

INTERNALIZING GOD'S REVELATION OF THE MANNA YEAR-ROUND

As we have seen, central to understanding the biblical story of the manna and the holiday of Shavuot is God's loving-kindness, and the biblical, ethical duty to emulate God through deeds of charity (*tzedaka*) and loving-kindness (*ḥesed*), not merely on Shavuot but throughout the year. Most of us no longer live in an agricultural economy that would permit us to care for and empower the poor and the stranger through the biblical commandments of leaving the corners of the fields and uncollected stalks unharvested. However, the laws of *tzedaka*, which command that Jews set aside a tenth of their income for the economically disadvantaged, operate along similar principles of empowering the poor person.

As Maimonides writes, the highest form of charitable giving is to offer the indigent a loan or gift, or establish a partnership with them, which will enable them to sustain themselves economically.[58] The traditions of *tzedaka* were so pervasive in Jewish communities that Maimonides states categorically, "We have never seen or heard of a Jewish community that did not set aside a repository for *tzedaka*."[59] Caring for the vulnerable and impoverished members of society by enabling them to earn their own living was the natural outgrowth of the revelation of God's saving presence in the story of the manna and the biblical, ethical laws associated with the holiday of Shavuot.

Over time, two lovely customs developed in Jewish communities to make the giving of charity a daily and weekly habit. The first is the practice to collect charity in the synagogue at the daily morning and afternoon prayer services. The second is to place a charity box in one's home adjacent to the Shabbat candlesticks and contribute to it before lighting Shabbat candles each Friday evening. Both of these customs

---

58. Maimonides, *Mishneh Torah*, Laws of Gifts to the Poor 10:7.
59. Ibid., 9:3.

are modeled on the manna, which rained down daily and was doubled on Friday in preparation for the Shabbat.

As to acts of loving-kindness, the rabbinic sages taught that the Jewish people can be identified by three character traits: modesty, compassion, and loving-kindness (Yevamot 79a). Loving-kindness, the attitude of generosity toward others through personal actions that extend beyond philanthropy, was made into a core pillar of Jewish identity. It is embodied in everything from welcoming guests and visiting the sick, to burying the dead with dignity and reaching out to their families.[60] These personal actions of *ḥesed* emerge from the consciousness of being in relation to an infinite God, who modeled these acts of kindness for the Jewish people.

In addition to these ethical actions, traditional Jews practice year-round rituals that reflect our gratitude to God for providing our sustenance. One of these is the separating of *ḥalla*, a symbolic offering of a portion of dough to God.[61] Unlike eating cheesecake, for example, which is a custom only on Shavuot, separating *ḥalla* is a biblically based "first fruit offering," mandated throughout the year whenever one kneads a substantial amount of dough. The amount of dough that requires such an offering is exactly one omer, derived from the amount of manna that fell for each person in the desert.

In addition to separating *ḥalla*, the custom to prepare for Shabbat by baking *ḥalla* and by making the blessing over two *ḥalla* loaves at all meals on Shabbat and holidays has its basis in the double portion of manna that God provided the people in anticipation of the Shabbat.

The attribution to God of our food and of the good land that produces it is also reflected in our liturgy throughout the year. Traditional

---

60. See Maimonides, *Mishneh Torah*, Laws of Mourners 13, 14.

61. Num. 15:18–21: "When you come to the land to which I am bringing you, and you eat of the bread of the land, you shall set some aside as a gift to the EverPresent God, as the first yield of your kneading dough you shall set aside." Biblically, the obligation of separating *ḥalla* is only for dough kneaded in the Land of Israel, and follows the logic of the Omer and the Two Breads offering. God provided our first bread to us in the desert so we offer God our first bread from the land. By rabbinic tradition, we continue to practice the separation of *ḥalla* even in the Diaspora.

Jews recite blessings before partaking of any food, and recite the Grace After Meals (*Birkat HaMazon*) (Deut. 8:10) or the shortened forms of Grace when a full meal has not been eaten.[62] These blessings come from our consciousness that God is the ultimate provider of all our sustenance, whether our food comes directly from heaven or appears to come from our own terrestrial efforts.

Theologically, the bringing of the Omer and the Two Breads to the Temple in biblical times taught the people that God was co-responsible for their success in the Land of Israel. This crucially important biblical insight, that our ability to sustain ourselves and even thrive is dependent on divine blessing, has huge ramifications. One often hears religious as well as secular people distinguish between what God does and what human beings do, as if what human beings are able to accomplish is independent of God. This dichotomy, between human attainment and divine beneficence, is alien to biblical Judaism. For the Bible, all that human beings achieve is ultimately attributable to God's grace.[63] This does not mean that human beings are not accountable for their actions or their successes. Human effort and striving is commanded and necessary; human agency is real and encouraged (Deut. 4:29–30). But given the infinite number of variables that can interfere with success, human will and proficiency alone are insufficient to explain human accomplishment. Moreover, an excessive belief in one's own powers often leads down a slippery slope toward arrogance and hubris. Balanced by a mature recognition of one's interdependence on God and on others, however, belief in oneself and one's abilities is a matter of both prudence and necessity.

Through all these approaches – ethical, ritual, liturgical, and theological – the principles which found expression through the Omer and the holiday of Shavuot were extended into Jewish thought and behavior throughout the year. Indeed, the powerful echoes of God's

---

62. Known in the tradition as the "Three in One" blessing ("*Al HaMihya*") and the blessing for God's creation of all forms of life and their needs ("*Borei Nefashot*").

63. This was not merely Moses' understanding in Deuteronomy but is embedded throughout the narrative of Genesis. See, for instance, Gen. 26:12, 28–30; 30:27; 39:5, 21–23. See also I Chr. 19:11–14, the first three verses of which are recited daily, 365 days a year, as part of the verses of song in the morning liturgy.

caring and concern as demonstrated by the manna continue to reverberate through all times and places in which the Jewish people find themselves.

TWO FINAL THOUGHTS ON THE CONTEMPORARY SIGNIFICANCE OF THE OMER

The giving of the manna represented the third time in the Bible that God emerged to meet the people and redeem them. But there is something of a tragic irony in the story of the manna which magnifies the importance of appreciating the miracle of the manna in our own time. For God's revelation to them in their distress, the people who were redeemed from Egypt should have been grateful. Moreover, God's raining down, day in and day out, of this wonderful, healing, white, honey-flavored food, intimating the wonderful, rich land flowing with milk and honey to which God was bringing them should have been cause for additional gratitude.[64] Yet, the Bible in the Book of Numbers tells us that the manna was spurned by these very people shortly before they rejected God's land (Num. 11:4 and ff.). The rejection of the manna by the first generation of Jews who left Egypt can be seen as both premonition and precursor to their rejection of the land in the incident of the spies (Num. 13–14).

Thirty-nine years later, in the Book of Numbers, the second generation of Jews seems not to behave much better, as they too found reason to complain about the manna (Num. 21:4–5). Given this history, learning and applying the lessons of the manna take on additional significance as a historical *tikkun*, a correction of our ancestors' double ingratitude. Today, when we in the Western world are blessed with abundant foodstuffs, the story of the manna can teach us not to take those blessings for granted, but rather to appreciate the privilege of our material well-being and use it to assist and empower those around us who are in need.

---

64. Saadia Gaon, in the introduction to *The Book of Doctrines and Beliefs*, argues that the manna was a greater miracle than all of the other miracles that the Jewish people witnessed, including the Exodus from Egypt, the splitting of the sea, and the revelation at Sinai precisely because, unlike these events which were "one-offs," the manna provided two million Jewish people with their basic sustenance, without which they could not have survived, for forty straight years (Kapach edition, Mossad HaRav Kook, Jerusalem, p. 26).

Second, the vessels with which God had hoped to preserve the memory and lessons of the manna – the jug and the meaning of the ritual laws surrounding the Omer – were shattered with the destruction of the Second Temple and lost in the course of the Jewish people's subsequent wandering in exile. The ordeal of nearly two millennia of exile severed the memory of the manna from the counting of the Omer and the holiday of Shavuot, which were supposed to recall it. Were it not for the Torah, which revelation we traditionally celebrate on Shavuot, providing the Jewish people with our historical memory, we would not know the story of the manna and the enormous kindness with which God blessed the Jewish nation in the desert.

Therefore, in addition to its intrinsic, spiritual significance, the custom of studying Torah on the night of Shavuot, and using that study to reestablish the link between the story of the manna, the rituals of the Omer, and the holiday of Shavuot, is an act of fulfilling God's desire to safeguard the memory of the manna in our collective consciousness. In the kabbalistic language of Rabbi Isaac Luria, whose contemporaries established the custom of all-night Shavuot study,[65] that mindfulness could help to spiritually gather the divine sparks and repair the "shattered vessels" of the manna and of our exile.[66] By doing so, and internalizing the manna's intended ethical and spiritual lessons, we can come closer to actualizing our nation's mission of being a blessing to the family of nations on God's good earth (Gen. 12:3).

---

65. The first *Tikkun Leil Shavuot* (lit., "the repairing of the night of Shavuot") occurred in 1533 and was led by Rabbi Joseph Karo (author of the *Shulḥan Arukh*) and Rabbi Shlomo Alkabetz (author of the *Lekha Dodi* prayer, sung on Friday nights). It is recounted in *Iggeret Alkabetz* written by the latter three years later. See Dr. Mor Altshuler, "Let Each Help His Neighbor: On the Origins of *Tikkun Leil Shavuot*," *Haaretz*, Literary Appendix (22.5.07).
66. For a basic introduction to the doctrine of the "shattered vessels" in the thought of Rabbi Isaac Luria, see Gershom Scholem, *Major Trends in Jewish Mysticism* (Schocken Books, 1961), 265–268.

Chapter Three

Rosh HaShana: Remembering the Forgotten Day[1]

Only take heed, and be very careful to guard the memory of the day you stood before God in Horeb all the days of your life, and teach about it to your children and your children's children. Do not forget the things which your eyes saw and do not remove the memory from your heart... when God spoke to you out of the fire and you heard the sound of words, but saw no image, only a sound.

(Deut. 4:9–10, 12)

Why do we commemorate the sacred day of Rosh HaShana? What revelatory event in the collective lives of the Jewish people is this holy day meant to recall and relive?

---

1. An earlier and much abbreviated version of this chapter ("Rosh HaShanah and Revelation") appeared in print on pp. 31–34 of the summer 1999 issue of the *Jewish Spectator*, vol. 64, #1, and online ("Remembrance of Trumpets Past") in the fall of 2014 on *Mosaic*, http://mosaicmagazine.com/observation/2014/09/remembrance-of-trumpets-past/.

The holiday of Rosh HaShana has always been something of an enigma. First, there seems to be no historical referent for the holiday in the Torah. Unlike Passover, which is about the Exodus from Egypt, or Sukkot, which the Torah links explicitly to the people's trek through the desert, Rosh HaShana, at first glance, seems to have no specific historical event in the Torah with which it is associated.

It is true that one rabbinic tradition and two or three lines in the liturgy teach that Rosh HaShana commemorates the creation of the world, or according to a parallel tradition, the conceiving, if not the creation, of humanity. But the question remains: Why didn't the Torah make overt the linkage between Rosh HaShana and creation? After all, the Torah states outright that Shabbat is a commemoration of creation: "Remember the Sabbath day to make it sacred .... For in six days the EverPresent God made the heaven and the earth and the sea, and all that is in them, and rested on the seventh day; therefore the EverPresent God blessed the Sabbath day and made it sacred." (Ex. 20:8, 11). If Rosh HaShana was supposed to commemorate creation as Shabbat does, why didn't the Torah say so?[2]

Second, the holiday of Rosh HaShana seems unaligned with the rest of the biblical Jewish holidays. The other holidays, it is conventionally taught, follow a historical, chronological sequence in the Torah: Passover represents the Exodus; Shavuot, which occurs fifty days later, corresponds to the Sinai revelation which took place about seven weeks later;[3] Yom Kippur symbolizes God's forgiveness of the Jewish people

---

2. The first day of Rosh HaShana is also the first day of the month of Tishrei, i.e., Rosh Ḥodesh. In the Jewish calendar, the first day of the month is so designated because it is when the new moon appears in the night sky, a monthly, recurring astronomical event. To the extent that this renewal of the cyclical order draws our attention to nature, it does remind us of the process of creation. This is why in the traditional liturgy, Psalm 104 (*Barkhi Nafshi*), which extols God's artistry in creation, is recited after the psalm of the day on Rosh Ḥodesh (ironically, on every new moon except Rosh HaShana). However, this association of the new moon with the act of creation is true of every new moon, not uniquely the new moon of Tishrei, that is, with Rosh HaShana. Therefore, the creation association of Rosh HaShana appears to be incidental, not essential, to the commemoration of the holiday.

3. Or the revelation of the manna, thirty days after the Exodus, as I argued in the previous chapter, "Not by Bread Alone: Why We Count the Omer and Celebrate Shavuot."

after the sin of the Golden Calf;[4] and Sukkot represents the journey through the wilderness which followed. In the middle of all this comes Rosh HaShana, which commemorates the creation of the world – an event that took place, traditionally speaking, at least 2,500 years before these other biblical stories.

Third, unlike all the other holidays that reflect the particular experience and collective memory of the Jewish people, Rosh HaShana as the commemoration of creation represents a universal moment common to all humanity. This universal story, while theologically important to Jews and non-Jews alike, is nevertheless neither one that the Jewish people personally experienced nor one they could collectively recall. Rosh HaShana seems inconsistent with the other biblical, seasonal holidays, which recollect milestones experienced firsthand by the Jewish people who left Egypt.

These first three difficulties are exacerbated by the commemorative formula used in the Kiddush of Rosh HaShana, *"zekher liyetziat Mitzrayim,"* a commemoration of the Exodus from Egypt. To put this question in context, consider the Kiddush that welcomes Shabbat. There, a double formula of *zikaron lemaaseh bereshit* and *zekher liyetziat Mitzrayim* – a commemoration of creation and of the Exodus – is used to explain the significance of the day. One would think that the Kiddush for Rosh HaShana, the holiday which commemorates creation, would certainly be *zekher lemaaseh bereshit,* a commemoration of the process of creation. Instead, the formula used in the Kiddush for Rosh HaShana, as well as in every *Amida,* every silent, devotional prayer during the holiday, is *zekher liyetziat Mitzrayim,* "a commemoration of the Exodus." This latter formula indicates that Rosh HaShana, like the other biblical holidays, is somehow linked to the post-Exodus cycle rather than to the story of creation in Genesis.

Fourth, there is the question of why we call this holiday by the appellation "Rosh HaShana," the beginning (lit., "head") of the year. In neither place in the Torah where the holiday is mentioned is the day called "Rosh HaShana," the head or the beginning of the year, i.e., the

---

4. Bava Batra 121a, and Rashi ad loc.

first day of the **first** month. Rather, the Torah in both places refers to this day as the first day of the **seventh** month:

> The first day of the seventh month shall be a day of rest, a remembrance of the *terua*, a sacred day. You shall not do any service work, and you shall bring a fire offering to the EverPresent God. (Lev. 23:24–25)

> The first day of the seventh month shall be sacred for you, no service work shall be done, a day of *terua* shall it be for you. (Num. 29:1)

This follows from what the Torah explicitly states in Exodus 12:1 regarding the month of Nisan, which precedes Rosh HaShana by seven months: "**This** month (i.e., Nisan) shall be for you the *rosh* (head) of the months, the first of the months for you in the months of the year." Following this logic, the first day of Nisan (i.e., the **first** day of the **first** month) should properly be called "Rosh HaShana," rather than the first day of Tishrei, the day that the rabbinic tradition has designated as such. Moreover, in the Babylonian Talmud, R. Yehoshua claims, in contrast to R. Eliezer and our liturgical tradition,[5] that the world was in fact created in Nisan. And the Talmud seems to rule in R. Yehoshua's favor.[6] Furthermore, in both Exodus 23:16 and Deuteronomy 31:11, the festival of Sukkot is referred to

---

5. For example, in the prayer recited after the sounding of the shofar, we recite the words "*Hayom harat olam* – Today the world was conceived."

    To reconcile the difference of opinion between R. Eliezer and R. Yehoshua as to when the world was created, the twelfth-century Tosafist known as Rabbenu Tam explains (Rosh HaShana 27a): "These and these are the words of the living God, and one can say that in Tishrei the thought occurred to God of creation but the universe was not created until Nisan." In other words, the **idea** of creation was **conceived** in Tishrei (much as a fetus is conceived several months prior to its birth), but the actual creation of the universe (or of the first human being) did not take place until Nisan.

6. Rosh HaShana 10b–11a, and see Rashi on 12a, "*Ḥakhamei Yisrael monin lamabul*," ad loc. It is also noteworthy that the blessing for the sun that is recited once every twenty-eight years to commemorate the anniversary of the fourth day of creation is recited in the Hebrew month of Nisan, not in Tishrei. Since the rabbinic sages were very careful not to recite blessings, and therefore God's name, in vain (what is

by the Torah as the "end of the year." It would hardly make sense to say that the first day of the Hebrew month of Tishrei marks the beginning of the year and the fifteenth day of Tishrei marks the end of the year.[7] Fifth, why is the mood on Rosh HaShana one of "fear and trembling"?[8] Birthdays are generally cause for rejoicing at having achieved another milestone. If Rosh HaShana is the birthday of creation or of humankind, as R. Eliezer suggests, then the holiday should be one of joy and celebration.

Sixth, one of the only things known about Rosh HaShana from the Torah, as per the verse in Leviticus above, is that the holiday is *zikhron terua* – a remembering of the blowing of the *terua*. What does that mean? When was the *terua* to be remembered first blown?

The final and related question about Rosh HaShana is why the shofar is sounded on this holiday. In fact, why is the shofar the central ritual symbol of the holiday? Presumably, the sounding of the shofar has something to do with "remembering the *terua*." But how precisely does the sounding of the shofar give expression to that remembering, and why is hearing the shofar the one and only biblical commandment of the holiday?[9]

---

termed in rabbinic parlance as a "*berakha levatala*"), one can deduce that as a legal matter the rabbis ruled that creation actually took place in the month of Nisan.

7. This, despite the noble and creative attempt of Rabbi Dr. Yoel Bin Nun to argue that very case. See "*BeRosh HaShana Yikatevun*" (Alon Shvut: Tevunot Press, 2003), 11–19. I am grateful to Dr. Jonathan Grossman for bringing Rabbi Bin Nun's thesis in that article to my attention.

8. *Fear and Trembling* is the name of a famous philosophical work written by Soren Kierkegaard, a Danish theologian, in 1843 about the *Akeda* – Abraham's offering of Isaac on Mount Moriah. The story of the *Akeda* is the Torah reading of the second day of Rosh HaShana.

9. Maimonides, *Mishneh Torah*, Laws of Shofar, preamble and 1:1.
   In fact, two of the most prevalent traditional historical reasons given for the sounding of the shofar on Rosh HaShana are misplaced. The first reason that we sound the shofar – to recall the ram that Abraham sacrificed as a surrogate for his son, Isaac, at the *Akeda* – begs the question of why the Torah portion of Isaac's near sacrifice is read on Rosh HaShana in the first place. On the surface, the story of the *Akeda* seems to have little to do with the story of creation other than that both of them appear in the Book of Genesis (however, see my explanation toward the end of this chapter as to why the rabbis chose this Torah reading for Rosh HaShana). Even if a connection between Rosh HaShana and the *Akeda* is substantiated, as it is in the Talmud, with the theory that our

Something appears to be amiss in our historical understanding of the holiday, an understanding which is essential to the meaningfulness of the actions – ritual and otherwise – unique to this awesome day.

ROSH HASHANA IN THE TORAH: REMEMBERING THE *TERUA* AND THE REVELATION AT SINAI

We saw in the fourth question above that the Torah does not call the first day of the seventh month by the name "Rosh HaShana." The Torah does refer to this day as "a day of rest," "a sacred day," "a day when no service work shall be done" – appellations that apply to nearly all the biblical holidays. What distinguishes Rosh HaShana

---

patriarch Abraham's merit at the *Akeda* is evoked to mitigate God's judgment of his descendants on Rosh HaShana, why is the shofar "sounded" rather than merely "taken" (as is the case with the lulav that is "taken")? After all, the ram at the *Akeda* was "taken" by Abraham and sacrificed in silence, without the staccato "sounding" of the sacrificed ram's horn (Gen. 22:13). Examining the Talmud carefully leads to the conclusion that the Talmud is not explaining why we blow the shofar, but only why the ram's horn is the preferred instrument for the blowing of the *terua* over the horn of another animal (Rosh HaShana 16a).

The second historical reason often suggested for the sounding of the shofar is that the broken sounds of the *terua* are meant to recall the sobs of Sisera's mother upon hearing of the death of her son (Judges 5:29–30). Sisera was a cruel tyrant who led the enemy Canaanite army that fought the Jewish people during the time of the biblical judges. This reason also seems to misunderstand the Talmud's purposes. It is one thing to say that Jews have empathy for the suffering of innocent people; another to say that the central religious commandment of one of the holiest days of the Jewish year found in the Book of Leviticus is derived from the suffering of the mother of a cruel tyrant, who took pride in the rapacious actions of her son in the later Book of Judges. In fact it is the actions of the Kenite woman, Yael, who brought about Sisera's death, that the judge and prophetess Deborah extols in her song of victory and whom we laud in our collective memory with the words: "Most blessed of women is Yael" (Judges 5:24–27).

The talmudic passage on which this explanation is based is not trying at all to answer the question of why we blow the shofar on Rosh HaShana. Rather the Talmud is trying to discern the nature of the *terua* sound that we are commanded to hear – does the *terua* resemble a long sigh or a short gasp? Using a philological analysis based on a single word in the aforementioned story in Judges and its cognate in *Targum Onkelos*, the Talmud tries to answer that question (Rosh HaShana 33b).

from all the other biblical holidays are, as we noted above in the sixth question, the terms "a remembrance of the *terua*" and "a day of *terua*." But what is a *terua*?

In the Book of Numbers, the Torah tells us that a *terua* is one of two musical notes produced by the trumpet or the shofar.[10] The *terua* was blown in two sets of circumstances: as a signal to the Jewish people to move their encampment from one place to another (Num. 10:5–6), and in the event of war, to "remind God" of their precarious plight, through the tremulous, staccato sound of their blowing (Num. 10:9). An alternative shofar sound, the *tekia*, was blown to gather (*"uvehak'hil"*) the people (Num. 10:7).

The one place in the Torah prior to Leviticus 23, the chapter of the holidays, where the blowing of the shofar on Rosh HaShana is mentioned, is in the Book of Exodus during the revelation of God's presence at Mount Sinai. There, the Torah speaks three times of the sounding of the shofar:

> And on the morning of the third day there was thunder (*kolot*), lightning, and a heavy cloud upon the mountain, and the sound (*kol*) of the shofar was very strong, and all the people in the encampment trembled. And Moses led the people out of their encampment toward God. (Ex. 19:16)
> And the sound (*kol*) of the shofar continued and was very strong. Moses would speak and God would respond with the sound (*bekol*). (Ex. 19:19)
> And all the people witnessed the thunder (*kolot*), the flames, the sound (*kol*) of the shofar, and the mountain smoking, and the people trembled when they saw it and kept their distance. (Ex. 20:15)

If Rosh HaShana, as described in Leviticus 23, is "a remembrance of the *terua*," and if the revelation at Sinai is the only prior place in the Torah that the shofar is mentioned, it follows that Rosh HaShana is, in fact, a

---

10. Num. 10:1–10; Ps. 47:6, 98:6.

commemoration of the revelation at Sinai.[11] And the *terua* sound, which the Torah prescribes for the holiday of Rosh HaShana, is also precisely the one, described in Numbers 10, that is used to move the people from their encampment. After the first sounding of the shofar at the Sinai revelation, Moses led the people out of their encampment to encounter God. Rosh HaShana, "a day of *terua*," therefore recalls this experience.[12]

Furthermore, the reason for the traditional sounding of the *tekia*, the long sound of the shofar, before and after the *terua*, can also be connected to the events surrounding the revelation at Sinai. Moses' description of the revelation in Deuteronomy includes God's command to "gather for Me (*hak'hel*) the people" (Deut. 4:10), an action accompanied by the blowing of a *tekia*. Hence, every time we sound the shofar on Rosh HaShana, we blow both the *terua*, symbolizing Moses' leading the people out of their encampment,[13] and the *tekia*, symbolizing Moses' gathering the people around Mount Sinai.[14]

---

11. The very brevity of the command to commemorate Rosh HaShana in Leviticus 23 (only three verses) as compared to the far more elaborate commands for the other holidays in that chapter indicates that to the listeners, the meaning and significance of this command was self-evident. In the chronology of the Torah, the Book of Leviticus is revealed while the Jewish people are still encamped around Mount Sinai (See Lev. 25:1, 26:46, 27:34 and cf. to Num. 10:11–12). Hence, the "remembrance of the *terua*" would have immediately been understood by the people as referring to the events that had occurred within the previous few months at the site of their encampment, Mount Sinai.

12. See also Rashi on Ex. 20:19, citing R. Yehoshua b. Levi in Shabbat 88b, saying the Jews moved their encampment twelve miles in response to the fearful events described in the third mention of the shofar blasts. According to this opinion, the third mention of the shofar blasts at Mount Sinai, like the first mention, involves the movement of the Jewish people from their encampment. In Num. 10:9, the Torah provides a second situation in which the *terua* is sounded – i.e., in times of imminent war. Interestingly, the language of Moses leading (*yotzei*) the people out of their encampment toward (*likrat*) God is reminiscent of the language used in Num. 20:18, 20 and 21:23 to denote the arraying of the people toward war (*yotzei, likrat*) – perhaps the war on behalf of civilized society that the Sinai revelation represents (on this latter point compare to Nahmanides' commentary on Lev. 23:24, beginning with the words, "*Al derekh haemet*," invoking war imagery from Jer. 4:19 and Ex. 15:3).

13. As per Num. 10:5, 6.

14. As per Num. 10:7.

The "sound" of the shofar carries additional importance in the events of the revelation. Along with the sound of the shofar, the sound (*kol*) of God's thunderous presence and the sound of God's revealed word were heard at Mount Sinai. All of these sounds – the shofar, the thunder during the Sinai theophany, and God's response to Moses – are referred to as "*kol(ot)*" in the Bible:

> On the morning of the third day there was thunder (*kolot*) ... and the sound (*kol*) of the shofar became stronger. Moses would speak and God would respond with the sound (*bekol*). (Ex. 19:16, 19)

This use of the word *kol* to denote not only the sound of the shofar, but also the sound of God's revealed word, is already evident in the prelude to the revelation: "If you will listen to My voice (*bekoli*) and keep My covenant, then you will be treasured to Me from among all the nations" (Ex. 19:5).

And in Deuteronomy, as if to drive home this very point, Moses reiterates the equation of "*kol*" with God's revelation at Mount Sinai: "God spoke to you out of the fire; you heard the sound (*kol*) of words, but saw no image; there was only a sound (*kol*)" (Deut. 4:12).

The sounding of the shofar on Rosh HaShana is therefore not only a reminder of the blasts but a reenacting of God's thunderous presence and covenantal word at Mount Sinai. Indeed, the sounding of the shofar plays such a prominent role in the earth-shaking events surrounding the Sinai revelation that the Torah positioned it as the centerpiece of the holiday.

And if the sounding of the shofar on Rosh HaShana is a reenactment of the frightening spectrum of sounds heard at Sinai, it is also clear why the mood of the day is one of fear and trepidation. Just as the Jewish people, and indeed the entire mountain, stood trembling before the spectacle of God's awesome presence and revelation at Mount Sinai,[15] so too do the Jewish people on Rosh HaShana stand in fear and trembling, reexperiencing God's revelation through the tremulous, shuddering *terua*

---

15. See Ex. 19:16, 18; 20:15.

sound from the shofar. It is no wonder then that Rosh HaShana inaugurates the ten-day period known in the Jewish tradition as the *Yamim Nora'im*, the Days of Awe.

There is additional biblical support for the thesis that Rosh HaShana commemorates the revelation at Sinai, from the Book of Nehemiah. The eighth chapter presents a dramatic account of the recovenanting ceremony led by Ezra the Scribe after the Jewish people's return from the Babylonian exile. At this ceremony, all the people – men, women, and children – gathered as one[16] and responded "Amen" in fear and trembling as Ezra, standing on a raised platform (suggesting a mountain), "revealed" to the confused and struggling returnees to the Land of Israel the Torah of Moses that they had forgotten. This "second revelation" of the Torah from a physically elevated point took place on the first day of the seventh month – that is, on the day we call Rosh HaShana. Apparently, Ezra too saw the linkage between the day of Rosh HaShana and the awe-inspiring revelation of the Torah to the Jewish people who stood at the foot of Mount Sinai.

ROSH HASHANA AND THE REVELATION: RITUALS

The relationship of Rosh HaShana to the divine revelation at Mount Sinai is acknowledged ritually in four ways.

First, the blessing recited prior to blowing the shofar recalls the various *kolot* or sounds of the revelation. The formulation is not "*litko'a bashofar*," to "blow" the shofar, as might be expected, or even "*al netilat shofar*," "to take the shofar," but rather "*lishmo'a kol shofar*," "to hear the sound of the shofar."[17] The verb "*lishmo'a*," "to hear," is taken from the revelation as described by Moses in Deuteronomy: "You **heard the sound** of words, but did not see an image, only the sound" (Deut. 4:12). In the biblical account of the revelation, moreover, the word "*kol*" precedes the word "*shofar*" in all three instances that it appears. It is not

---

16. On the unity of the people, cf. Neh. 8:1, Ex. 19:2, and Deut. 33:5.
17. The biblical command is not to blow the shofar, but to hear the sound of the shofar. Thus one who blows the shofar but stops up his ears from hearing the sound has not fulfilled his legal obligation (see the responsa of Maimonides, *Mishneh Torah*, Laws of Shofar 1:8 and 3:10).

surprising then that the language of the blessing stresses hearing the sound of the shofar, rather than the simpler *"lishmo'a et hashofar,"* to listen to the shofar.[18]

Second, according to Jewish tradition, those listening to the blowing of the shofar may not interrupt by speaking from the first shofar blast until the last. Since listening to the sound, the *kol*, of the shofar is tantamount to reexperiencing the revelation of God's voice at Mount Sinai, it would be sacrilegious to interrupt God's "speech" with human speech. And like the Jewish people, who stood together at Sinai (Ex. 19:17) to hear God's word, the synagogue congregation stands up as one before each set of shofar sounds.

Third, as noted above, the sound of the shofar is mentioned three times in the story of the revelation, and the word *"kol"* also includes three different sounds (*kolot*) – the sound of the shofar, the sound of the thunder, and the sound of God's voice. It is therefore not surprising that according to rabbinic tradition, the biblical obligation is to sound a minimum of three *terua* blasts with the shofar; indeed almost everything related to the sounding of the shofar is in sets of three:[19]

- Each *terua* blast is flanked by a *tekia* blast on either side for a total of three notes.[20]

---

18. This formulation of the blessing also has practical ramifications in Jewish law. Because the commandment is simply to hear the sound itself, rather than to take or blow a physical object, one can fulfill its observance even with a borrowed or stolen shofar. This is in contrast to a lulav, where the blessing of *"Al netilat lulav"* denotes the command to acquire the physical lulav, and where one cannot fulfill the command with a borrowed or stolen lulav (cf. Maimonides, *Mishneh Torah*, Laws of Shofar 1:3 to Laws of Lulav 8:1). The rabbis who formulated the blessing in this particular manner were apparently aware of the significance of the words *"lishmo'a"* and *"kol"* in relationship to the sounding of the shofar at the Sinai revelation (see also my comments below on the *"Shofarot"* section of the liturgy).

19. See Mishna Rosh HaShana 4:9: "The order of the blasts is thrice three threes."

20. This despite the fact that the word *"terua"* is found only twice in the Torah in reference to Rosh HaShana (once in Leviticus and once in Numbers). This numerical anomaly forced the rabbinic sages in Rosh HaShana 33b to search – some might say "stretch" – for another mention of *terua* in the Torah – the sounding once every fifty years of the shofar on the Yom Kippur of the Jubilee year – with which to support a threefold biblical obligation to sound three *teruas*: "All the *teruot* of the seventh month are one." Our explanation above obviates the necessity for such an exegetical stretch.

- Three separate types of musical notes are sounded – *tekia, shevarim,* and *terua.*
- The shofar is blown three times during the *Musaf* (supplemental) service – before the *Amida,* during the *Amida,* and after the *Amida.*
- Within the *Amida* itself, the shofar is also blown three times – during the *Malkhuyot* (Kingship), *Zikhronot* (Covenantal Memory), and *Shofarot* (Divine Revelation) sections.

All these "threes" reflect the threefold sounding of the shofar and the three different forms of "sound" experienced at Sinai.

Finally, there are two individuals involved in the sounding of the shofar, the *"baal makri,"* who calls out the notes to be sounded, and the *"baal toke'a,"* who blows the shofar notes. The *baal makri* is customarily the spiritual head, or most learned individual, of the community. These two roles are modeled after the roles of Moses and God at Mount Sinai, where we are told, *"Moshe yedaber, vehaElohim yaanenu bekol"* (Ex. 19:19) – Moses would speak and God would respond with a *"kol"* (sound).

ROSH HASHANA AND THE REVELATION: LITURGY

The liturgical link between Rosh HaShana and the revelation is also unmistakable. The *Amida* for *Musaf,* the supplemental, silent devotional service, is built around three distinct parts – *Malkhuyot* (Kingship), *Zikhronot* (Covenantal Memory), and *Shofarot* (Divine Revelation) – which contain the organizing themes of the holiday and relate to the revelation in several interconnected ways.

The *Malkhuyot* section proclaims the kingship of God and recalls both the preamble and the actual revelation at Mount Sinai. In the prelude to the revelation in Exodus, God says, "If you listen to My sound (*koli*), and you keep My covenant (*beriti*), then you will be to Me a **kingdom** of priests (*mamlekhet kohanim*)" (Ex. 19:5–6).

If the Jewish people are God's kingdom, then God must be the people's king. The blasts of the shofar at Mount Sinai announced God's coronation as sovereign of the Jewish people. The rabbinic commentary the *Mekhilta,* on the first of the Ten Commandments, makes this explicit:

"I took you out of the land of Egypt and I have earned My right to be your king and your ruler."[21]

The thirteenth-century Spanish exegete Nahmanides makes a related point in his commentary on the verse in Deuteronomy: "It was in Yeshurun that God became king, when the leaders of the people gathered together, all the tribes of Israel" (Deut. 33:5). He explains that this refers to the bestowing of God's kingship at Mount Sinai. This verse from Deuteronomy is, in fact, one of the proof texts used in the *Malkhuyot* (Kingship) section of the *Musaf* of Rosh HaShana.[22]

In the second section of the *Musaf* service, *Zikhronot*, the central theme is remembering the *berit*, the covenant. In the preamble to the revelation, God predicates the chosenness of the Jewish people on their adhering to God's voice (*"bekoli"*) and their guarding God's covenant (*"beriti"*). This covenantal agreement at Sinai is the subject of the culminating proof text of the *Zikhronot* prayer:

> Fulfill for us, God, that which You promised in the Torah through Moses Your servant, straight from the mouth of Your divine glory, as it says: "And I will remember for them the covenant (*berit*) with the first generation whom I took out of Egypt before the eyes of the nations [of the world] to be their God, I, the Lord." (Lev. 26:45)

The covenant that God made with the first generation of Jewish people that left Egypt, to which the verse from Leviticus refers, was the Ten Commandments, which begin with the words, "I am the Lord, your God, who has taken you out of the land of Egypt" (Ex. 20:2). Thus on Rosh HaShana, not only is the proclamation of God's kingship reenacted, but the covenantal agreement between God as king and the people as God's kingdom is recalled. That covenantal agreement is embodied in the Ten Commandments that both **begin with** and are **predicated upon** the Exodus from Egypt. No wonder that the formula of *"zekher*

---

21. *Mekhilta*, Ex. 20:5.
22. See also I Sam. 10:24 and I Kings 1:39 for the pairing of the word *"terua"* with the blowing of the shofar in the coronation rituals of King Saul and King Solomon.

liyetziat Mitzrayim" – in commemoration of the Exodus from Egypt – is used both in the Kiddush, as discussed above, and the *Amida* of Rosh HaShana. The holiday indeed recalls the Exodus from Egypt itself and revolves around the period following the Exodus.

The commemoration of the revelation of the Ten Commandments also explains why Rosh HaShana is referred to in rabbinic tradition as *Yom HaDin*, the Day of Judgment.[23] During the revelation at Mount Sinai, God assumed sovereignty over the people and legislated the constitutional law that was to govern the Godly kingdom. Jews today continue to be judged, as the Jewish people who stood at Sinai and later fashioned the Golden Calf were judged, by the Ten Commandments that God as king set forth in the covenant.[24] This covenant, contingent on keeping God's commands, set the standard or benchmark for judging the Jewish people for all time.

The Ten Commandments also reflect God's attribute of *din* in an additional sense, that of uncompromising judge. God, as depicted in the Ten Commandments, is described as a strict, harsh, and unforgiving judge; a vengeful God – *"Kel kana"* – who imputes hate to those who sin – *"poked avon avot, leson'ai"* – and who will not forgive those who take God's name in vain – *"lo yenakeh."*[25] The Ten Commandments establish the high legal standard and describe the stern divine Judge to which the Jewish people are held accountable.[26] Hence our continued trepidation today at the approach of the holy and awesome day.

---

23. The designation of the day as the "**The** Day of Judgment" – using the Hebrew *heh hayedia* – points to the singular, foundational nature of the divinely revealed law encapsulated in the Ten Commandments that serves as the basis of divine judgment. Similarly, the *heh hayedia* in the rabbinic designation of the day as *Yom HaZikaron* – "**The** Day of Remembrance" – points to the central importance of remembering the events of this day as encapsulated in Deut. 4:9–12 at the head of this chapter.

24. See Ex. 32:8 where God delineates the violation of the first two – perhaps three – of the Ten Commandments.

25. Ex. 20:5–7. See, in contrast, God as depicted in the thirteen attributes, a God of "mercy, compassion, and long suffering (Ex. 34:6)" – the covenant with a forgiving God for which we celebrate Yom Kippur, the Day of Atonement.

26. Although the Ten Commandments were revealed only to the Jewish people at Mount Sinai, they can be said to have raised the bar for what constitutes civilized living for all of humanity. The Jewish people were simply the vanguard ("To Me belongs all of

Nor is it accidental that each of the three sections of the Rosh HaShana *Musaf* quotes a total of ten verses from the various parts of the Bible, several each from the Torah, the Prophets, and the Writings (*Ketuvim*), as proof texts for its theme. Each group of ten biblical verses, representing divine speech, parallels the "*Aseret HaDibbrot*," literally the "Ten Statements," or Ten Commandments that God uttered at Sinai.

In addition, in the first paragraph of the *Shofarot* section, the root word "*kol*" is repeated ten times, alternately describing God's voice, God's thundering presence, and the punctuating sound of the shofar during the Sinai revelation:

> You revealed Yourself in the Clouds of Glory to speak to Your holy people. From the heavens You made them hear Your voice (*kolekha*) and You revealed Yourself in pure, thick clouds. The whole world trembled at Your presence; all the creatures were in awe before You, when You, our King, revealed Yourself on Mount Sinai to teach Your people Torah and commandments, and they heard Your majestic voice (*kolekha*), and Your holy words in flashes of fire. Amid thunder (*kolot*) and lightning did You reveal Yourself to them, and with the sound (*kol*) of the shofar did You appear to them, as it is written in Your Torah: "And on the morning of the third day there was thunder (*kolot*) and lightning and a heavy cloud upon the mountain, and the sound (*kol*) of the shofar was very strong, and all the people in the encampment trembled.... And the sound (*kol*) of the shofar continued very strong; Moses would speak and God would respond with the sound (*bekol*).... And all the people saw the thunder (*kolot*), the flames, and the

---

the earth, and you will be a kingdom of priests and a holy nation" – Ex. 19:5–6 – that is, a people meant to serve as teachers and role models for all of humanity's civilized and moral living). It is thus not surprising that the second mishna in chapter 1 of Tractate Rosh HaShana depicts Rosh HaShana as the day when all of humanity is judged by God. Then again, according to the Jewish traditional belief that all of the Torah was revealed at Sinai, the seven Laws of Noah that govern all of humanity (which significantly overlap the Ten Commandments that govern the Jewish people) were revealed at Sinai no less than the Ten Commandments.

sound (*kol*) of the shofar, and the mountain smoking, and the people trembled when they saw it and kept their distance.

This tenfold repetition of the root word "*kol*" in the *Shofarot* section, like the tenfold use of the biblical proof texts in each of the three sections of the *Musaf Amida*, are meant to symbolize the Ten Commandments "sounded" by the divine voice at the Sinai revelation.[27]

In sum, the *Musaf* liturgy of Rosh HaShana is comprised of the three central themes of the revelation at Sinai: God's kingship **of** the people, covenant **with** the people, and thunderous revelation **to** the people, or what our liturgical tradition calls *Malkhuyot, Zikhronot,* and *Shofarot.*

All three of these elements, noticeably present at the revelation at Sinai, were absent at creation, the event traditionally associated with Rosh HaShana. First, kingship is a political term – it presupposes a mass of people to be led and governed. There was no such mass of people present at creation, nor in the entire Book of Genesis. There was such a mass at Sinai, and, as Nahmanides notes in his commentary on Deuteronomy 33:5, it is there that the united body of the people of Israel verbally accepted upon themselves God's kingship.

Second, no covenant was made at creation. The first recorded covenant of any sort was with Noah, some ten generations and 1,600 years

---

27. There are two other Rosh HaShana rituals that emphasize the tenfold theme of Rosh HaShana. The first is the supplementary Torah reading of the day from Numbers 29 describing the ten sacrifices brought in the Tabernacle on this day: two rams as total burnt offerings, corresponding to the first two commandments and the two days of Rosh HaShana in which we totally commune with God; seven sheep as wholeness offerings, corresponding to commandments 3–9 and the seven days between Rosh HaShana and Yom Kippur; and one goat as a sin offering, corresponding to the tenth commandment and the day of Yom Kippur, the day on which the sins of the Jewish people are forgiven. Second, the number of trumpet blows sounded by the shofar has evolved to the number one hundred. Although three soundings of the staccato *terua* flanked on each side by a *tekia* are the minimum that are biblically required, for a total of nine soundings of the shofar, that number evolved upward first to thirty, and then to ninety, all multiples of the number three. The final Jewish tradition of one hundred soundings of the shofar is actually difficult to account for unless one recognizes that $100 = 10 \times 10$, recalling, again, the centrality and exponential power of the Ten Commandments.

after creation. The first covenant with the Jewish people as a people took place, as we saw, and as the verse in Leviticus makes plain, after the Exodus from Egypt, at Sinai (Lev. 26:45).

Third, at creation, there was no sounding of the shofar and no accompanying coronation ceremony.

Finally, several of the blessings said on Rosh HaShana seem connected specifically to the Sinai revelation. In Jewish liturgy, the closing words (known in rabbinic parlance as the *ḥatima*) of a blessing underscore its general theme. The closing of the blessings for the Kiddush, the *haftara*, and the *Amida* on Rosh HaShana – and only on Rosh HaShana – end with the distinctive words, *"udevarkha emet vekayam laad,"* "Your **word** is true and lasts eternally." The Hebrew root word for "Your word" is the same root as that used for the word "statement" in the *Aseret HaDibbrot – dalet-beit/vet-resh*. Were this blessing referring to the words that God uttered at creation to bring the universe into being, the appropriate Hebrew root would be A-M-R (as in *vayomer*), used repeatedly in the chapter describing the creation of the world.[28] Never is the root word D-B-R used in the story of creation. For the rabbinic sages who composed the language of the blessing, the true and eternal words that mark the holiday of Rosh HaShana were those uttered by God during the revelation at Sinai.

ROSH HASHANA AND THE REVELATION: CUSTOMS

Two holiday customs resonate with the identification of Rosh HaShana as a reenactment of Sinai. The first is the custom of Jewish men to immerse in a *mikve*, ritual pool, on the day prior to Rosh HaShana. Since the Jewish people, prior to the revelation at Sinai, also immersed in water to prepare for their encounter with the Divine (according to the rabbinic commentary on Ex. 19:10 and 19:16), traditional Jews similarly prepare for the day that reenacts God's revelation.[29]

The second custom is the dipping of bread in honey. The revelation at Sinai took place in the desert only twenty-one days after the

---

28. "With ten *maamarot* was the world created," Mishna Avot 5:1.
29. See *Leading the Passover Journey*, 24–26, for why the immersion in water precedes the revelation of God's presence.

beginning of the falling of the manna, the heaven-sent bread, which the Torah describes as being white in color and tasting like "*tzapiḥit bidevash*," wafers dipped in honey (Ex. 16:31). We thus eat *ḥalla*, and apples, dipped in honey on Rosh HaShana to reexperience the miraculous (white) food eaten by the Jewish people in the desert as they camped around Mount Sinai. This is similar to why we eat matza, "poor man's bread," during the holiday of Passover, reenacting the flat bread that our ancestors ate both during the Egyptian bondage[30] and in the days immediately after they left Egypt (Ex. 12:39). Through the most basic foods that we eat we relive what our ancestors ate during each of these peak experiences in the Jewish people's journey from Egypt.[31]

THE ROSH HASHANA ENIGMA SOLVED

Linking Rosh HaShana to the revelation at Sinai solves almost all of the difficulties raised at the beginning of this chapter. Although the date of Rosh HaShana may coincide with the anniversary of creation of the world or of human beings,[32] creation is apparently not the holiday's primary theme in the Bible. Rather, this holiday commemorates God's revelation at Mount Sinai. Like the other biblical revelatory events commemorated by the Jewish festivals, this particular redemptive event was experienced collectively by the Jewish people after they left Egypt. And like the other biblical holidays, Rosh HaShana is therefore "*zekher liyetziat Mitzrayim*," a commemoration precipitated by and predicated upon God's liberation of the Jewish people from Egypt (Ex. 20:2). The holiday occurs in proper chronological sequence: after the holiday of Passover commemorating the Exodus, and the Omer

---

30. "This is the bread of poverty that our ancestors ate in the land of Egypt" – the first words of the *Maggid* section of the Passover Haggada.
31. Significant also in this regard is the placement of the jug of manna in the Sanctuary immediately adjacent to the Ark of Testimony containing the covenantal Ten Commandments (Ex. 16:33, 34). Both in the sacred space of the Sanctuary, the *Mikdash*, and in Jewish homes, our *mikdashei me'at*, our "miniature sanctuaries," on the sacred day of Rosh HaShana, the covenant and the symbol of the manna are experienced as adjacent to one another. God's commanding presence and physical nurturance of the people coexist side by side.
32. As R. Eliezer claimed, which explains why one of several names given to the holiday is Rosh HaShana (see below).

period and holiday of Shavuot commemorating the falling of the manna, but before the holiday of Yom Kippur commemorating God's forgiveness of the Jewish people for the worship of the Golden Calf. The mood of awe and trepidation in anticipation of judgment by the divine King reenacts the mood of the Jewish people standing at Sinai during the revelation. Finally, the holiday is called *zikhron terua* and the shofar is sounded, to remember the sounding of the shofar and the sounds of God's revelation at Mount Sinai.

SHAVUOT AND ROSH HASHANA: TWO HOLIDAYS COMMEMORATING THE SAME EVENT?

But wait a minute: there seem to be two biblical holidays, Shavuot and Rosh HaShana, commemorating the same event. After all, the conventional understanding is that Shavuot already commemorates the revelation at Sinai! Among the many approaches to sorting out this puzzle, several rely on distinctions between Shavuot and Rosh HaShana to explain why having both holidays commemorate the Sinai revelation might make sense. After all, there are two biblical sacred days that celebrate the Exodus from Egypt – Passover and Shabbat[33] – with only the former, the holiday of Passover, corresponding to the actual time of the year in which the Exodus took place. Similarly, in commemorating the revelation, the other of the two most important theologically significant events that the Jewish people experienced, the Torah may have legislated two holidays by which to recall it, one at the onset of summer – the season in which the event occurred – and one at the conclusion of summer to remind us of that event as we begin a "new year."[34]

---

33. Ex. 12:14 and Deut. 5:15.
34. Reappropriating the meaning of Rosh HaShana as the commemoration of God's revelation at Sinai in addition to our common understanding of the meaning of Rosh HaShana as commemorating God's creation of the world would also parallel the way Shabbat commemorates both the Exodus from Egypt (a particularistic event) and the creation of the world (a universal event). Both Rosh HaShana and Shabbat would then signify the celebration of *Hashem Elokeinu*, the God of the Jewish people, and *Melekh HaOlam*, the King of the universe, the two components which dialectically comprise every Jewish blessing. Linking the particular and the universal in this way deepens and mutually reinforces the spiritual meaningfulness of this holiday.

Another way of understanding the seeming redundancy of the holidays of Shavuot and Rosh HaShana is by distinguishing between the anniversary of the act of **divine revelation** that Shavuot commemorates (i.e., *Zeman **Matan** Toratenu*) and the **people's acceptance** of God's kingship and covenant that Rosh HaShana commemorates (i.e., *Kabbalat Ol Malkhut Shamayim* and ***Kabbalat** HaTorah*).[35]

The case for adopting this distinction between God's act of giving and the people's recollection (***zikhron** terua*) and acceptance of what was given is strengthened by the fact that there were two separate and distinct acts involving the Ten Commandments – God's verbal communication of the Ten Commandments in the third month of the year (Ex. 19:1), the month of Sivan, and the Jewish people's receipt of the engraved Tablets of the Law with the Ten Commandments several months later on Yom Kippur, the tenth day of the month of Tishrei.[36]

The need for two separate holidays was necessitated by the fact that while the Jewish people heard the Ten Commandments communicated orally in the month of Sivan, they never took actual receipt of the first set of divinely engraved tablets. Those first tablets were shattered by Moses when, descending the mountain, he witnessed the people worshiping the Golden Calf and blatantly violating the first two commandments. All that remained of the first tablets were shattered fragments.[37] The people were privileged to receive only the second set of God's tablets, brought down intact by Moses, on the tenth day of Tishrei (according to rabbinic tradition).

The holiday of Shavuot in Sivan therefore commemorates God's spoken communication of the commandments. The holiday of Rosh

---

35. I have heard this distinction used by the "Brisker tradition" (an analytic school of Torah study associated with the nineteenth-century talmudist Rabbi Chaim Soloveitchik) to explain the difference between the biblical holiday of Shavuot and the later rabbinic holiday of Simḥat Torah, each of which celebrates a different aspect of the Torah.

36. According to the reckoning of the sages. See for example, Rashi on Ex. 34:29.

37. In this regard I have conjectured, using a midrashic sensibility, that the "*adi*" that the people used to demonstrate their loyalty to God after the Golden Calf (Ex. 33:4–6) were those very shattered fragments that the people gathered. The letters *ayin-dalet-yud-mem* can be read, not as *edyam*, but as *eidim* – witnesses – namely, the two tablets – *Luḥot HaEdut* – that testified to the covenantal agreement between God and the Jewish people.

HaShana in Tishrei, on the other hand, recalls and recreates that revelation in preparation for the acceptance of the physical, engraved commandments on Yom Kippur.

A third possible explanation for why there are two holidays celebrating approximately the same event is based on the insight of Rabbi Samson Raphael Hirsch, the founder of Neo-Orthodoxy in nineteenth-century Germany. His commentary on Leviticus 23:21 argues that Shavuot actually commemorates the preparatory day leading up to the revelation of the commandments at Sinai rather than the day of the revelation itself:[38]

> It is not the fact of the revelation of the Torah but our making ourselves worthy to receive it that our festival celebrates. It is the day before the Law Giving…the day on which the nation finally presented itself as ready and worthy for the great mission to the world…it is that day which the fiftieth day of the counting of the Omer [i.e., the holiday of Shavuot] represents.[39]

Hirsch is prompted to adopt this unusual explanation by the talmudic opinion of R. Yossi, who claims that the verbal revelation actually took place on the seventh day of Sivan, not the sixth day of Sivan, the day on which we celebrate Shavuot (Shabbat 86b). This position later seems to become the authoritative one in the rabbinic tradition.[40]

Hirsch's opinion is an extension of the kabbalistic tradition that views the forty-nine days of the counting of the Omer as days in which the Jewish people rose in levels of holiness in preparation for encountering God's presence on Mount Sinai. Shavuot, the fiftieth day, would then represent the peak day of preparing for the Sinaitic revelation, while Rosh HaShana would represent the recollection and reliving of the actual revelation.[41] Although Hirsch does not make this claim regarding

---

38. Ex. 19:11, 15 – "be **prepared** for the third day."
39. Samson Raphael Hirsch, *The Pentateuch*, Book of Leviticus 2 (Gateshead: Judaica Press, 1982), 670–671.
40. See Rabbi Abraham Gombiner, footnote 49, p. 100 below.
41. Using yeshiva terminology, the "*hakhana*" for the revelation and the "*ḥazara*" of the revelatory event.

Rosh HaShana, doing so is a logical extrapolation of his essential insight regarding Shavuot.[42]

A variation of Hirsch's insight in combination with the second hypothesis above could lead to yet a fourth way of understanding what each holiday represents. Shavuot, as Hirsch says, commemorates the **preparation** for the **verbal revelation**, while Rosh HaShana, which recalls this revelation (*"zikhron terua"*), commemorates the **preparation** for receiving the **physical tablets** ten days later on Yom Kippur.[43] This would then explain why Rosh HaShana falls precisely ten days before Yom Kippur: the Ten Days of Repentance correspond to the Ten (covenantal) Commandments[44] that the Jewish people had to prepare for and internalize before receiving the physical tablets.[45]

All the accoutrements of the original revelation – the sounding of the shofar, the state of fear and trembling, the hailing of God's kingship, and the embracing of the covenantal obligations – were recalled and relived on Rosh HaShana to prepare the people for the acceptance of the second set of physical tablets on Yom Kippur.[46] This was done to arouse

---

42. As to the timing of the holiday on the first day of Tishrei, please see the comment of Rabbenu Nissim below in footnote 47, p. 99 below.

43. As in the third explanation above, there is some philological support for viewing Rosh HaShana as the day commemorating the preparation for the receiving of the engraved tablets. In Ex. 34:2, God says to Moses, who is about to go back up the mountain to receive the second tablets, "Be **prepared** in the morning." Moses, as per God's command, used the same language when he instructed the people to "prepare themselves" for the verbal revelation at Sinai in Ex. 19:11, 15.

44. *"Divrei HaBerit,"* Ex. 34:28.

45. One might then flesh this out further by arguing that the first two days of these days of awe, the days of Rosh HaShana in which the people accepted upon themselves the kingship of God, correspond to preparing to receive the first two of the Ten Commandments which are written in the first person: "I am the Lord…You shall have no other gods before Me"; the seven days that follow prepare the people to receive the next seven commandments, written in the third person; while the day of Yom Kippur, the day of forgiveness for sin, prepares the people to accept the tenth commandment – "Do not desire/covet" – arguably the animating cause of all sins between people. It is fitting that Yom Kippur, the Day of Atonement, and the tenth day of the ten days of awe/repentance, corresponds to the commandment warning against these primal, motivating forces of human sinfulness – i.e., desire (greed) and lust.

46. Ex. 34:1–4 and Rashi on 34:1. In Ex. 34:3, the Torah sets up the same restrictions regarding proximity to the mountain for the receipt of the second tablets as for the

---

the people toward repentance as well as to testify to the divine origin of the second tablets even though the latter tablets, written by God, were chiseled by Moses. Moreover, since the people, by worshiping the Golden Calf, breached their original, verbal acceptance of the first set of tablets (which explains why Moses shattered them), the Ten Commandments were in effect neither genuinely, nor physically, accepted by the people until the month of Tishrei. Today, to reenact the preparations for the receiving and faithful acceptance of those commandments in writing, the Jewish people recall the revelatory encounter at Mount Sinai on Rosh HaShana, and spend a total of ten days in contrition and repentance before reenacting receiving them – and God's forgiveness – on Yom Kippur.[47]

---

first. These restrictions imply that a second revelation of God's presence took place during the writing of the second tablets as indicated by God descending upon the mountain in Ex. 34:5 (cf. God's descent on the mountain in 19:18). However, this revelation was a private one to Moses (Ex. 34:6–7) rather than to all the Jewish people. See also Nahmanides' commentary on the Torah, Ex. 34:27: "God commanded Moses that he write a book of the covenant and read it in the hearing of the people and they should accept it upon themselves by saying, 'We will do and we will obey' as they had done with the first tablets; **for He wanted that the whole procedure with the first tablets should now be repeated with the second tablets. There is no doubt that Moses actually did repeat it.**"

47. This aligns well with the explanation of R. Yehoshua's position offered by the fourteenth-century talmudic commentator Rabbenu Nissim of Gerondi (popularly known as "the Ran"). As mentioned previously, R. Yehoshua in Rosh HaShana 10b–11a argued (and the sages in the Talmud apparently ruled in accordance with his view) that the world was created in the Hebrew month of Nisan. That being the case, why, he asks, was the first of Tishrei chosen by God to be the day of judgment? Rabbenu Nissim answers:

God wanted the Jewish people to be worthy as they were being judged and desired to judge them during a period set aside for forgiveness and atonement. [In the Bible] God became reconciled with the Jewish people on Yom Kippur and that day was established as a day of forgiveness for all generations.... Therefore, God benevolently set the day of judgment ten days before the day of divine forgiveness...because the Torah wanted to give the people time to examine their actions and to return to God during this propitious period for divine forgiveness and atonement. Also, beginning with Rosh HaShana until Yom Kippur, God began to get reconciled with the people and on Yom Kippur God became fully reconciled. Therefore, God chose to judge His creatures during this period already established for forgiveness and atonement. (*Ḥiddushei HaRan* on Rosh HaShana 16a)

An alternative approach to understanding the seeming redundancy between Shavuot and Rosh HaShana is to decouple the linkage between the holiday of Shavuot and the Sinai revelation altogether. This approach is most strongly supported by the fact that the Torah does not link the revelation at Mount Sinai to the holiday of Shavuot in any of its five descriptions of the holiday, even though the Torah dates the revelation at Sinai to sometime early in the third month, the month of Sivan.[48]

This omission is the most persuasive argument for us as well not to presume a connection between the two. In fact, the fifteenth-century Spanish biblical exegete Abrabanel did just that in his commentary on Leviticus 23. Troubled by the Torah's failure to mention the revelation at Sinai in connection with the holiday of Shavuot, he repeatedly comments (ad loc.) that although Shavuot apparently falls on or near the day of the Sinai revelation, as per the Written Torah, the holiday was not meant to commemorate the Sinai revelation at all. Rather, as alluded to in the Bible every time that it is mentioned, the holiday of Shavuot was meant as an agricultural, new-grain, thanksgiving festival "to the one who provides bread to all His creatures"(Ps. 136:25). For Abrabanel, the overlapping between the holiday of Shavuot and the original date of the Sinai revelation was nothing more than mere happenstance.[49]

While Rabbenu Nissim does not connect the recollection and reenactment of the revelation at Sinai with the first day of Tishrei, he provides a rationale for the close proximity of Rosh HaShana, representing divine judgment, and Yom Kippur, representing divine forgiveness. This rationale is even more pronounced in the thesis advanced above, where Rosh HaShana, the day recalling divine judgment, and Yom Kippur, the day celebrating divine forgiveness, commemorate historically and geographically proximate events: the recollection of the revelation of the Ten Commandments at Mount Sinai (the day called by the sages *Yom HaDin*, the Day of Judgment) and God's forgiveness of the Jewish people at the foot of Mount Sinai after their worship of the Golden Calf (the day called by the Torah *Yom HaKippurim*, the Day of Forgiveness [Lev. 23:27]).

48. See Ex. 19:1 and compare to Ex. 23:16; 34:22; Lev. 23:16; Num. 28:26; and Deut. 16:10.
49. Abrabanel's argument is also strengthened by the disagreement in the Talmud between the rabbis and R. Yossi alluded to previously, as to what day precisely the revelation took place (Shabbat 86b). Rabbi Abraham Gombiner, the *Magen Avraham*, a seventeenth-century Polish commentator on the *Shulḥan Arukh*, the code of Jewish Law authored by Rabbi Joseph Karo (*Oraḥ Ḥayim* 494), states

If Abrabanel is correct, and Shavuot is the thanksgiving festival celebrating God's physical sustenance of His creatures, then we can again
extrapolate, though Abrabanel does not, that Rosh HaShana is the sole
biblical holiday with which the Torah commemorated God's revelation
to the Jewish people at Mount Sinai.[50]

While satisfying in terms of not having to split hairs, this decou-
pling alternative seems quite disturbing to those of us raised to think
differently. The Torah's failure to link the day of the revelation to the
holiday of Shavuot seems not merely to be an act of benign omission but
a conscious decision **not** to recall the revelation of the Ten Commandments close to, if not on, the anniversary of its occurrence. Why would
it choose not to do so?

Perhaps God could not fully forgive the people for their orgiastic worship of the Golden Calf just forty days after the revelation – and
rightly so.[51] In effect, that idolatrous worship – an apparent betrayal,[52]
if not rejection of the God who rescued them from Egyptian bondage
and gave them the Ten Commandments – combined with the shattering

---

categorically in agreement with R. Yossi's opinion in the Talmud that the revelation
took place on the seventh day of Sivan, and not on Shavuot, which commences
on the sixth day of Sivan. Following R. Yossi's opinion means that either Shavuot
is celebrated on the "wrong" day (at least in Israel where the holiday is only
celebrated for one day) or the holiday is celebrating something other than the
revelation at Sinai.

50. A contemporary Orthodox scholar, Rabbi Mosheh Lichtenstein, also makes this
argument: "The upshot of all these calendar calculations is that Shavuot is essentially
independent of *Matan Torah* and its essence must be sought elsewhere" (http://
etzion.org.il/vbm/english/shavuot/shv60ml.htm). Another Orthodox scholar,
Dr. Elchanan Samet (*Studies in the Weekly Torah Portion*, First Series, "*Parashat Emor*,"
p. 104 and footnote 22 [Yediot Achronot Books, Chemed Press, 2009]), points out
further that not only is there no linkage in the Torah of Shavuot to the giving of the
Torah, but there is virtually no linkage of the two in Second Temple sources either
(e.g., Philo, Josephus, or even the Mishna). See also the previous chapter, "Not by
Bread Alone," for my interpretation of the historical significance of the Shavuot
holiday in the Torah.

51. To support this contention see Rashi on Num. 14:33, "Forty years," in which he argues
that the decree of forty years of desert wandering was for both the sin of the spies
and for the not-fully-requited sin of the Golden Calf.

52. See the opinion of Ulla in Shabbat 88b.

of the tablets, annulled the first covenant between God and the Jewish people at Sinai. It was as if Moses, upon seeing the people worshiping the calf and violating their commitment of fidelity to God (Ex. 19:8; 24:3, 7), ripped up the "marriage contract," already metaphorically ripped apart by the people's actions.[53] It is no wonder that the Torah does not link the holiday of Shavuot to the Sinai revelation. Given the people's subsequent actions, there was nothing to celebrate on that day. It was not until the people repented and God agreed – following Moses' repeated pleadings – to "rejoin and recovenant" the Jewish people with a second, replacement marriage contract (the second set of covenantal tablets)[54] in the month of Tishrei, that the covenantal relationship was reconstituted.[55]

If this reading of the Torah is correct, the holidays of Rosh HaShana and Yom Kippur reenact both sides of the reconstituted relationship. Rosh HaShana represents the Jewish people's second, and this time, faithful acceptance of God's kingship, covenant, and revelation while Yom Kippur represents God's forgiveness of the Jewish people after their worship of the Golden Calf. Linking the two are the Ten Days of Repentance reflecting the Jewish people's contrition for their idolatrous behavior.

SHAVUOT AND ROSH HASHANA: A RABBINIC REFRAMING

The question which now cries out for a response is why the talmudic sages relinked Shavuot with the Sinai revelation and grounded Rosh HaShana in the story of creation. We can only speculate as to their motivation. Here are two different, perhaps complementary, theses, which attempt to do so.

The rabbis were living in a period of immense social and historical upheaval. With the Roman conquest in the first century CE, the Land of Israel stood barren and desolate, the holy Temple lay in ruins, and the Jewish people were exiled, unable to fulfill their celebratory rituals.

---

53. See Rashi on Ex. 34:1.
54. Ex. 34:10, 27, 28.
55. For a more benign view of the meaning of the Golden Calf, see Yehuda Halevi's interpretation in his classic book, *The Kuzari*, 1:97.

Scattered in the Diaspora far from God's land, the people had neither first fruits to offer nor the Temple to which to bring them. To associate Shavuot with the bringing of these crops, the fruit of the land's bounty and of God's providence, would have evoked immense psychological pain among an already demoralized people.

Instead, our sages emphasized the tradition associating the date of Shavuot with the revelation at Sinai, which took place at approximately the same time (apparently, during the first week of the month of Sivan). The Sinai revelation was far more meaningful for the exiles, since it took place outside the land, in the wilderness, which was where the Jewish people metaphorically found themselves again; its product, the covenant, was one the Jewish people could, and indeed needed to, wholeheartedly embrace if they were to remain a distinct nation living in the Diaspora.[56] One motive for the rabbis then was, simply put,

---

56. Rabbi Elchanan Samet, cited above, puts it this way: "In the consciousness of the later generations that were removed from the original meaning of the days of the harvest because of their residing in exile and their distance from working the land, the festival of Shavuot acquired the central meaning of being 'the period of the giving of the Torah.'" In another essay ("The Parasha of the Festivals: Its Structure and Significance," May 8, 2003, http://www.vbm-torah.org/parsha.63/31emor.htm), Rabbi Samet makes an even more audacious claim based on a close reading of the biblical text in Lev. 23: "Not only are the waving of the Omer and the bringing of the 'Two Loaves' mitzvot that apply only in *Eretz Yisrael*, but the very days upon which these sacrifices were brought were not commemorated in the desert. The festival of Shavuot, after all, is altogether dependent on the counting of the fifty days from the waving of the Omer, **and when there is no day of waving then clearly there can be no festival of Shavuot!**" Based on Rabbi Samet's close reading, the holiday of Shavuot had no biblical leg to stand on once the Jews were exiled and the Temple destroyed, since there was no Omer or Two Breads to bring. Therefore, perforce, the rabbinic sages had to find a different foundation on which to premise this holiday.

Rabbi Arthur Waskow makes a similar point (*Jerusalem Report*, May 20, 2013, p. 45, "Her as Holy"):

The rabbis of the Talmud could no longer celebrate Shavuot by bringing sheaves of newly sprouted grain and two loaves of leavened bread to the Temple after its destruction by the Romans. Indeed as the Jewish community became more and more dispersed, the food offering connection with any piece of earth grew weaker. To replace food and land, the rabbis sought to make words of prayer, words of Torah, and words of reinterpretive Midrash ways of connecting with God. So they sought to create a festival when all Israel in every generation

to save the Jewish people from further trauma and save the holiday of Shavuot from oblivion.

Having done so, the rabbis then searched for an additional, universal meaning to Rosh HaShana as a commemoration of creation, which could buttress observance of the holiday by Jews in the Diaspora. Since they had an ancient oral tradition from R. Eliezer linking the creation of the world and of Adam to this day (Rosh HaShana 10b), they emphasized that tradition, and called the day by the appellation "Rosh HaShana," to lock in the new understanding of that day.[57] Despite having done so, they still left discernible vestiges of the day's original significance as *zikhron terua*, the recollection of the Sinai revelation, within the liturgy and rituals of the day. This might be called the "domino" theory of how the rabbis reinterpreted these two holidays: the necessity of reframing

---

could stand at Sinai to receive the words of the Torah and speak new words of Torah, as on Passover all Israel in every generation could walk away from Egypt's Tight and Narrow Space [a literal translation of the Hebrew word for Egypt, *Mitzrayim*].

57. See the first, second, and third mishnas of Tractate Rosh HaShana. Note that the first mishna refers to the first day of Tishrei as only one of four Rosh HaShanas in the course of the year:

> There are four Rosh HaShanas: On the first of Nisan is Rosh HaShana for calculating [Jewish] kings and festivals; on the first day of Elul is Rosh HaShana for tithing of animals; ... on the first day of Tishrei is Rosh HaShana for [purposes of calculating] years [the start date of contractual documents according to the reign of non-Jewish monarchs], the [heralding of the] Sabbatical and Jubilee years [when no planting or reaping is permitted], for planting [calculating the age of fruit trees, whose fruit are not permitted during the first three years after planting], and for [tithing] vegetables; and on the first day of Shevat is Rosh HaShana for trees.

However, the common assumption, one which the Mishna apparently wanted its readers to make, was to conflate the first mishna with the second mishna that designates (this third) Rosh HaShana as "Rosh HaShana – when all people pass before God as God's legions, as it says (Ps. 31:15), 'who has formed their hearts together (*yahad*), who understands all of their actions.'" Since the second (and third) mishna of the tractate refers only to this day as "Rosh HaShana," and associates the day with God's judgment of His creatures, a concept that speaks to the core of our existential human condition, we, like the second mishna in the tractate, have come to refer to this day in the Jewish calendar as Rosh HaShana as well. This answers the last of the seven questions posed at the beginning of this chapter as to why this day is called Rosh HaShana.

the meaning of Shavuot led to the reframing of the meaning of Rosh HaShana as well.

A second consideration that may have contributed to the rabbinical shift in the meaning of Shavuot and Rosh HaShana was the grave threat that early Christianity posed to rabbinic Judaism. As part of their fierce polemic against early Christianity's transmutation of the manna, heavenly bread, into a symbol for the body of Christianity's savior – which his disciples were instructed to consume through the ritual of the Eucharist[58] – the rabbis cleared from Shavuot its biblical association to both the manna[59] and bread generally and instead used these as metaphors for Torah.[60] Thus the holiday of Shavuot, in which the Bible celebrated God's **physical** nurturance of His people through the manna with the first fruits offering,[61] was decisively reinterpreted by the rabbis into the holiday celebrating God's **spiritual** nurturance of His people through the bestowing of the Torah.

Then, to counter Christianity's critique of Jewish particularism and chosenness, the rabbis backed off from explicitly associating Rosh HaShana with the Sinai revelation and covenant, in which the Jewish people's special status is given its most emphatic articulation (Ex. 19:4–6). Instead, they associated the holiday with the most universal story of the Jewish tradition, the story of the creation of the universe. They drove home the universal character of the day by naming it "Rosh HaShana" and positing that all human beings, not merely the Jewish people, were judged on that day.[62]

---

58. See especially John 6:30–58 and Matthew 26:26.
59. See chapter 2, "Not by Bread Alone: Why We Count the Omer and Celebrate Shavuot," above.
60. See, for instance, *Sifrei* on Deut. *Parashat Ekev*, 48; Exodus Rabba 5:9.
61. See chapter 2: "Not by Bread Alone."
62. See the rabbis' proof text of Psalms 33:15 in Mishna Rosh HaShana 1:2. In this regard, it is worth noting that Rabbi Nachman Cohen, author of the *Master a Mesikhta* series on the Talmud, in his volume on Rosh HaShana, interprets the second mishna's statement that "all human beings are judged on Rosh HaShana" as following the opinion of R. Yehuda. However, this was not a universally accepted opinion. Two other rabbinic sages disagreed – R. Yossi, who says that human beings are judged every single day, and R. Natan, who says that people are judged at every moment. See Rosh HaShana 16a for the proof texts that are cited to support each position.

Following through on this interpretation, the rabbis may have further utilized Rosh HaShana as a polemic against early Christian teachings through their choice of the biblical and prophetic readings for the holiday. To counter the claim of Christian supersession, the rabbis chose as the Torah readings for the first day of Rosh HaShana the banishment of Ishmael (Gen. 21: 9–21), the rejected son, as it were, of Abraham. This choice of biblical reading by the rabbinic sages may have functioned as a hidden, polemical allusion by the rabbis to their rejection of Jesus and later of Mohammed.

On the second day, the rabbis chose as the Torah reading the next chapter in the Book of Genesis, the *Akeda* of Isaac, the near-sacrifice of the progenitor of the Jewish people by his father Abraham. In the Bible, Abraham's willingness to sacrifice his son evokes eternal divine blessing on Abraham's future progeny. Rather than read the revelation of the Torah at Sinai, the rabbis chose this biblical story, full of pathos, as the day's reading. One cannot fail to notice that this story, which preceded the New Testament by nearly two millennia, was in effect rabbinic Judaism's response to the passion of the New Testament's story of Jesus' Crucifixion.[63]

In addition, the rabbis chose two prophetic readings that reinforced this anti-Christian polemic. The first day's reading – Hannah's prayer from I Samuel 1 and 2 – foretells Davidic kingship and represents a pointed jab at early Christianity's claim that Jesus was the messianic descendant of King David and his true spiritual heir. On the second day, the prophetic reading from Jeremiah 31 evokes the figure of the weeping matriarch Rachel and her beloved son Ephraim, as a possible counterpoint to and refutation of the later Christian matriarch Mary and her son Jesus. The rabbinic selection of these biblical and prophetic texts for Rosh HaShana is striking in this polemical context.[64] This thesis

---

63. In the latter, Jesus' "Father" (in heaven) chooses to sacrifice (and later, resurrect) His "son" to bring salvation to mankind (see John 3:16). The prophetic reading of the first day of Rosh HaShana, in which Hannah "offers" her son to God for a lifetime of divine service is yet another example of this sacrificial impulse preceding Mary's offering of her son to divine service.

64. See Leo Strauss, *Persecution and the Art of Writing* (University of Chicago Press, 1952).

might be called the "self-defense" theory of the rabbinic reinterpretation of the holidays.[65]

The rabbinic reinterpretation of the biblical holidays captured the imagination and allegiance of the Jewish people who, for nearly two millennia, lived in exile. They had never seen the Temple and the pageantry of the first fruit ritual, and barring the coming of the Messiah, would not see it in their lifetimes. They felt beleaguered by Christian triumphalism and embraced the Rabbinic defense of their religious identity. Thus, the rabbis' understanding took hold over time and became authoritative.

Now that the Jewish people have returned to their land, if not quite to the Temple, and the need for anti-Christian polemics has largely dissipated in the early twenty-first century, it is time to resurface the original, biblical meaning of these holidays side by side with their later rabbinic significance, in order to deepen our religious understanding and experience.

INTERNALIZING ROSH HASHANA THROUGHOUT THE YEAR

Our post-modern world posits that all narratives are legitimate expressions of the human condition; no narrative, and no ethical system deriving from it, is inherently privileged.

The collective memory of Sinai, reenacted through the commemoration of Rosh HaShana, is, at least as far as the Jewish people are concerned, a counter-cultural critique of this post-modern position. We privilege certain texts, such as the narrative of the revelation at Mount Sinai, which we dramatically reenact, and we privilege a set of norms, like the Ten Commandments, a set of non-negotiable moral demands which we unconditionally accept. Indeed, civilization as we know and cherish it is impossible without adherence to these ethical norms (witness the barbarian atrocities being committed in the Middle East by those who do not accept these norms, or the flagrant abuse of many of these norms of decency even within Western culture). The divine source of these norms, embodied in the revelation of God's kingship

---

65. In this regard, see Israel Jacob Yuval, *Two Nations in Your Womb: Perceptions of Jews and Christians in Late Antiquity and the Middle Ages* (University of California Press, 2006).

and covenant at Mount Sinai, anchors our ethics in absolute terms and is a necessary corrective to the rootlessness of our age and the moral relativism of our times.[66]

And it was not only the Ten Commandments that were revealed at Mount Sinai. The covenant between God and the Jewish people forged at Mount Sinai included all the civil, criminal, and ethical laws found in the Torah portion of *Mishpatim*, immediately following the Ten Commandments in the Book of Exodus.[67] In fact, the rabbinic tradition roots the authority of **all** the Torah's commandments, a large percentage of which have a strong social and ethical basis, to the revelation at Mount Sinai.[68] Moses himself, in the Book of Deuteronomy, his ethical will to the Jewish people, repeatedly emphasizes the divine source as well as the ethical, social values of the covenant and the commandments.[69] Thus, the divinely sanctioned ethical principles embedded in the revelation of the covenant at Mount Sinai, commemorated by Rosh HaShana, overflowed into the consciousness and behavior of the Jewish people throughout the year.

Liturgically, the primary way that we carry forward the theme of God's kingship and God's covenant from Rosh HaShana on a daily basis is through the mandated twice-daily recitation of the *Shema*. In the Torah scroll and in many of our prayer books, the first verse of the *Shema* contains a peculiar anomaly: the last letter of the first word, the *ayin* of the word "*Shema*," and the last letter of the last word, the *dalet* of "*ehad*," are written in an enlarged font. Together, these two letters form the Hebrew word "*ed*," meaning witness. The purpose of the recitation of *Shema*, Judaism's credo, is to bear witness to God's sovereignty and uniqueness in the world. By reciting the three sections of the *Shema*,

---

66. See also David Hazony, *The Ten Commandments: How Our Most Ancient Moral Text Can Renew Modern Life* (Scribner, 2010).
67. Ex. 24:3–7. See also the commentaries of Ibn Ezra and Nahmanides, ad loc.
68. See, for instance, Maimonides, Introduction to *Mishneh Torah*.
69. Moses reiterates the revelation of the Ten Commandments in Deuteronomy 5. Throughout the Book of Deuteronomy, Moses repeatedly uses the term "*ah*," "brother," to refer to one's fellow Jew, a reflection of the social solidarity that emerges from the covenantal experience at Sinai.

we in effect proclaim the kingdom of heaven, the obligation to fulfill the commandments, and the memory of the Exodus as the basis of our belief in God and way of life.

In Temple times, the Ten Commandments were also recited publicly as part of the morning prayer service, immediately prior to the reading of the *Shema* (as the two appear together in Deuteronomy, with the Ten Commandments appearing in chapter 5 and the *Shema* following it in chapter 6). This practice of reciting the Ten Commandments prior to the reading of the morning *Shema* was discontinued when early Christians claimed that the Ten Commandments were the only commandments of God that were still valid.[70] Nevertheless, there are still traditional Jews whose custom it is to privately recite the Ten Commandments daily, after the conclusion of the entire morning prayer service, as well as the passage from Deuteronomy 4 (quoted at the beginning of this chapter) mandating that we remember the day of the Sinai revelation.[71]

A second piece of liturgy used to reinforce the principle of divine kingship on a daily basis is "*Alenu*." This prayer, recited at the conclusion of each of the three daily prayer services for the past several hundred years, has its roots as the opening prayer of the Kingship section of the Rosh HaShana *Amida* for perhaps the last 1,800 years. The key motif of the prayer is found as the congregants bow down: "And we kneel and prostrate ourselves before the King of all kings, The Holy One, Blessed Be He."

By instituting this prayer at the conclusion of our prayer services every day, the rabbis were able to instill the core principle of the kingship of God into the congregants' consciousness thrice daily, all year round.

The Shabbat prayers provide additional liturgical reinforcement of the kingship of God on a weekly basis. *Kabbalat Shabbat*, the series of six psalms welcoming Shabbat before the singing of *Lekha Dodi* ("Come my Beloved, let us welcome the Shabbat queen"), has at its core the idea of the divine King.[72] The final psalm recited before the Shabbat evening

---

70. See Berakhot 12a; Y. Berakhot 81.

71. As part of the six "commandments to remember" that Jews are biblically commanded. Both are found in traditional prayer books at the conclusion of the morning service.

72. Ps. 95:3; 96:10; 97:1; 98:6; 99:1; 29:10.

service climaxes with an image of this King enthroned on high: "The Lord reigns, He is robed in majesty, the Lord is robed, girded in strength. The world is firmly established; it cannot be moved. Your throne stands firm as of old, You are eternal" (Ps. 93:1–2).

The theme of the kingship of God is carried through in the Shabbat morning *Amida* prayer as well. There, in the third stanza of the *Kedusha*, recited aloud responsively by the prayer leader and the congregation, we read:

> Reveal Yourself from Your place, O our King, and reign over us for we are waiting for You. When will You reign in Zion? May it be soon in our days and may You dwell there forever and for all time…. May our eyes see Your kingdom, as is said in the songs of Your splendor, written by David, Your righteous, anointed one: The Lord shall reign forever and ever.

Immediately following the *Kedusha* proclaiming God's kingship, the central blessing of the Shabbat morning *Amida* then refers to the revelation of the Ten Commandments at Sinai:

> Moses rejoiced at the gift of his portion when You called him "faithful servant." A crown of glory You placed on his head when he stood before You on Mount Sinai. He brought down in his hands two tablets of stone on which was engraved the observance of the Sabbath.

This sequence of prayers on Shabbat thus mirrors the *Amida* for *Musaf* on Rosh HaShana, in which the section proclaiming the kingship of God (*Malkhuyot*) is followed by the section about remembering of the covenant (*Zikhronot*) – embodied in the Ten Commandments – and the section describing God's revelation on Mount Sinai (*Shofarot*).

Through the inclusion of these liturgical pieces every Shabbat, the acceptance of the kingship of God and the revelation of the Ten Commandments are reinforced on a weekly basis throughout the Jewish calendar year.

STANDING TOGETHER AT THE REVELATION

The nearly universal synagogue attendance of world Jewry on at least one day of Rosh HaShana reflects a sort of Jungian "collective unconscious" memory of Rosh HaShana as the reenactment of the revelation at Sinai.[73] Like the biblical Jews who stood together at the revelation as "one nation with one heart"[74] and responded to God's voice with the words *"naaseh venishma,"* "we will obey and listen," without fully knowing what they were getting themselves into, contemporary Jews often obediently come to synagogue en masse on Rosh HaShana to listen to the sounding of the shofar without quite fully understanding, or at least being able to articulate cogently, why they are there.

This unconscious memory of standing as a single, united, community-nation before God at Sinai needs desperately to be brought back into the Jewish people's collective consciousness. This would restore the intended meaning of the term *"Yom HaZikaron,"* the "Day of Remembrance," which Rosh HaShana is aptly called in the rabbinic tradition. As currently understood, based in large part on Numbers 10:1–10, *Yom HaZikaron* is primarily about God remembering us, His creatures. But God does not really have memory problems;[75] it is human beings who are prone to forget and whom the Torah admonishes to remember the day of God's revelation at Mount Sinai:

> Only take heed, and be very careful to **guard the memory of the day you stood before God in Horeb** all the days of your life, and teach about it to your children and your children's children. **Do**

---

73. Freud, too, proposed the possibility of a collective unconscious memory:

    The masses too, retain an impression of the past in unconscious memory traces…. It seems to me convincing enough…that the archaic heritage of mankind includes not only dispositions, but also ideational contents, memory traces of the experiences of former generations…. There exists an inheritance of memory – traces of what our forefathers experienced, quite independently of direct communication and of the influence of education by example. (Sigmund Freud, *Moses and Monotheism* [Vintage Books, 1939], 120, 127)

74. See Ex. 19:2 and Rashi ad loc., and Ex. 19:17; see also Nahmanides on Deut. 33:5.

75. We testify to that truth twice, once toward the beginning and once in concluding the recitation of *Zikhronot*, the section on covenantal memory in the *Amida* in *Musaf*, when we say, "There is no forgetfulness before Your glorious throne."

**not forget the things which your eyes saw and do not remove
the memory from your heart**...when God spoke to you out
of the fire and you heard the sound of words but saw no image,
only a sound.[76]

On Rosh HaShana, by consciously remembering and reexperiencing
what the Jewish people experienced at Mount Sinai, we can reestablish
the day as it was in the time of Ezra and apparently as it is meant to be
in the Torah: the holiday on which the Jewish people come together to
reaffirm God's kingship, covenant, and revelation at Mount Sinai.

---

76. Deut. 4:9, 10, 12. Nahmanides, in his commentary to Deut. 4:9, states that to forget
the day of the revelation and the experience of awe that accompanied it is a violation
of a negative biblical commandment.

Chapter Four

Yom Kippur: "Return and Forgiveness"

Return to Me and I will return to you,
says the EverPresent God.
(Mal. 3:7)

Until now we have examined four events in which God revealed the Divine Presence to the entire Jewish people: the Exodus, the splitting of the sea, the raining down of the manna, and the communicating of the Ten Commandments at Mount Sinai. Each event represented some form of redemption – freedom from slavery, rescue from danger, physical sustenance, and the bestowal of a civilizing set of laws to prevent anarchy and inculcate sanctity. For each of these redemptive events, the Bible set aside a sacred day, the first and seventh days of Passover, Shavuot, and Rosh HaShana. Furthermore, as we saw, the rabbis sometimes had to shift the meaning of the biblical holidays in order to deal with the historical challenges that the Jewish people faced after the destruction of the Second Temple.

Yom Kippur, too, commemorates a redemptive biblical event in which the Divine Presence became manifest before the entire Jewish people. However, the redemption was not physical or political as in the first four sacred days, but spiritual, defined by God's forgiveness for the sin of the Golden Calf. The people learned that even when they erred and violated one or more of the Ten Commandments, there was a way back – the way of repentance – that led to atonement, "at-one-ment" with God, and divine acceptance of the human condition. The rabbis, perhaps even the Bible itself, expanded this spiritual redemption after the worship of the Golden Calf to encompass other biblical violations that required God's compassionate forgiveness, so that the day became the day of atonement for all misdoings.

THE MYSTERIOUS NATURE OF YOM KIPPUR

Unlike the other biblical holidays, which are celebratory in nature, Yom Kippur is anything but a celebration. Here is the Torah's prescription for this day:

> On the tenth day of this seventh month is the Day of Atonement; it shall be a sacred holiday to you, and you shall afflict your souls; and you shall bring a sacrificial offering to the EverPresent God. And you shall do no work on that day, for it is a day to make atonement for you before the EverPresent, your God. For any soul that shall not be afflicted on that day shall be cut off from his people. And any soul that does any work on that day, that soul will I destroy from among his people. You shall do no work; it is a statute forever throughout your generations in all your dwellings. It shall be a Sabbath of Sabbaths for you, and you shall afflict your souls; on the ninth day of the month at evening, from evening unto evening, you shall keep your Sabbath. (Lev. 23:26–32)

Rather than revel in good food and drink as we do on all the other biblical holy days including Shabbat, traditional Jews, following the interpretation of "affliction" in the Mishna (Yoma 8:1), refrain for twenty-five hours from all food and drink, bathing, wearing leather shoes, anointing themselves with skin creams and lotions, and sexual relations. And unlike all of the other seasonal holidays, when traditional Jews do use fire to prepare food for the holiday, on Yom Kippur one does not use fire to cook. Indeed, the Torah, in laying out the restrictions for Yom Kippur, seems almost obsessive in its focus on "afflicting" oneself and on avoiding any work, repeating these admonitions three times each within the space of seven verses. This is hardly what one would think of as a holiday!

Because of its stringencies, Yom Kippur, of all the holidays in the Torah, is perhaps the most physically uncomfortable to observe. And yet, it is observed in Israel, where I live, more so perhaps than any other holiday in the course of the year.

Additionally, in what seems like a particularly strange observation, the final mishna in Tractate Taanit records that, historically, the two most joyous days in the Jewish calendar were the fifteenth day of Av[1] and Yom Kippur. What could the rabbis of the Mishna have intended in characterizing the day as an especially joyous one?

Aside from the biblical afflictions and prohibitions from any sort of work, the day is marked by unusual prayers and customs uniquely tied to the day. The morning Torah reading and supplemental *Musaf* service chosen by the rabbis are chock-full of mysterious symbolism, whose meaning is difficult to fathom and whose description of sacrificial rites is even more difficult to relate to. During the *Minḥa* (late afternoon) service, the rabbis have us read the Torah portion from Leviticus about forbidden sexual relationships, followed by the prophetic reading (*haftara*) depicting the fantastic tale of Jonah and the whale. What could a moralizing biblical chapter and a story about a prophet being swallowed by a fish possibly teach us on this most solemn day of the year?

The prayers of the day also beg to be explored. In the run-up to Yom Kippur and at both the opening and close of the holiday, traditional Jews recite *Seliḥot*, penitential prayers for forgiveness, with God's thirteen attributes repeated over and over. Why the mantra-like repetition of these attributes? The holiday formally begins with the recitation of *Kol Nidrei*, a legal formula for annulling vows normally reserved for a

---

1. The biblical equivalent of Sadie Hawkins Day, when young women would go out to the fields in their finery and woo the young men.

court of law, and concludes with *Ne'ila*, a prayer service that lacks the individual confession of the other Yom Kippur prayer services. Neither *Kol Nidrei* nor *Ne'ila* has a parallel in Jewish prayer services throughout the year. Why then do these prayers uniquely frame this day?

And then, there are the distinctive Yom Kippur customs that have developed over the ages. Many men wear a white robe (*kittel*) to synagogue services and many women have the custom of wearing all white and removing gold jewelry on this day. Traditional Jews of both genders prostrate themselves repeatedly during the *Musaf* portion of the Yom Kippur prayer service. What do these rituals, liturgical rites, and customs mean?

THE GOLDEN CALF, AFFLICTION, AND ATONEMENT

To understand the meaning of these ritual and liturgical details we must return to the point in the biblical narrative when the Jewish people were encamped in the desert at the base of Mount Sinai. God had revealed the Ten Commandments to them and then asked Moses to ascend to the top of the mountain – without specifying how long he would be there – so that God could teach him many of the other laws of the Torah (Ex. 24:12). Because Moses had not taken along any food or water to this private tutorial (Deut. 9:9), and because he was gone for such a long time in the middle of the desert's summer heat, the people became anxious that he would not return. Moses was, for the people, their only physical connection to God. In fact, from their perspective, the line between God and Moses was blurred, to say the least:

> And the people saw that Moses was delayed from coming down the mountain so the people surrounded Aaron and said to him: "Get up! Make us a god to go before us because we don't know what happened to that man, Moses, who brought us up from the land of Egypt." (Ex. 32:1)

For the masses, God and Moses were synonymous. Though they had heard God utter the first commandment – "I am the EverPresent God, your God who took you out of the land of Egypt, the house of bondage" (Ex. 20:2) – as far as the *hoi polloi* were concerned, it was Moses, not some invisible, terrifying God, who had led them out of Egypt. Without Moses, they were afraid, no one would provide for them, protect them, or lead them through the vast expanse of the desert to the proverbial Promised Land, the Land of Israel.[2]

In Exodus 32, we read that the people convinced Aaron to help them make a golden calf – a physical object to replace Moses. Aaron agreed, apparently hoping to channel the people's anxiety until Moses would return. He melted down golden earrings, donated by the men from their wives' jewelry, and molded them into the form of a calf. Trying to stall further, and prevent a betrayal of God, Aaron proclaimed: "**Tomorrow** we will have a festival for the **EverPresent God**" (Ex. 32:1–5).

But, as the text records, the people pointed to the calf and said: "**This** is your god, O Israel, who has taken you up from the land of Egypt" (Ex. 32:4). They arose early in the morning, offered sacrifices to their new god and bowed down before it, and then "sat down to eat and drink, and they rose to play" (Ex. 32:6) in what was probably some form of wild sexual orgy.[3]

These actions of the Jewish people were a blatant violation of at least the first two of the Ten Commandments. The first commandment states: "**I am the EverPresent God, your God who took you out of the land of Egypt.**" The people said that the **Golden Calf** was the god that took them out of Egypt. The second commandment states: "You shall make no image of anything…that exists on this earth" (Ex. 20:4). The people made a golden image of something that walks on this earth to represent God.[4] The second commandment also states that such an object should not be bowed down to or worshiped, and the Jewish people prostrated themselves and offered sacrifices to the Golden Calf.

God told Moses, who was still on the top of the mountain, what the people had done, and instructed him to go down to them. On his

---

2. See Ex. 16:2–8, 20:15–18, and *supra*, "Where is Moses?" in the chapter on Passover.
3. The disappearance of Moses' brother-in-law Ḥur, who was supposed to be in charge of the people along with Aaron in Moses' absence (Ex. 24:14), led the sages in *Midrash Tanḥuma* 20 to speculate that he was assassinated during this orgy. See also Rashi's commentary on Ex. 32:6.
4. The calf was an Egyptian idol, "Apis."

way, Moses met Joshua who was awaiting him halfway up the mountain. Joshua, hearing the tumult in the camp below, said in distress: "*Kol milḥama bamaḥaneh*," "There is the sound of war in the camp!" Moses, knowing what had actually happened, replied sadly: "*Ein kol anot gevura, ve'ein kol anot ḥalusha, kol anot anokhi shome'a*," "This is not the sound of affliction of the victor, or the sound of affliction of the loser, it is just the sound of affliction that I hear" (Ex. 32:17–18). Given the situation, Moses might very well have meant, "It is the sound of **God's** affliction that I hear."

What sounds did Joshua and Moses hear that might have afflicted God? They heard the partying of the people, eating, drinking, and engaging in inappropriate sexual "play" before the Golden Calf. This was a betrayal of their commitment made at Mount Sinai to "do and listen" (Ex. 24:7) to God and to God's commandments. Moses, when he saw the orgiastic partying and dancing before the calf, threw down the tablets inscribed with the Ten Commandments in a fit of rage, shattering them into small fragments. In effect, he ripped up the marriage contract that bound God and the Jewish people. With the symbol of their covenant with God literally in pieces, what could the Jewish people do to restore their shattered relationship with the Divine?

One of the greatest scholars who explained the traditions of repentance and atonement in Judaism is Maimonides. In his twelfth-century code of Jewish law, he teaches that one of the key ways to successful repentance is to avoid those means which led to sin in the first place.[5] Applying this insight to the story of the Golden Calf, the Jewish people "afflicted God" by eating, drinking, and engaging in inappropriate sexual behavior as part of their worship. God therefore commanded that they, and all future generations of Jews, avoid eating, drinking, and sexual intimacy on the day of the year that they were ultimately forgiven, in order to repent and gain forgiveness. Therefore, on Yom Kippur, Jews afflict themselves, and avoid the very actions that led to the worship of the Golden Calf, which afflicted God. In so doing, they demonstrate their commitment to not repeating the mistakes of their ancestors.

---

5. *Mishneh Torah*, Laws of Repentance 2:4.

A similar line of reasoning helps us understand the Bible's thrice-emphasized prohibition of work on Yom Kippur. Unlike the other seasonal holidays on which the use of fire to prepare food is permitted, on the holiday of Yom Kippur, like on the Sabbath, it is traditionally prohibited. In fact, the Bible describes Yom Kippur as a "Sabbath of Sabbaths," as we saw in the text from Leviticus above.

The one example given in the Torah of the traditional thirty-nine categories of work prohibited on the Sabbath is the kindling of fire. This particular prohibition was commanded by Moses immediately after he came down from the mountain with the second set of tablets on Yom Kippur, the day of forgiveness for the Golden Calf. And the timing is no coincidence; fire, and its inappropriate usage, was on God's and Moses' minds:

> And Moses assembled all the congregation of the Jewish people, and said to them: "These are the words which the EverPresent God has commanded, that you shall do: 'Six days shall work be done, but on the seventh day shall be a holy day to you, a Sabbath of solemn rest to the EverPresent God; whoever does any work on it shall be put to death. You shall kindle no fire throughout your habitations upon the Sabbath day.'"(Ex. 35:1–3)

Although all work is prohibited on the Sabbath – and on the Sabbath of Sabbaths – Moses specifies the prohibition of kindling fire perhaps because the use of fire facilitated the creation of the Golden Calf in the first place. We know this from Aaron's attempt to deflect responsibility for his pivotal role in fashioning the calf:

> And Moses said to Aaron: "What did this people do to you, that you brought such a great sin upon them?" And Aaron said: "Let not my lord be angry; you know that the people are set on evil. So they said to me: 'Make us a god that will lead us, for this man, Moses, who took us out of Egypt, we do not know what has become of him.' And I said to them: 'Whoever has any gold, let them break it off'; so they gave it me; **and I cast it into the fire, and out came out this calf.**"(Ex. 32:21–24)

Since fire was used to create the calf, either magically, as Aaron implied, or consciously, as the Torah seems to record, telling us that Aaron formed a molten calf (Ex. 32:4), the Torah thrice emphasizes the prohibition of work – whose most prominent example is fire – on this Sabbath of Sabbaths.

We now understand not only why the Bible vehemently insists that Jews afflict themselves (by not eating, drinking, or engaging in sexual relations) but also why the Bible repeats the prohibition of working on this day in such intensive fashion: both are responses to the sinfulness of the Golden Calf. But why, according to our sages, do traditional Jews also afflict themselves on Yom Kippur by not wearing leather shoes, bathing for pleasure, and anointing themselves with moisturizing oils or lotions?

Back in the narrative of the Golden Calf, even though Moses persuaded God not to destroy the people, and granted them provisional forgiveness (Ex. 32:34), God still felt deeply wronged by the people's misdirected worship. So God told Moses that **he** should lead the people to the land of Canaan, accompanied by a heaven-sent angel who would help them conquer the land. God would not accompany them lest He consume them during the journey:

> And the EverPresent God spoke to Moses: "Depart, go up, you and the people that you brought up out of the land of Egypt, to the land – the land flowing with milk and honey – which I swore unto Abraham, to Isaac, and to Jacob, saying, 'To your descendants will I give it; and I will send an angel before you and I will drive out the Canaanite, the Amorite, and the Hittite, and the Perizzite, the Hivite, and the Jebusite; but I will not go up in your midst for you are a stiff-necked people; lest I consume you on the journey.'" (Ex. 33:1–3)

The people were very upset by the news that God would not accompany them. Feeling genuinely contrite for what they had done, they mourned deeply and demonstrated their mournful remorse by removing the jewelry that they had from the mountain of Horeb/Sinai, as recorded in the Torah:[6]

---

6. It is odd that there is no mention of the people wearing jewelry at Mount Sinai. Although it may refer to the "finery" – the clean clothes that they prepared in

And when the people heard these evil tidings, they mourned; and no man put on his jewelry. And the EverPresent God said unto Moses: "Say to the Jewish people: 'You are a stiff-necked nation! If I go up in your midst, in one moment of wrath, I might consume you! As for now, keep off your jewelry, that I may know what to do with you.'" And the Children of Israel stripped themselves of their jewelry from Mount Horeb. (Ex. 32:4–6)

To reconcile with God, on our Day of Atonement, we imitate our ancestors' mourning behavior and engage in the traditional rituals of bereavement: not wearing leather shoes, bathing, or anointing ourselves. For the same reason, the custom is for women not to wear gold jewelry on Yom Kippur. Like the Jewish people in the biblical narrative, we remove our jewelry to persuade God of our contrition and remorsefulness.

Additional customs demonstrate our contrition and remorse. Like the High Priest, who on Yom Kippur wore simple, white, linen garments instead of his customary gold-embellished clothing,[7] we too

---

preparation for God's revelation on the mountain (see Ex. 19:10, 14), I would suggest a different interpretation. The word for "their jewelry" in the verse is spelled *ayin-dalet-yud-mem*, usually pronounced "*edyam*." Those letters, with different vowels, spell the word "*eidim*" – witnesses, reminiscent of how the Torah describes the tablets: "Tablets of testimony, tablets of stone…written with God's forefinger" (Ex. 32:18). To paraphrase a hermeneutic technique often used in rabbinic parlance: do not read the word as denoting "jewelry" (*edyam*) but as denoting "witnesses" (*eidim*). When Moses came down from the mountain and saw that the people were worshiping the Golden Calf, he threw down the tablets from halfway up the mountain, shattering them into what must have been thousands of small fragments of precious stones (according to one rabbinic opinion, the tablets were made of sapphire – see Ex. 24:10). The Torah does not tell us what happened to the fragments of these tablets whose letters were hand-written by God's forefinger. I would suggest that as part of their remorse for worshiping the Golden Calf, the people gathered up these invaluable fragments and wore them on their persons as jewelry – hand-carved, "custom-made" jewelry from God, as it were, of Mount Sinai. Once Moses informed them that God would no longer dwell among them, they removed these covenantal jewels as they were now emptied of their significance as a symbol of their covenantal relationship.

7. Because as the Talmud tells us (Rosh HaShana 26a): "The prosecuting attorney cannot at one and the same time be the defense attorney." That is, since the people donated their gold to create the Golden Calf, it would be inappropriate for the High

dress in simple white clothes. Traditional men wear a *kittel*, a plain white garment that recalls a shroud, the simplest, least ornamental form of clothing. Many women dress in plain, all-white clothing as well. We show thereby that on this day at least, we do not pay attention to ourselves, to our own vanity, but redirect our attention and devotion to God.

RETURN AND REVELATION

Returning to the biblical narrative, God was now, as it were, in a quandary. God wanted to keep a distance from the Jewish people, but recognized their contrition through their mourning and their actions, and saw how much they wanted to reconcile and restore their former intimate relationship. So God encouraged them to continue to show their remorse by not yet adorning themselves with their jewelry, and in turn, tells them that He will rethink his plan.

And this proves to be the tipping point in the biblical narrative – the moment when the people literally re-turn to God as the Divine Presence is revealed, even if still from something of a distance, to all the Jewish people. This revelation of the Divine Presence, the fifth such revelation in the Jewish people's first year of freedom, is indeed the basis for the sacredness of the day of Yom Kippur:

> Now Moses took the tent and pitched it outside the camp, far away from the camp; and he called it the "Tent of Meeting." And it came to pass, that everyone who sought the EverPresent God went out to the Tent of Meeting, which was outside the camp. And whenever Moses went out to the Tent, all the people rose up, and stood, every person at his tent door, and gazed after Moses, until he entered into the Tent. And whenever Moses entered into the Tent, **the pillar of cloud descended** and stood at the door of the Tent; and [the EverPresent God] spoke with Moses. And **when all the people saw the pillar of cloud stand at the door**

Priest, representing the people, to wear his customary gold clothing when performing the rituals to gain atonement for that sin.

of the Tent, all the people rose up and every man bowed down at his tent door. (Ex. 33:7–10)

In contrast to their earlier behavior when they rose up to play and bow down to the Golden Calf, all the people now rise to honor God and, when they see the divine cloud, bow down and prostrate themselves before God's visible presence. So like the Jews who prostrated themselves before God's presence in the Bible, traditional Jews today stand up and prostrate themselves four times before God in the *Musaf* service on Yom Kippur in a dramatic reenactment of the events in which the Divine Presence became manifest to the entire Jewish people.[8]

In the biblical narrative, the people now know that God's presence is returning, even if the relationship is still distant and mediated through Moses. God returned because the people, first figuratively and then physically, turned back toward God.[9] Several verses later, God succumbs to Moses' entreaties and agrees to rejoin the Jewish people on their journey to the Promised Land (Ex. 33:11–18). This willingness to rejoin the people was the cause of great joy then, and in all subsequent generations that relive this tale of ignoble sin and spiritual redemption, of separation from and then reunification with God. And this joy explains the otherwise startling mishna which teaches that "Yom Kippur was one of the two most joyous days of the Jewish year."

We now understand the biblical admonition to afflict ourselves the way we do, the biblical command to abstain from all forms of "work," and the source of the joy that the rabbis spoke of in relation to Yom Kippur. We also understand the reason for the customs of not wearing

---

8. This explains why we repeatedly prostrate ourselves during the *Musaf* service on Yom Kippur. The timing (in three of the four prostrations), however, corresponds to the points in the Yom Kippur service in the Temple that the people would prostrate themselves upon hearing God's name pronounced by the High Priest. Our *Musaf* service describes the Temple service in which we reenact the actions of the Jewish people in Temple times.
9. For a similar reading see Chanoch Waxman, "The Jewelry and the Tent" on *Parashat Ki Tissa* (1999), http://etzion.org.il/en/jewelry-and-tent.

gold jewelry, wearing plain white robes, and repeatedly prostrating our-selves during *Musaf*.

DECODING THE YOM KIPPUR PRAYERS

We have not, however, addressed the Yom Kippur Torah readings and liturgy. Let us begin with what the rabbinic sages considered the high point of the day: the Yom Kippur service performed in the Mishkan, described in both the morning Torah reading and the supplemental *Musaf* prayer.

Understanding the Yom Kippur Service in the Mishkan

In Leviticus 16, the Torah describes the unique service in the Mish-kan, led by the High Priest on Yom Kippur. This service, in which the holiest person entered the holiest place on the holiest day of the year, would be merely of antiquarian interest to us today were it not for the fact that the rabbinic sages chose this chapter as the Torah reading on the morning of Yom Kippur. The sages then doubled the importance of this ancient ritual service in the Temple by making the Mishna's elaborate description of this service, full of mysterious rites, the centerpiece of *Musaf*. Clearly, the sages, who lived after the destruction of the Second Temple, saw something of enduring meaning in this chapter even after the Mishkan and its successor, the Temple in Jerusalem, were gone.

To understand the Yom Kippur service described in Leviticus, we return to the biblical narrative and specifically to the aftermath of the Golden Calf. God had provisionally forgiven the Jewish people, had decided to recovenant with them, and had agreed, in principle, to journey with them to the Promised Land. However, God's presence, although made visible to the people from a distance, was still outside the Jewish people's encampment. To bring God's presence inside the encampment, God instructs the Jewish people to build a home within the camp in which God's presence can dwell. Almost the first thing that Moses does after he comes down for a third time from the moun-tain is to assemble the Jewish people and request that they voluntarily contribute the materials necessary to build a Mishkan to house God's presence.[10] The Mishkan was to be constructed according to the exact specifications given by God through Moses. From a list of raw materials needed to construct the Mishkan and its furnishings, gold was among the most valuable (Ex. 35:5, 22).

These two elements – following God's instructions precisely, and donating the gold necessary to honor God's presence – were tests of the Jewish people's follow-through of their *teshuva*/return to God after the sin of the Golden Calf. At the Golden Calf, in direct violation of God's commandments, the men had given to Aaron their wives' golden earrings to make a god of their own imagination. Now the men went well beyond donating these,[11] and did so enthusiastically, following God's instructions:

> And they came, everyone whose heart stirred him up, and everyone whose spirit made him willing, and brought their contribution to the EverPresent God for the work of the Tent of Meeting and for all the service to take place in it and for the holy garments. And they came, both men and women, all who were willing-hearted, and brought brooches, and earrings, and rings, and pendants, all jewels of gold; every man that brought a contribution of gold objects of every kind to the EverPresent God…. The Jewish people brought a voluntary contribution to the EverPresent God; every man and woman, whose heart made them willing to bring… as the EverPresent God had commanded by the hand of Moses. (Ex. 35:2–22, 29)

Maimonides distinguishes in Laws of Repentance between repentance and complete repentance.[12] The former is marked by an individual recognizing his or her wrongdoing, feeling genuinely contrite, verbally

---

10. The first thing that he did was to prohibit "work" – and specifically as we mentioned the use of fire – on the Shabbat. However important it was to create a sacred space for God to inhabit, it was more important to set aside the Sabbath as a sacred time in which no work would be done – including the creative work necessary to build the Mishkan.
11. Exodus Rabba 48:5.
12. *Mishneh Torah*, Laws of Repentance 1:1, 2:1.

confessing, and making a sincere, internal commitment not to commit the sin again. "Complete repentance" on the other hand, includes all of the former and one, additional, crucial element: encountering the opportunity to sin again in a similar way, under similar circumstances, and turning away from that sin toward God. Maimonides' inspiration for this distinction may very well have been the Jewish people's "complete repentance" after the Golden Calf. By investing their most valuable resources and enthusiastic efforts in building a Mishkan for God, as God had commanded, the Jews demonstrated their "complete repentance" for the sin of the Golden Calf.

The Mishkan thus became the vehicle for returning God's presence among the Jewish people in two senses, both as a physical place where the presence became visible in the desert encampment of the Jewish people, and in a spiritual sense by embodying the people's complete return to God and to following God's will. Hence, it is not surprising that the Mishkan plays such a pivotal role in what transpires on Yom Kippur.

However, one piece of unfinished business from the Golden Calf incident lingered. That was Aaron's pivotal role in fashioning the Golden Calf. In retelling the story in the Book of Deuteronomy, Moses tells the people, "And God was very angry with Aaron, intending to utterly annihilate him, so I also prayed for Aaron at that time" (Deut. 9:20). Indeed, the original chapter in Exodus describing the sin of the Golden Calf ends with the ominous words, "And God smote the people who had made the calf that was made by Aaron" (Ex. 32:35).

Aaron's name (and role) is literally the last word of the chapter, signaling that in the biblical narrative Aaron is held responsible for what transpired. And yet, there is no explicit punishment meted out to Aaron in the Book of Exodus. It seems that Aaron's involvement was glossed over by God at the time, perhaps because of Moses' intervention.

But the suggestion of Aaron's culpability returns implicitly in Leviticus, the next book of the Bible. There, several months after the sin of the Golden Calf, immediately after the Mishkan is inaugurated and the Divine Presence settles within, the following tragic tale transpires:

> And Nadav and Avihu, the sons of Aaron, each took his censer, put fire inside, laid incense on it, and offered a strange fire before

the EverPresent God, which He had not commanded. And there came forth fire from before the EverPresent God, and devoured them, and they died.... Then Moses said unto Aaron: "This is what the EverPresent God spoke, saying: 'Through them that are close unto Me I will be sanctified, and before all the people I will be glorified.'" And Aaron was silent. (Lev. 10:1–3)

God's forgiveness of the Jewish people for the Golden Calf was, as the narrative indicates,[13] and as I have characterized it above, a provisional one.[14] Apparently, the same was true for Aaron and his family. When his sons followed in their father's footsteps and acted on their impulses instead of on God's instructions, bringing a cloud of incense not commanded by God into the Holy of Holies, they were immediately consumed by fire, the very medium that Aaron used in fashioning the Golden Calf. Aaron, perhaps understanding that he had received his comeuppance for his role in the Golden Calf, is silent.[15]

This tragic narrative is crucial in understanding Aaron's central role in the Yom Kippur service in the Mishkan, which occupies such a pivotal place in the traditional Yom Kippur liturgy. The chapter in Leviticus describing that service begins as follows:

And the EverPresent God spoke to Moses after the death of Aaron's two sons, when they drew near before the EverPresent God and died. And the EverPresent God said to Moses: "Tell Aaron, your brother, that he should not come at all times into the holy place within the curtain, before the Ark cover which is upon the Ark, so that he should not die; for only in the midst of a cloud [of incense] will I appear above the Ark cover. This is how Aaron shall come into the holy place..." (Lev. 16:1–3)

---

13. Ex. 32:34 – "And on the day that I remember, I will visit upon them their sins."
14. See also *The Genesis of Leadership*, 180–186.
15. See Leviticus Rabba 10:5 and *Sifra, Milluim* 19 cited by Rashi on Lev. 9:23. For a similar reading of this incident, see also Rav Yair Kahn, "The Death of Aaron's Sons and the Priestly Service on Yom Kippur," http://etzion.org.il/en/ death-aarons-sons-and-priestly-service-yom-kippur.

The biblical text introduces the Yom Kippur service in the Mishkan as a response to the death of Aaron's two sons. Specifically, Aaron, unlike his two errant sons, is not to come into the Holy of Holies on a whim whenever he pleases, but only on one day of the year, on the day of forgiveness, and only according to God's precise instructions. The chapter then gives in elaborate detail the instructions to effect atonement for Aaron and his household, Aaron's children, the Jewish people, and the Mishkan itself, which may have become defiled in the course of the year.[16] Toward the conclusion of the chapter, to sum up the purpose of the elaborate service, the text tells us: "Because on this day you will be forgiven for **all of your sins,** before God will you be purified" (Lev. 16:30).

It was specifically Aaron, who was intimately involved in the sin of the Golden Calf, and through his sons, the sin of trespassing God's domain, who enacted the service repenting for those sins. Indeed, through him, the Yom Kippur service in the Mishkan brought atonement to the entire Jewish people for all the major sins that marred the people's relationship with God and each other in the course of their history. These sins, which were serious in and of themselves, were also emblematic of the sort of sins that we, as human beings generally, Jewish or not, are inclined to commit. Thus the service was meant to bring

---

16. While contemporary readers may understand why all these people have to achieve atonement, we are usually puzzled as to why the Mishkan itself requires atonement. How can a thing, which has not sinned, require atonement? What does that mean? However, when we understand that the Mishkan itself was crucial to the return of the Divine Presence among the Jewish people, the preoccupation with restoring the pristine purity of the Mishkan from ritual defilement becomes clear. God's "home," the Mishkan, no less than God's "mate," the Jewish people and its selected representatives, the High Priest and the priestly family, must all be deemed worthy, properly prepared, and spiritually receptive, for the Divine Presence to continue to dwell amongst them. If anyone committed an egregious sin or came into the Mishkan, whether intentionally or inadvertently, in a ritually impure state (e.g., he had accidentally come in contact with a corpse – death being a contagious, spiritual "contaminant" in the Bible), the Mishkan itself would absorb some of that sin or ritual impurity and make it unsuitable for God's presence to dwell within. On Yom Kippur, the accumulated sinfulness and ritual impurity were spiritually purged from the Mishkan through the sin offerings brought in the unique, annual service.

atonement for all the major categories of sins which human beings tend to commit no less today than in biblical times.

The Components of the Yom Kippur Service in the Mishkan

What was the meaning of each of the Yom Kippur rituals performed in the Mishkan? The first sacrifice brought by Aaron on Yom Kippur was a bull, as a sin offering. Biblical commentators point out that the bull was brought by Aaron as an offering of atonement for the sin of the Golden Calf.[17] As we saw, according to the description of the Golden Calf episode, the biblical text held Aaron responsible for that sin because he facilitated the process of forming the calf. Hence, as the great eleventh-century biblical interpreter Rashi puts it in talking about the red heifer purification ceremony in the Book of Numbers, Aaron offers the "parent," the bull, to God, in order to clean up the mess of the "child," the Golden Calf, and achieve atonement for the calf that Aaron fashioned.[18] On Yom Kippur, this sin offering brought atonement for Aaron and his household.

The second activity in the Yom Kippur service was the offering of fiery incense by the High Priest in the Holy of Holies. The Torah itself offers us a clue as to why. In the prelude to the Yom Kippur chapter, the Torah begins, as pointed out above, with the words, "After the death of the two sons of Aaron, when they came close before God and died." By introducing the Yom Kippur service in the context of the deaths of Aaron's two sons, Nadav and Avihu, the Torah is telling us that this part of the service is meant to expiate their sin of offering fiery incense in the Holy of Holies, which God had not commanded. For trespassing in the divine sanctum without being summoned, Aaron's sons were consumed by divine fire. Notwithstanding Moses' attempt to console Aaron by labeling their lives as "sanctified," God was clearly displeased with their actions. The episode threatened to ruin the inauguration day of the Mishkan and could have led to the removal of the Divine Presence, thus effectively terminating the recently renewed relationship between God

---

17. Rashi, quoting the *Midrash Tanhuma* on Ex. 29:1, *Dibbur hamathil "par ehad"*; and Nahmanides, quoting *Torat Kohanim* (*Sifra*) 4 in his commentary on the priestly consecration service, the *"miluim"* in Lev. 9:2.

18. Rashi on Num. 19:2 quoting *Midrash Tanhuma* 8.

and the Jewish people. Moreover, it brought human death, the highest form of spiritual defilement, into the Holy of Holies.

Therefore, to atone for the sins of his sons and to spiritually cleanse the Holy of Holies, each year on Yom Kippur Aaron brought over from the Altar of Incense a cloud of incense which permeated the Holy of Holies with its fragrant mist and sweet scent. Just as the bull sacrifice atoned for the sin of the Golden Calf, the incense, brought by Aaron as God commanded, atoned for the sins of Aaron's sons.[19]

The incense was brought after Aaron's offering of the bull but before the people's sin offerings because the offerings were brought in concentric circles – first for the High Priest himself and his household, then for his children, "the sons of Aaron," and finally for the people as a whole.

Next, the blood of Aaron's bull sin offering was sprayed before the Ark cover in the Holy of Holies. Both the sacrifice and the spraying of the blood constituted acts of "substitution." First, the sacrificed animal and its blood, equated by the biblical text with its physical life (Lev. 17:11, 14), was to act as a substitute for Aaron and his household to atone for their sins. Second, in the Mishkan, the Divine Presence "sat" enthroned before the cover of the Ark, the place from where God's voice communicated with Moses. Therefore, the cover of the Ark also served as the substitute for God in receiving the blood of atonement.

Having effected atonement for himself and his sons, Aaron then brought the sin offering for the Jewish people, consisting of two goats. One was offered as a sacrifice to God and the other was sent out to "*Azazel*" in the desert.

The first goat offering was apparently an expiation for the people's collective participation in the Golden Calf episode. This sacrificial offering is consistent with the prescribed goat sin offering whenever the

---

19. This is why the second confession that the High Priest offered was for "the sons of Aaron." It is interesting to note that later in the Torah, following the rebellion of Korah, Aaron uses the incense to atone for the sins of the people (Num. 17:11, 12). Apparently having learned from the Yom Kippur service that properly offered incense can atone for improperly offered incense, Aaron as High Priest uses his own incense to expiate the sin of Korah and his followers, who also offered incense which, as Levites, they were not qualified to bring.

collective Jewish people inadvertently sin[20] (which, according to some interpretations, was the case with the Golden Calf[21]). The blood of the goat sacrificed as a sin offering was sprayed before the Ark cover in the Holy of Holies, then on the curtain in the Tent of Meeting,[22] and then on the Incense Altar,[23] just as the blood of Aaron's sin offering was sprayed

---

20. Num. 15:26. See Yair Kahn, above. The last verse of the *Kol Nidrei* service is in fact taken from this hypothetical case: "And the entire community of Israel shall be forgiven as well as the proselyte who lives among them, because the entire people [sinned] inadvertently." I will offer a different reason for the use of this verse in explaining the *Kol Nidrei* service, below.

21. The Jewish people's collective sin at the Golden Calf, unlike their leaders', was apparently unintentional, because it was somehow either coerced by the leaders of the episode who were executed after Moses returned, or came about as a result of some sort of inner compulsion because of the anxiety they felt at Moses' sustained absence and the *hoi polloi* seeking a substitute leader rather than a substitute God (see *The Genesis of Leadership*, 172–178). Although the plain reading of the episode does not support the latter view, the eleventh-century medieval philosopher Rabbi Judah Halevi offers a similar reading in his magnum opus, *The Kuzari*, 1:97, to exculpate the Jewish people from the sin of idolatry. Alternatively, we might cite the talmudic sage Resh Lakish who said that "repentance is great because one's intentional acts are transformed into unintentional acts" (Yoma 86b). The psychological basis of this remark is that one's later remorse for one's actions is understood to mean that had the person who sinned known earlier (when he sinned) what he knew later (after he repented) he would not have sinned in the first place – thereby making his original sin retroactively unintentional. Since the Jewish people repented after the sin of the Golden Calf, their intentionality in worshiping the calf was retroactively nullified and could be atoned for with a sin offering of the goat as prescribed in Numbers.

Finally, the use, specifically, of a goat to act as the paradigmatic sin offering of the people to God in the Yom Kippur service (Lev. 16:5), the inauguration service of the Mishkan (Lev. 9:3), and throughout the year (Num. 15:26), may itself be due to the selling of Joseph into slavery by his brothers and their dipping his coat into the blood of a goat that they slaughtered to hide their crime from their father (Gen. 37). Kidnapping is a sin not only against one's fellow human beings, but against God who outlaws it in the eighth of the Ten Commandments (Rashi, based on *Mekhilta* on Ex. 20:13). The brothers' sin was the first and paradigmatic sin of the "children of Israel." The goat and its blood therefore became the symbol of the collective sins of the Jewish people that required sacrificial atonement (see also below regarding the goat sent to "*Azazel*").

22. That had the picture of the cherubs, symbolizing God's throne, woven into it.

23. That had been defiled by Aaron's sons who took incense from it into the Holy of Holies without being instructed to do so. According to the rabbinic Oral Tradition, the blood of the bull and the goat were mixed and sprayed together, apparently because

and dabbed in those places. As with Aaron's bull, here too, the goat and its sprayed blood acted as a substitute for the lives of the collective Jewish people who had sinned before the divine "throne."

The process of expiation from the sin of the Golden Calf on Yom Kippur evoked, in turn, other associations of sin and sacrifice in the Jewish collective memory that also required forgiveness in this annual service.[24] If the Golden Calf is the archetype of the people's abandonment and betrayal of God in the Book of Exodus, then the sin of Joseph's brothers, who sold him into slavery, is the archetype of the collective guilt of fraternal abandonment and betrayal in the Book of Genesis.[25] The ritual of marking and sending away the second goat into the wilderness seems to echo the sin of Joseph's brothers selling him into slavery.[26]

---

the sins of Aaron and the people were mutually dependent: without Aaron's skill in fashioning the idol, the people could not have sinned and without the people's pressure upon him, Aaron would not have sinned.

24. The rabbis followed this pattern embedded in the biblical service to add later sins in the collective Jewish memory to the centerpiece Golden Calf incident. They did so by fashioning the liturgy of *Kol Nidrei* to repent for the spies and by the choice of Torah reading for the afternoon service to repent for the sin of Baal Peor (Num. 25). These sins were part of "all the sins" with which the text in Leviticus sums up the atonement service on Yom Kippur.

25. This act of betrayal may be a specific instance of what Nahmanides referred to generally as "the acts of the ancestors are a blueprint for the acts of their descendants" (Nahmanides, Commentary on the Torah, Gen. 12:6). See also *Midrash Tanḥuma, Parashat Lekh Lekha* 9 (Mossad HaRav Kook edition).

26. The evidence for this is based on the *Sifra*, a halakhic Midrash to the Book of Leviticus, cited by Nahmanides in his commentary on Lev. 9:2. The *Sifra* suggests that the goat sacrifices offered at the inauguration of the Mishkan were an atonement for the Jewish people for kidnapping and selling Joseph into slavery. The same is arguably true here in the Yom Kippur service, modeled closely on the inauguration service. According to the Book of Jubilees (Jub. 34:18, 19), a pseudepigraphical work of the second century BCE, Jacob's sons slaughtered a goat, dipped it into the goat's blood, and then sent Joseph's blood-stained coat to Jacob on the tenth of Tishrei (i.e, the day that we commemorate as Yom Kippur). Apparently, the author of the Book of Jubilees, basing himself on Leviticus, also connected the goats featured in the Yom Kippur service to the story of Joseph. See also Calum Carmichael, *Illuminating Leviticus* (Johns Hopkins University Press, 2006), who makes a similar argument.

The compelling literary parallels between the Joseph story and the Yom Kippur service indicate how the latter might atone for the former. Immediately prior to the kidnapping of Joseph, the Torah tells us that an anonymous *"ish"* (man), found

That pernicious act led to the enslavement of the whole Jewish people for hundreds of years and to God's visible absence from the lives of the

---

Joseph "*to'eh basadeh*," wandering in the field (Gen. 37:15), and directed him to his brothers. When Joseph finally located his brothers and they spotted him from a distance, his fate was initially unclear. First, they thought to kill him; then they voted to just throw him into a pit and let him die of natural causes; finally, they decided to sell him into slavery and doomed him to what might be charitably described as "an uncertain fate" in the hands of Midianite/Ishmaelite slave traders. This uncertain fate entailed a journey through the desert linking Canaan to Egypt where he was sold as a slave, a virtual death sentence in biblical times. To cover up their crime, the brothers then slaughtered a male goat, dipped Joseph's coat in it and sent it to their father, Jacob. The blood of the goat was used by the brothers as the surrogate for Joseph's blood. Indeed, Jacob cried out upon seeing the blood-sprayed coat: "A wild animal has devoured Joseph!"

In the Yom Kippur service, two goats were selected – the first to be offered to God in the Mishkan and the second to be sent out to "*Azazel*" in the desert. The goats were designated for their respective fates via lottery, which necessarily implies an unknown result. The first goat was slaughtered and brought as a sin offering to God in the Mishkan. The Torah describes the man who escorted the second goat to *Azazel* as an "*ish iti*" ("a designated man"), almost certainly a play on the words "*ish ... to'eh*" ("a man ... wandering") in the story of Joseph. (The letters *taf, ayin, heh* spell out *to'eh*, while the letters *ayin, taf, yud* spell out *iti*. In the Bible, *yud* and *heh* are interchangeable [as in the change of name of Sarai to Sarah in Gen. 17:15]). The word "*Azazel*," to which the goat was sent, may itself be a compound of two words: *eiz azal* (lit., "goat left" – where to, no one knows.). According to *Sifra, Aḥarei Mot* 2:4 and Yoma 67a, the goat met a bloody death after it was thrown off a steep cliff. Alternatively, in a reading suggested by Carmichael, "*Azazel*" was a term for a demonic wild force that lurked in the desert – a parallel to the illusionary "wild animal" that the brothers wanted Jacob to believe had devoured Joseph.

The goat ritual in Leviticus and the story of the selling of Joseph in Genesis both use the root word SH-L-Ḥ (sent) four times. In the Joseph story, Joseph was twice described as being "sent" by his father, Reuben urged the brothers not to "send" their hands against the lad, that is, not to murder him, and the blood-filled coat was "sent" by the brothers to their father. In our reading in Leviticus, the first goat is repeatedly described as being sent into the desert. Apparently the Bible wanted us to understand that the scapegoat was being "sent out" on Yom Kippur to dramatically evoke and symbolically atone for the Children of Israel **sending out** (i.e., recklessly abdicating responsibility for and "scapegoating") their brother.

Appropriately, the rabbis tell us that when the goat sent to *Azazel* perished in the desert to complete the process of atonement, the red string that was hanging in the Mishkan miraculously turned white (Yoma 67–68). This is a reversal of Joseph's brothers dipping the coat into blood and turning it red (I am indebted to Dr. Yaakov Ugowitz for this insight).

Jewish people from the time that Jacob/Israel journeyed down to Egypt (Gen. 46:1–4) until God remembered His covenantal promise hundreds of years later (Ex. 2:22–25). This collective sin left a spiritual vacuum in the collective lives of the Jewish people and an indelible, bloody stain not merely on Joseph's coat, but on the Jewish nation as a whole.

Like Joseph, upon whom the brothers projected their own troubles and inadequacies, and whom they blamed for the lack of their father's love, the second goat, sent to *Azazel*, had all the sins of the people symbolically placed on its head by the High Priest (hence the term "scapegoat"). The goat was then sent out of the camp and escorted through the desert to an uncertain fate, just as Joseph, after he was sold into slavery, was escorted through the desert by the Midianite/Ishmaelite traders who brought him to an uncertain fate in Egypt.

This ritual, which reenacted Joseph's experience, was sure to evoke a sense of guilt and deep contrition in those who understood the symbolic meaning of these acts. Like the blood of the goat in the Joseph story which became the surrogate for Joseph's blood, in Leviticus the lifeblood of the goat sent to *Azazel* acted as the surrogate for the blood-curdling kidnapping and selling of Joseph into slavery.

When the Jewish nation left Egypt, they had an additional material reminder of this collective sin. As per Joseph's dying wish, Moses carried his forefather's remains with him out of Egypt and throughout the forty-year sojourn in the desert.[27] Moses, the people's leader, lifted Joseph's bones out of his grave and bore his casket out of Egypt to reverse the earlier leaders' responsibility for throwing Joseph into the pit that would have been his grave, and selling him to a slave caravan bound for Egypt. The annual Yom Kippur service led by the High Priest, representative of their descendants, brought further atonement for the twelve tribes, the nation's ancestors, before the Divine Presence.

This understanding of the meaning of the goat sent to *Azazel* helps to explain why in the *Musaf* service, after the description of the Temple service performed by the High Priest on Yom Kippur, the rabbinic sages inserted the martyrology, the searing liturgical poetic description of the ten great Jewish sages in the second century who were executed by the

---

27. Ex. 13:19; see also Joshua 24:32.

Romans. According to this liturgy, the wicked Roman tyrant Hadrian seized upon the lack of any overt punishment for Joseph's ten brothers for kidnapping their younger brother as a pretext to sentence the ten great rabbinic leaders of his time to cruel and unusual deaths. By placing the Temple service and martyrology in sequence, the sages who composed the Yom Kippur prayers were telling us that, after the destruction of the Temple and the disappearance of the animal sin offerings on Yom Kippur, these ten martyrs were cynically used by the pagan Hadrian, as **human** sin offerings, for the Jewish people's sins in the Joseph story.[28]

To sum up: the first four parts of the service – the offering of the bull, the incense, the goat offering, and the spraying of the blood – collectively expiated the two primal sins of the Jewish people **against God** up until this point in the Torah's narrative (the Golden Calf and the offering of fiery incense by Aaron's sons). Once atonement was made with God for these two sins, then the second goat, which symbolized Joseph's ordeal, was sent out to *Azazel* to atone for the Jewish people's earlier sin **against their brother**. This helps to explain the repeated use of the words "*kol ḥatotekhem*," "the atonement for **all** your sins," achieved with this service on Yom Kippur – the two sins against God and the sin against Joseph by his brothers.

The fifth substantive part of the Yom Kippur service was the offering of two rams as communion offerings (*olot*),[29] one for the High Priest and one for the Jewish people. The rams symbolized the offering by Abraham of Isaac as a wholly burned communion offering at the *Akeda* (Gen. 22:2, 13). Having "made up" with God for the three primal sins of the collective Jewish people, the people could achieve total communion with God by reenacting Abraham's wholehearted offering of his son. The priest's ram symbolized Abraham's sacrificial devotion while the people's ram symbolized Isaac's willing surrender (Isaac was the first Jewish child and hence the progenitor of all the Jewish people).

---

28. The bitter irony is that this vicious pagan act by the Roman Emperor Hadrian was a reversal of, and a regression from, the biblical *Akeda* story read on Rosh HaShana, where animal sacrifice replaces human sacrifice.

29. An "*ola*" (singular) is a "closeness offering" (*korban*) in which the entire animal is sacrificed, symbolically offering the giver's entire self, as it were, to the Divine. The person "communes," aspires to be one, with God. The translation "burnt offering" conventionally used, fails to capture the telos of this sacrificial offering.

The symbolic acts of willing devotion and surrender to God embodied in these communion offerings sealed the covenantal relationship between God, the priesthood, and the people. They assured that God's presence would continue to dwell among them in the center of the camp for another year.

The Torah reading and the *Musaf* service of Yom Kippur, then, are intended to help us relive (Taanit 27a) the sacrificial service that atoned for the primal sins in the history of the Jewish people, and thus seek atonement for the way those sins of betraying God and our fellow human beings may be manifested in our own personal lives (Menaḥot 110a). Once we have atoned for our sins, we read about how the Jewish people were restored through the communion offerings to a state of wholeness with God and each other. Today, when we no longer have the Temple, our prayers, which have taken the place of Temple sacrifices,[30] can restore us to the state of spiritual redemption achieved by our biblical ancestors. This in turn leads us to why we recite the *Seliḥot* prayers in the run-up to, and on, Yom Kippur.

The Role of the *Seliḥot*

Seliḥot are prayers for forgiveness recited in the period leading up to, and on, Yom Kippur.[31] The *Seliḥot* consist of liturgical poems, *piyutim*, from the late rabbinic and early medieval periods. Each poem leads to the repeated public chanting of God's thirteen attributes from the Bible, followed by God's promises to forgive the Jewish people for their sins.

There are different customs as to when in the Jewish calendar the recitation of these prayers for forgiveness begins. As far back as Maimonides in the twelfth century, the custom was to recite the *Seliḥot* prayers only between Rosh HaShana and Yom Kippur.[32] However, as time passed, two different customs evolved: the Sephardic, Middle Eastern tradition developed the custom to recite *Seliḥot* from

---

30. See Hos. 14:3: "We shall compensate for [the offering of] bulls with our lips."
31. The first appearance of *Seliḥot* is in the prayer book of Rav Amram Gaon in the ninth century.
32. Maimonides, *Mishneh Torah*, Laws of Repentance 3:4.

the first day of the Hebrew month of Elul – forty days before Yom Kippur – until Yom Kippur.[33] The Ashkenazic, European tradition developed the custom to begin the recitation of *Seliḥot* several days (between four and eight, depending on what day of the week Rosh HaShana falls) before Rosh HaShana and continue that recitation through Yom Kippur.[34]

The reason for reciting *Seliḥot* goes back to Moses' third forty-day sojourn on Mount Sinai. Recall that after the sin of the Golden Calf, Moses achieved provisional forgiveness for the Jewish people. But he realized that God's provisional forgiveness for the worship of the Golden Calf was only a temporary solution to a crisis in the relationship between God and the Jewish people that would likely recur, perhaps in altered form, later on. Moses has just been through a harrowing experience negotiating for the very survival of his people after their sin. Wishing to avoid the process in the future, he sought a deeper understanding of

---

33. This corresponds to Moses' third forty-day stay on Mount Sinai. There he continued to pray for the forgiveness of the Jewish people and ultimately came down from the mountain on Yom Kippur with the second tablets – a concretization of that forgiveness. See Deut. 10:1–11. By reciting the *Seliḥot* for forty days, we reenact Moses' prayers on the mountain for the Jewish people and God's response in the form of the thirteen attributes.

34. One reason for the latter custom, which requires at least a four-day run-up of reciting *Seliḥot* before Rosh HaShana, is based on the description of the sacrificial offerings of the holidays found in Num. 28–29. There, the Torah, in describing the communion sacrifice, which is brought for all the holidays, says that one should "bring" a communion offering. However, for the holiday of Rosh HaShana, the Torah says one should "make" a communion offering. On this, the twentieth-century codifier Rabbi Israel Meir Kagan, in his law code the *Mishna Berura*, says (Laws of Rosh HaShana, chapter 581:6, commenting on Rabbi Moshe Isserles's gloss in 581:1 and citing the *Eliya Rabba*): "That we should 'make' means we should 'make ourselves' into a communion offering. Like the communion sacrifice which was offered totally to God, we should become one with God on Rosh HaShana." How can we become one with God? The commentary continues: "Therefore we require [at least] four days beforehand to check for imperfections." Just like a sacrificial offering requires that it be designated as a sacrifice and set aside at least four days before it is offered to God, so that it can be inspected for any possible imperfections, so too, through the recitation of *Seliḥot*, we prepare ourselves for at least four days before Rosh HaShana and then through Yom Kippur, inspecting and repairing the imperfections in our own characters and personalities so that we can commune with God on the High Holy Days.

"what makes God tick," so that he could work more closely with God and not feel tossed about between God on the one side and the Jewish people on the other, every time the people misstepped. Living constantly on the verge of losing the people was something Moses wanted desperately to avoid (see Ex. 33:3).

Moses therefore asked God for two things in addition to provisional forgiveness for the people. First, that God, who had originally told him he would not lead the people in their journey to the Promised Land, "change His mind." Moses' argument was that if God was not going to accompany the people, there was no point in proceeding to the Promised Land; a home not shared with the Divine Presence was no home at all (Ex. 33:15–16). Second, in order that God not explode again in anger when the people violate another one of the commandments, he requested that God reveal to him the nature of the Commander, "the wizard behind the curtain," as it were, of the commandments:[35] "Let me know Your ways, so that I may know You, in order that I find favor in Your eyes, and see that this nation is Your people" (Ex. 33:13).

Commentators galore have tried to understand what precisely Moses was asking of God. Maimonides' reading in the *Guide for the Perplexed* seems persuasive.[36] In the context of the thirteen attributes with which God responded, Maimonides understands Moses to be asking how God governs humanity, and particularly the Jewish people. If Moses and God are to be partners in leading the Jewish people, then Moses, the "junior partner," is seeking to better understand his "senior partner's" deeper, internal values and subjective processes for relating to the world. When, and on what basis, does God forgive people and when does God not? Why does it seem that the righteous sometimes go unrewarded and the wicked often go unpunished? How does God balance justice on the one hand with compassion on the other?

Just as he sought to know God's name at the burning bush, Moses here wanted to know what to expect from God, "God's ways," (Ex. 33:13) in the future. In effect, Moses was saying: "You revealed to me and to the people, with the Ten Commandments, what it is You want and expect

---

35. An allusion to the American classic film *The Wizard of Oz*.
36. Maimonides, *Guide for the Perplexed* I:54.

from us. But to more deeply understand Your will, I must understand You, the commander – who You are, or at the very least how You relate to humanity and, in particular, to Your people. If I am really special to You, then reveal something more of Yourself to me than merely the commands that You revealed to all the people."

So when Moses goes back up Mount Sinai for a third time, God reveals to him the thirteen attributes (*Shelosh Esreh Middot*), a somewhat different and more complex picture of God than the side that came through in the Ten Commandments. There, God described Himself as a "zealous God who visits the sin of the parents on the children of those who hate Him … who will not forgive." Later on, in the section of civil laws immediately following the Ten Commandments that Moses reads to the people (Ex. 24:3), God warns them that they must obey God's messenger (Moses?), "as he will not postpone [punishment] for your sins because My Name is in him" (Ex. 23:21). In contrast, here God describes Himself as:

> The EverPresent, the EverPresent, a compassionate and gracious God, slow to anger, full of kindness tempered by truth; treasuring loving-kindness for thousands of generations, holding back from punishing sin, transgression, and iniquity; forgiving [those who eventually repent] but not forgiving [those who do not repent] – visiting the sins of the fathers on their children, grandchildren, on the third and fourth generation [if they continue in their fathers' sinful ways]. (Ex. 34:6–7)[37]

We see here a more nuanced, compassionate, gracious, forgiving, patient side to God as compared to the stern, more demanding, even uncompromising side that came through in the revelation of the Ten Commandments and the set of civil laws that Moses received on Mount Sinai.[38]

---

37. Words in brackets are as per the interpretations of the sages cited by Rashi, ad loc.
38. Not for naught is this day called *Yom HaKippurim*, the Day of Atonement, in contrast to Rosh Hashana, commemorating the Sinai covenant which the rabbis called *Yom HaDin* – the Day of Judgment. See p. 90 in the previous chapter on Rosh Hashana.

Moses immediately seizes upon this revelation to plead that God behave as the God He says He **is**: "Therefore, please EverPresent God, walk among us even though the people are stiff-necked – and [if they sin], forgive their sins and transgressions, and make us Your permanent possession" (do not abandon them even if they do sin) (Ex. 34:9). In fact, later on, in the Book of Numbers, Moses successfully uses God's more forbearing and compassionate self-description to save the people from immediate annihilation after the sin of the spies.[39]

God's revelation of the thirteen attributes had a transformative effect on Moses. On the day that he came down the mountain after this personal revelation, with the second set of tablets, Moses' face was aglow with such radiance that the people were afraid to approach him (Ex. 34:30). By rabbinic reckoning and tradition, that day was Yom Kippur.[40] For some time afterward, Moses had to wear a mask, which was a metaphor for the fact that the collective people, and even their leadership,[41] could not absorb the unmediated, complex truth of what Moses had learned about God. Unlike Moses, they needed to have this truth filtered so that they could internalize the otherwise blinding light of God's governance at their own pace and in their own way.

After the destruction of the Temples, the rabbinic sages did with the thirteen attributes what they did with much of Jewish practice that had previously been observed by an elite group only.[42] They democratized their recitation. The rabbis in the Talmud reinterpreted God's personal revelation to Moses on Mount Sinai as a way for all members of the Jewish people to win forgiveness in their future encounters with God. In a graphic midrashic teaching, they had God, robed in a *tallit* as leader of the prayers, telling Moses, "Whenever Israel sins, let them do this order [of the thirteen attributes] before Me, and I will forgive them" (Rosh HaShana 17b).

See also Menachem Leibtag, "God's Thirteen Middot HaRaḥamim for Seliḥot, Rosh HaShana, and Yom Kippur," http://www.tanach.org/special/13mid.txt.

39. Num. 14:17–19. See also my explanation for *Kol Nidrei*, below.
40. Bava Batra 121a, and see Rashi ad loc.
41. "Aaron and all the tribal heads," Ex. 34:31
42. See the chapter in this book on Shabbat, below.

In alignment with this midrash, the rabbis placed the thirteen attributes in the center of the *Seliḥot* prayers, empowering every synagogue prayer leader to invoke them to gain God's forgiveness for his congregation, as Moses had after the sin of the spies. They did this, not because they thought the thirteen attributes was some sort of magical formula, which, recited repeatedly by the synagogue leader in a quorum of ten, could in some mystical way influence – even coerce – God to reconcile with and always forgive the Jewish people. They did not believe that the prayer leader was a magic talisman.

Rather, they wanted the thirteen attributes to become so internalized into our basic character that we would consistently act toward other human beings the way God does. That's why the Midrash in Tractate Rosh HaShana used the language of "they should do before Me this order" and not "they should recite before Me this order." It was not reciting the thirteen attributes, per se, that could bring forgiveness – it was enacting these attributes in our lives, and becoming more forbearing, compassionate, and gracious that would reconcile and unite us with God.[43] The purpose of the multiple repetitions of this portion of the service was to create a mantra-like effect, not coercing God, but transforming ourselves, to become more God-like, more like God's thirteen attributes.

Indeed Maimonides, at two pivotal points in the *Guide for the Perplexed*, also interprets the biblical revelation to Moses of the thirteen attributes[44] as a directive to us to imitate God so that we become

---

43. As Rabbi Kagan says (see footnote 34, p. 137 above): We should "make ourselves" worthy of being a communion offering for God – of being one with God.

44. We have shown why it has been considered sufficient to mention only these [thirteen attributes] out of all His acts ... for the chief aim of man should be to make himself, as far as possible, similar to God, that is to say, to make his acts similar to the acts of God, or as our sages expressed it in explaining the verse, "You shall be holy" (Lev. 19:2). As He is gracious, you also should be gracious; as He is merciful, so you should also be merciful (*Sifrei* to Deut. 10:12) (Maimonides, *Guide for the Perplexed* I:54).

My object [in saying this] is that you should practice loving-kindness, judgment, and righteousness on the earth. In a similar manner we have shown that the object of the enumeration of God's thirteen attributes is the lesson that we should acquire similar attributes and act accordingly. The object of the above passage is therefore to declare that the perfection in which man can truly glory is attained by him when he has acquired – as far as this is possible for man – the knowledge

more compassionate and forgiving.[45] Moreover, it is not enough to superficially imitate those behaviors. Rather we need to understand and internalize the thirteen attributes so that they become an essential part of our inner world, our character, and therefore our behavior.

But the rabbis did more than democratize and internalize God's attributes revealed to Moses. They also "edited" them so that, when recited by the prayer leader and the congregation, they would come across as expressing even more compassion and mercy than they did when God recited them. In the Bible, God concluded His self-revelation to Moses by saying, "forgiving [those who eventually repent], but not forgiving [those who do not repent], visiting the sins of the fathers on their children, grandchildren, on the third and fourth generations" (if they continue in their fathers' ways). But in the rabbis' edited version, the list concludes with, "God … forgives." Period. Without qualifications. Nothing about not forgiving those who do not repent, nothing about visiting the sins upon future sinning generations. This despite the talmudic principle that do we not edit biblical verses in order not to quote part of the verse out of context.[46] There appears to be no more glaring

---

of God, the knowledge of His providence, and the manner in which it influences His creatures in their production and continued existence. Having acquired this knowledge he will then be determined always to seek loving-kindness, judgment, and righteousness, and thus to imitate the ways of God (Maimonides, *Guide for the Perplexed* III:54).

45. Maimonides bases his interpretation of the purpose of the thirteen attributes on a whole slew of rabbinic texts. For instance, in Shabbat 133b, explaining the words "This is my God and I will adore Him" (Ex. 15:2), the Talmud asks: "What does it mean to adore Him? Abba Shaul said: 'I shall adore Him' means be like Him – just as He is compassionate and gracious, you too should be compassionate and gracious!" Then there's the Talmud in Sota 14a commenting on the words, "You should walk after the EverPresent God your God" (Deut. 13:5), asking how does one "walk after God"? R. Ḥama said in the name R. Ḥanina, "This means to follow the attributes of The Holy One, Blessed Be He. Just as He clothes the naked, so should you clothe the naked; just as God visited the sick, so should you visit the sick; as He consoled mourners, so you too shall console mourners; as He buried the dead, so too should you bury the dead, etc."

46. Taanit 27b. "*Kol pesukei delo paskei Moshe annan lo paskinan.*" This is why my teacher, Rabbi Joseph B. Soloveitchik, would begin the Friday night Kiddush with the words, "And God saw all that He made and it was very good," before continuing with the

a violation of this principle than the rabbis having us proclaim something that appears to be not entirely faithful to what God said to Moses.

But understanding that the purpose of reciting God's thirteen attributes is to teach us to embody them explains why in the *Seliḥot* the rabbis had the temerity to edit the words revealed to Moses. If we are to become like God, the rabbis wanted us to emulate only God's most positive characteristics. They did not want us to bear a grudge or be vindictive toward others as would be required if we imitated God "who does not forgive and visits their sins upon the third and fourth generations." The Torah itself, in Leviticus, commands us: "Do not bear a grudge and do not take vengeance" (Lev. 19:18). Since we cannot be God-like in our understanding of other human beings and know whether they have engaged in true repentance, we need to strive to be better than the way God described Himself to Moses in order to come close to achieving God's goodness in actuality.[47]

Moses himself modeled for us a selective recitation of the thirteen attributes after the sin of the spies, editing out God's name "*El*," which is associated with judgment, as well as "*emet*," His attribute of "Truth," as those attributes were not those he wished to emphasize to God when he was praying on behalf of the Jewish people.[48] This editorial decision served as a precedent for the rabbis in reformulating the thirteen attributes for the *Seliḥot* service.

The rabbis' intentions also help us understand the timing of the *Seliḥot* services. During the days leading up to Rosh HaShana and Yom Kippur, the time recommended by rabbinic authorities for reciting *Seliḥot* is the middle of the night. This period is known as "a pleasing time,"[49] not merely for God to accept our prayers but for us, as human beings, to internalize the thirteen attributes and mold our own personalities to become more God-like. In the middle of the night, our defenses come down and our subconscious, our deepest self, is open to

---

remainder of the verse that normally begins Kiddush, "And it was the evening, and it was the morning of the sixth day." See *Nefesh HaRav* [Hebrew edition], 159.

47. See also Maimonides, *Mishneh Torah*, Laws of Repentance 2:10.

48. Num. 14:18. Jonah, following Moses' lead, also (albeit sarcastically) edits out many of God's attributes in the prophetic book we read on Yom Kippur afternoon (Jonah 4:1).

49. Rabbi Israel Meir Kagan, *Mishna Berura*, Laws of Rosh HaShana 681:1.

autosuggestion and to change. The most tender and fulfilling moments between two people who love each other often take place deep into the night, when our guard comes down and when we are most receptive to our beloved.[50] Therefore, the rabbis of the geonic period instituted the custom of reciting the thirteen attributes at this time, when we are most likely to be profoundly impacted by what we hear and what we say.

This same rationale explains why the repeated recitation of the thirteen attributes marks both the evening service that begins Yom Kippur and the *Ne'ila* service that closes it. Yom Kippur is a day when the afflictions that we endure cause us to drop our usual defense mechanisms and open up wholeheartedly to God. Like the middle of the night, which is a "pleasing time" for God and for us, Yom Kippur is the ultimate "pleasing time" for Jews to reunite with God. The *Seliḥot* at the beginning and end of the day serve as a frame for all five Yom Kippur prayer services, encapsulating within their liturgical borders the entire purpose of the day: to come as close to God as is humanly possible.

In sum, the *Seliḥot*, which have as their centerpiece God's thirteen attributes, are meant to transform us as they transformed Moses and to empower us as they empowered him to win forgiveness for our sins. Embodying God's attributes and "becoming holy as God is holy" (Lev. 19:2) is the covenant of the thirteen attributes, in whose merit, according to rabbinic imagination, God promises that our prayers will not go unanswered.

Moses' use of the thirteen attributes to save the Jewish people after the episode of the spies segues into why the rabbis instituted the *Kol Nidrei* prayer on Yom Kippur eve.

Kol Nidrei

Recited as the holiday begins, *Kol Nidrei* is a legal formula for the nullification of vows.[51] Across Jewish denominations, the *Kol Nidrei* service

---

50. That's also why in hasidic circles, "*yeḥidus*" – the one-on-one counseling session with the Rebbe – usually takes place in the middle of the night, when the possibility of fundamental personality change is most acute.

51. The formula for nullification of vows is normally recited by an individual supplicant before three individuals who together comprise a court of Jewish law.

is regarded as one of the most solemn and sacred prayers of the year. But each year I am intrigued as to why, and look for answers to myriad questions that grow out of the prayer:

- Why does the nullification of vows, the function of a Jewish court of law, commence the holy day of Yom Kippur?
- On what basis does the court nullify these vows? Even a court has to have a legal basis for absolving individuals of their commitments![52]
- In the *Kol Nidrei* service, we seem to switch from annulling vows to seeking communal forgiveness from God. What is the relationship between annulling vows and receiving forgiveness?
- Are we not seeking forgiveness for our own individual sins? Then why the emphasis on the collective throughout? Why does the prayer book say, "And You should forgive the **entire community** of the Children of Israel" and "Please forgive the sin of this **people**." What sin did the entire people engage in that requires forgiveness?
- Finally, where do all these verses that conclude the *Kol Nidrei* come from?

Kol Nidrei truly is a unique service. The key to unlocking its meaning may come from answering the final question above.

Three verses conclude the *Kol Nidrei* service:

> And they shall be forgiven, all the congregation of the Children of Israel, and also the stranger who resides among them, because the entire people sinned inadvertently. (Num. 15:26)
>
> Please forgive the sin of this people as Your great kindness demands, and as You have forgiven the sin of this people from the time of Egypt until now. (Num. 14:19)
>
> The EverPresent God said: "I will forgive them as you spoke." (Num. 14:20)

---

52. See Joseph B. Soloveitchik, *On Repentance* (Jerusalem: Orot Press, 1980), 206ff.

All three verses come from the aftermath of the biblical story of the spies. The prelude to that story finds the Jewish people in the desert. After spending almost an entire year at the base of Mount Sinai – receiving the Ten Commandments, worshiping the Golden Calf, being forgiven by God, and building the Mishkan – they finally begin the long-awaited journey to the Land of Israel on the twentieth day of the second month of the second year after leaving Egypt (Num. 9:11). Ironically, at this moment, their anxiety – the same sort of anxiety that they felt when Moses was up on the mountain – resurfaces.

This time the anxiety comes not from Moses' absence, but from the people's uncertainty about the future and their fear of having to wage war in order to conquer the Promised Land.[53] At the outset, their feelings are inchoate – even to themselves. It is only the marginal people, those on the outskirts of the camp, who are heard grumbling (Num. 11:1). Then some of the people in the camp begin to complain about the food, and before Moses knows what has happened, everybody is up in arms complaining about the manna, recalling the days in Egypt when they had onions and garlic and fish "for free" (Num. 11:4–15). Finally, just when God sends a wave of quail to feed the carnivorous mass and Moses seems to get the situation under some control, his sister and brother begin to verbally slander their younger brother and undermine his unique stature: "Who does he think he is?" they ask. "Separating himself from his wife as if he is holier than we are! What, he thinks that only he is a prophet – we too are prophets and yet we do not separate ourselves from our spouses!"[54] What begins as low-level, anxiety-driven grumbling among the margins of society deteriorates into dissatisfaction at the uppermost, innermost sanctum of power and political leadership.

Underlying all of these diverse complaints is the looming challenge of conquering the Promised Land. With virtually no supporters left except his young disciple Joshua (Num. 11:28), Moses has no choice but to acquiesce when the people demand that a fact-finding mission of twelve tribal representatives be sent to ascertain whether this land is

---

53. See *The Genesis of Leadership* (Jewish Lights, 2006), 197–202.
54. Num. 12:1–3. This reading follows that of Rashi ad loc.

really all that Moses has said it is, that it is worth conquering, and conquerable by this ragtag group of former slaves (Deut. 1:22).

The heads of each of the twelve tribes are sent to the Land of Israel for forty days and come back with the following scouting report. "Yes," they all agree, "there is a Promised Land, and it is dripping with milk and honey, just like Moses said." There's just one problem, ten of the twelve conclude: "There is absolutely no way that we're ever going to be able to conquer it!" They then launch into a tirade: "You should have seen the giants there! Why, you know, they were **all** giants and their cities were big and fortified! And we, we were just a bunch of grasshoppers compared to them and don't think that they didn't know it! And you know what else about the so-called Promised Land? That place is really dangerous – it's a land that swallows up its inhabitants! It's because God hates us that He took us out of Egypt, because He wants to annihilate us at the hands of those Amorites! We will never be able to conquer that land," they predict. Instead, the ten spies suggest, "Let us appoint a new leader, and return to Egypt."[55]

The people, hearing this hysterical report, are terrified. They were anxious and on edge to begin with, and now the spies confirm their worst fears and send them over the emotional brink. All night long they cry in their tents. The next morning, despite the best attempts by Joshua and Caleb, the two dissenting spies, to convince the people that with God's help they can overcome all these obstacles and succeed in conquering the Promised Land, the people are simply too far gone. Referring to Joshua and Caleb, the mob cries out in a spirit of desperation and bloodlust: "Let's stone them!" At this point, God has heard enough. The Divine Presence appears to the whole people to restore order.

What were the sins of the spies and their generation? They did not violate any of the Ten Commandments as their predecessors at the Golden Calf did. They didn't make an idol; they didn't bow down or offer sacrifices to one; they didn't hold a feast in honor of an idol and engage in a frenzied, sexual orgy. They didn't do any of these things. All they did was talk. They used words, first to grumble amorphously, then to complain about God's food, then about God's leader, then about

---

55. This description follows Num. 13–14 and Deut. 1:22–27.

God's land, and finally, directly about God. They used words to slander and to reject God's many gifts to them. They also used words to belittle themselves. "We were like grasshoppers in their eyes and in our own," the spies said (Num. 13:33).

Why did they say these things? Because of the human proclivity to project blame for their own inadequacies onto others – to "scapegoat" rather than assume responsibility for themselves and for their future. This tendency is part and parcel of the human condition. It goes all the way back to Adam and Eve, who blamed each other for eating from the Tree of Knowledge rather than acknowledging and taking responsibility for their own desires and culpability. It harkens back to Cain who shirked responsibility for slaying his brother by replying to God's question, "Where is your brother, Abel?" with the disingenuous words, "I don't know, am I my brother's keeper?" And it reminds us of Joseph and his brothers where words – first Joseph's tattling and then the brothers' plotting to harm him (Gen. 37:2, 19–27) – led the Children of Israel into hundreds of years of exile from God's land and from God's presence.

The people were afraid after they heard the spies' report. In one sense, they had every right to be. But instead of acknowledging their fears and anxieties and praying to God to help them as God had done so many times in the past, they projected their fears outwards. The ten spies described insurmountable obstacles and imputed hateful, destructive motives to God to avoid the challenge of leading the people in conquering the Promised Land. They frightened all the Jewish people through their distorted descriptions. And they did all this with mere words. The spies spoke with malice and the people reacted and spoke out of fear.

Despite the fact that they only spoke, God was understandably enraged with this generation of renegades. To reject God's land (Lev. 25:23), where God's presence permanently dwelled (Num. 35:34), and to yearn to return to Egypt meant rejecting living as free people with God in God's land in favor of living as slaves in bondage to the Egyptians in Pharaoh's land. If the people did not want to live with God, then God no longer had any need for them; God threatened to wipe them out in one fell swoop and to recreate the Jewish people from scratch through Moses.

Only Moses' appeal to God's thirteen attributes based on compassion, graciousness, patience, and loving-kindness stopped God from following through on His first impulse to wipe out the people. Moses quelled God's anger by arguing that it would look bad in the eyes of the world if God, who described Himself as slow to anger, suddenly wiped out all His people in a fit of divine rage. Moses causes God to reconsider His first, destructive impulse. So God says to Moses, "*salaḥti kidevarekha*," "I will forgive them as you have spoken." In other words, **your words, quoting My words, will cancel out and annul their words.**

But there is a price that they will have to pay. The price is "measure for measure" – since they do not want My land, they will not get it. Instead, they will die natural deaths in the desert over a forty-year period and their children will be the ones to enter the land. Since they perceived themselves as grasshoppers, they are clearly not up to the challenge of conquering the land; instead, like grasshoppers, they will be interred in the desert sands. This generation will fade away, and their place will be taken by a new, more courageous generation raised in the spartan wilderness and capable of fighting for their ancestors' homeland.

Although the people are spared immediate death, they are still crestfallen. Some try to advance to conquer the land, and meet a stunning defeat at the hands of the Canaanite and Amalekite natives. The rest of the people must have been wondering, will even our children ever get to this land?

Moses responds to their new anxiety with two passages, which begin with the words, "When you come to the land." He reassures them that they, through their children, **will** one day inherit the land. Then, in a follow-up passage, Moses talks about what to do when the whole people sin unintentionally. Moses instructs the people to bring certain sacrifices so that the priest can effect atonement and forgiveness on their behalf.

By placing these passages immediately following the incident of the spies, the Torah seems to be engaging in self-commentary. Unlike the ten spies who intentionally, and with premeditation, distorted what they saw in their report to the people, the people of that generation were not premeditated sinners. They were inadvertent sinners, caught in an anxious frenzy based on false information, who responded to the spies' report based on human instinct and not malicious forethought. They also expressed deep regret and tried to repent by setting out to fight for the land on their own. Therefore, unlike the ten spies whom

God summarily executed, the people were saved and promised a future through their children, thanks to Moses' intercession on their behalf using God's thirteen attributes.

This is why every year at *Kol Nidrei* we recite these three passages that recall the sin of the generation of the spies and Moses' efficacious intercession. That is also why the *Kol Nidrei* service is voiced in the collective. It is the sin of the people's "voice," their collective words at the incident of the spies that we recall.

By evoking this episode as we begin Yom Kippur, we recall our own sins committed not only through actions, but also through words. We recall our propensity as human beings to project our anxieties and fears onto others rather than take responsibility for our own weaknesses and vulnerabilities. We remind ourselves of the way we distort and limit ourselves through words – whether by making vows and commitments that we are unable to fulfill, or by belittling our capabilities in order to lower the expectations which others have of us and which we have of ourselves.

We no longer have a Temple in which we can bring sacrificial offerings to God as penance for unintentional sins. We no longer have an active priesthood or a Moses to effect atonement on our behalf for our mis-speech. So instead, we use the post-Temple rabbinic court of three to annul our vows and all of our misguided words for the past year and the coming year. In the *Kol Nidrei* service, the cantor and the two *tallit*-draped "congregant-judges," both holding Torah scrolls, constitute a makeshift Jewish court of law. They effect the nullification of vows and atonement on our behalf in place of the priest and sacrificial service in Temple times, and in place of Moses, flanked as he was by Joshua and Caleb, the biblical court of three, at the time of the spies.

The basis for the annulment and atonement is that all our words, past and future, like the words of the generation of the spies, were and are uttered without premeditation, on the basis of distorted or incomplete information, without comprehending the full consequences of what we might have said. In effect, we are pleading, "Forgive us God, annul our words, because we did not know what we were saying. If we really knew the consequences of our spoken words, if we really could overcome our propensity to project blame rather than assume responsibility, then we wouldn't have said what we did in the first place. We have genuine remorse and regret. Alas, we are human and therefore we often fall victim to the human condition – the same condition which ensnared Adam and Eve, Cain and Abel, Joseph and his brothers, and the generation of the spies."

At *Kol Nidrei*, we ask God to respond to our intercessors, as God responded to Moses with the message, "I will forgive as you have spoken." Yom Kippur is our opportunity to redeem ourselves by regretting our sins, expressing remorse, and committing ourselves to do better in the future. And Yom Kippur is the reenactment of the day when God said: "It's okay – I know you didn't really mean to sin. I know, and have come to accept, that you're only flesh and blood subject to anxiety and impulsiveness. Yom Kippur is My acceptance of your humanity. I acknowledge your heartfelt regret, accept your sincere repentance, and extend to you My forgiveness. Because to err is human, but to forgive is divine."

The Late Afternoon Services

The Torah portion read in the late afternoon *Minḥa* service, as the day of Yom Kippur begins to ebb, is chapter 18 from the Book of Leviticus, which lists the forbidden sexual relationships. It is understandable why the rabbis chose Leviticus 16 for the morning Torah reading on Yom Kippur. It describes the service that took place on Yom Kippur in Temple times. But what motivated the rabbis in their choice for *Minḥa* is far more puzzling. What were they thinking about when they selected this reading about sexual impropriety?

Perhaps they were remembering another sin, recorded in the Book of Numbers, committed by the next generation of Jewish people some thirty-nine years later. That sin of Baal Peor recalled the sin of the Golden Calf and can be reasonably called "Golden Calf II." Here is what transpired:

> The Jewish people dwelled in Shittim, and the people began to commit harlotry with the daughters of Moab. And they called the people to the sacrifices of their gods; and the people ate, and bowed down to their gods. And the Jewish people joined themselves to Baal Peor; and the anger of the EverPresent God was

kindled against Israel [and God sent a plague against the people].
And the EverPresent God said to Moses: "Take all the heads of the
people, and hang them before the EverPresent God in full public
view, so that the fierce anger of the EverPresent God may turn
away from Israel." And Moses said to the judges of Israel: "Kill
every one of your men that have joined themselves to Baal Peor."
And behold, one of the Jewish people came forward and brought
before his brothers a Midianite woman in the sight of Moses, and
in the sight of all the congregation of the Jewish people, who were
weeping at the door of the Tent of Meeting.... And those that
died by the plague were twenty-four thousand. (Num. 25:1–6, 9)

The rabbinic sages apparently instituted the reading of the chapter on forbidden sexual relationships with "Golden Calf II" in mind as a cautionary
tale. Here, again, is a sin of idolatry, like the sin of the Golden Calf. But
it is idolatry with a couple of twists – not the new creation of an Egyptian idol but the worship of an existing Canaanite deity, not the implied
sexual orgy in the euphemism "they rose to play" before the Golden Calf,
but the explicit sexual licentiousness of the people, which leads inexora-
bly to orgiastic idol worship. In the narrative, Moses is so distraught and
devastated by what unfolds before his eyes (he and the other leaders are
literally in tears) that he does not invoke the thirteen attributes to try to
save the people from God's plague. The result is especially tragic: twenty-
four thousand dead, the largest single loss of Jewish lives in the five books
of the Torah. Only the vigilante action of Moses' great-nephew, Pinḥas,
prevents the plague from spreading further (Num. 25:11).

The rabbis knew that what happened to the new generation of
Jewish people encamped on the borders of the Land of Israel could
happen again, to anyone, in any place, and in any generation. The sexual
instinct is among the strongest – perhaps the strongest – of all human
instincts, as our survival as a species is dependent on it. To satisfy it, one
might trespass all moral and spiritual boundaries[56] – even the explicit
prohibition on idol worship.

---

56. See Rabbi Joseph Karo, *Shulḥan Arukh, Even HaEzer* 22:15: "In sexual matters there
are no trustworthy guardians" (*"ein apitropsun le'arayot"*).

The Torah reading from Leviticus warns that if the Jewish people cannot set boundaries to their sexual appetites then they too will suffer dire consequences. They will be "cut off from the people," and the Land of Israel, animated by God's presence, will "vomit out" the Jewish people just as it expunged the non-Jewish idolators who engaged in these illicit sexual practices prior to the arrival of the Jewish nation:

> Do not defile yourselves in any of these things [sexual transgressions], for in all these the nations are defiled, which I cast out from before you. And because the land was defiled, I visited its sins upon it, and the land vomited out her inhabitants. Therefore you shall keep My statutes and My ordinances, and shall not do any of these abominations ... for whoever shall do any of these abominations shall be cut off from among his people. (Lev. 18:24–30)

There is a chilling message in this choice of Torah reading for the late afternoon of Yom Kippur. While God forgave the Jewish people for the worship of the Golden Calf thanks to Moses' intervention, and while the day of Yom Kippur helps every sincere penitent achieve some measure of atonement for his/her sins, some sins – sexual licentiousness intertwined with recidivist idol worship among them[57] – are so egregious that they erode the divine image in human beings and undermine the foundational mission of the Jewish people to be God's people in history. Yom Kippur stands for the proposition that God forgives, but as this Torah reading suggests, sometimes the price paid to earn God's forgiveness is very, very steep.[58] To help the people remember that sobering lesson, the rabbis mandated this reading as Yom Kippur draws to a close.

The *Haftara* Reading

Yom Kippur is an intensely particularistic holiday. In its rituals and liturgy, it recalls many of the defining sins of the Jewish people – events that nearly brought Jewish history to a premature end. But the challenge

57. The other two are murder and desecrating God's name.
58. See Maimonides, *Mishneh Torah*, Laws of Repentance 1:4.

of people sinning and then feeling the need to repent for those sins is universal – common to all humanity. What is the connection between God's relationship to the Jewish people and the divine relationship with the rest of humanity? Do the same principles that apply to God's governance of the Jews apply to the way God governs all human beings and the nations they inhabit? To answer these questions, the rabbinic sages chose the Book of Jonah as the prophetic reading for the late afternoon service of Yom Kippur.

The Book of Jonah tells the story of the Jewish prophet, Jonah the son of Amitai (lit., the "son of my truth"), who is commissioned by God to warn the residents of the Assyrian city Nineveh of their pending doom. Resisting his mission, Jonah charters a seat on a ship headed in the opposite direction. God brings a storm, and the sailors must ultimately throw Jonah overboard into the raging sea, where he is swallowed by a large fish. Inside the cavernous fish, Jonah repents for resisting God's mission and, once released, delivers the message to the residents of Nineveh. Much to his chagrin, the citizens of Nineveh immediately repent, and God spares them from destruction. Jonah is unhappy about God's mercy to the very end, saying accusingly to God, "I know that You are a gracious and compassionate God, slow to anger, with great kindness and have remorse for bringing evil" (Jonah 4:2). In other words, he selectively quotes, as did Moses, from the thirteen attributes to explain why he tried to run away from God.

It is not clear why Jonah is upset by this turn of events – after all, his mission has been an unqualified success. Perhaps he is concerned that his credibility as a prophet will be undermined for predicting a catastrophe that never transpired. Perhaps he is disconsolate that the future enemy of Israel, who several decades later will ultimately conquer the Land of Israel and exile its inhabitants, has been spared God's wrath despite its evil deeds. Or maybe he is a prophet who, as his father's name implies, believes in absolute truth and justice and does not subscribe to the possibility of repentance leading to the pardon of sin. Any and all of these are plausible interpretations.

What is clear, however, from this fantastic tale is that the rabbis wanted us, the readers, to focus on the universal possibility of repentance – perhaps as a corrective to the intense particularity of the rest of Yom Kippur, or perhaps as a spur to the Jewish people, to repent of their sins as did the gentile citizens of Nineveh. Jonah is a symbol of the mission that each of us and the Jewish people have to be a blessing to all the nations of the world.[59] Despite our resistance to play this role as God's agent, whether out of our own narrowly perceived self-interest ("why is this **our** problem?") or because we think it is a violation of some deeply entrenched principle of justice ("they deserve what they get"), the story asks us to reconsider the meaning and direction of our lives in light of this mission. Do we engage only with the members of our own particular, tight-knit community, or do we reach out to those outside of our communities to help repair God's world?

Whether Jonah liked it or not, the thirteen attributes teach that God is a compassionate being who is indeed slow to anger with all of God's creatures.[60] This was part and parcel of the revelation to Moses after the Golden Calf, which allowed God to rejoin His people on their journey through history to the Promised Land. Our understanding of who God is, as Maimonides points out regarding the thirteen attributes, is the educational impetus for us to be likewise – compassionate toward all of God's creatures on God's good earth. What Jonah failed to understand, we the readers, through distance and hindsight, and through the prophetic reading of the Yom Kippur *Minḥa* service, come to appreciate deeply.

Ne'ila: Back to the Future

The *Ne'ila* (lit., "Closing of the Gates") service that concludes Yom Kippur, like the service that begins the day, is unique among Jewish prayers. On no other day of the year is there a communal prayer service inserted between the late afternoon and evening services. It is also unlike the other prayers of the day; while it includes the communal confession ("We are guilty, we have betrayed ...") that we recite at every Yom Kippur prayer

---

59. See Gen. 12:3, 22:19.
60. This extending of God's mercy to all His creatures is summed up in the final verse of the book (Jonah 4:11): "Should I not be compassionate toward Nineveh, the great metropolis, that has more than 120,000 persons who cannot tell the difference between their right and left hands, and many domesticated animals as well?!"

service, it omits the private individual confession ("for the sin I have committed...") which is part of every other Yom Kippur prayer service. Instead of the private confessional prayer, the rabbis include in *Ne'ila* two generic paragraphs: "You reach out Your hand to transgressors" and "You have set apart human beings from the beginning." In both of these paragraphs, only one specific sin is mentioned, and confessed to: "the robbery/violence/oppression/exploitation of our hands." If *Kol Nidrei* is about achieving forgiveness for the abuse of words, *Ne'ila* is about achieving forgiveness for our abusive actions, those done "with our hands."

These prayers reflect many of the sins that punctuate the Torah, some of which are of special concern on Yom Kippur day. They recall Joseph's brothers, who abducted Joseph and threw him into a pit to die; Aaron, who took the gold from the people and fashioned it into a golden calf; and Aaron's sons, who took incense that God had not commanded, offering it in the Holy of Holies.

These sins are not merely historical – they are typological – they symbolize different kinds of oppressive actions over others in our everyday lives. In these sins, we confess to taking the energy and passion due God, who has provided us with everything in this world, and misdirecting it to harm others, both human and divine. So as the sun begins to set on the day of Yom Kippur, we ask God to give us the strength to desist from actions that prevent us from finding true oneness with God and with our fellow human beings created in God's image.

We conclude the *Ne'ila* prayer service with the rousing recitation of the first and second lines of the *Shema*[61] and the proclamation made by the people of Israel after Elijah's victory over the prophets of the Canaanite deity – "The EverPresent God is God."[62] The communal recitation of these verses announces loudly and clearly to ourselves, to God, and to each other, our absolute fidelity to God. We then blow the shofar,

---

61. "Listen O Israel, the EverPresent God is God, the EverPresent God is One" and "Blessed be the name of Your glorious kingdom, forever and ever."

62. I Kings 18:39. For the parallelism between Moses' confrontation at the Golden Calf at Mount Sinai and Elijah's confrontation with the prophets of Baal at Mount Carmel see *Leading the Passover Journey*, 141–142.

symbolically proclaiming, as we do on Rosh HaShana, our acceptance of God's kingship,[63] and sing aloud, "Next year in the rebuilt Jerusalem," proclaiming our fidelity to God's land and capital city.

These two proclamations of fidelity to God and God's land correct two of our biblical ancestors' primal sins, their betrayal of God in the Golden Calf and betrayal of God's land through the sin of the spies. So while during *Ne'ila*, at the conclusion of Yom Kippur, we ask for atonement for sins of action, we also atone in *Ne'ila*'s conclusion with our stirring words for the sin of words against God and God's land evoked in the *Kol Nidrei* service that opened the day. Both during and at the end of *Ne'ila* we "go back to the future" – remembering our people's earlier sins as we commit ourselves to a better, more fulfilling future.

INTERNALIZING YOM KIPPUR THROUGHOUT THE YEAR

The repentance and forgiveness that mark Yom Kippur overflow into the way we practice Judaism throughout the year.

Theologically, Judaism is distinguished from other religions by its approach to repentance, viewed as essential for God's forgiveness. While God's abundant grace is one of Judaism's working assumptions,[64] as it is in Christianity, in Judaism it is largely predicated on human beings first beginning the process of *teshuva*, repentance, to which, if sincerely offered, God responds favorably. God's grace is tied intimately to human deeds. Indeed, so important is *teshuva* in the system of Judaism throughout the year that Maimonides devotes an entire ten-chapter section to it in the first book of his code of Jewish Law, the *Mishneh Torah*.

In those ten chapters, Maimonides delineates three stages to the process of *teshuva*: First, recognition of the sin; second, expressing remorse for having committed the sinful act; and third, committing oneself not to repeat the same act in the future. An integral part in this

---

63. Sounding the shofar every Yom Kippur is an extension of Lev. 25:9. The shofar was sounded on Yom Kippur inaugurating the Jubilee year. In fact, the term "Jubilee" to denote the fiftieth year is derived from this shofar sounding (see Ex. 19:13), which proclaims, every fifty years, God's kingship over the Jewish people (Lev. 25:55) and the Land of Israel (Lev. 25:23).

64. In the thirteen attributes repeatedly recited on Yom Kippur, God is described as being "*rav ḥesed*," "full of grace."

three-stage process is verbal confession.[65] For a sin committed only against God, one makes the confession to oneself – no intermediary is needed, or even desired.[66] Verbalizing it to oneself makes it real enough and makes the likelihood of self-deception less likely. In the final analysis, however, as Maimonides points out, one only knows if one has fully repented if, when faced in the future with a similar situation and set of circumstances, one chooses not to sin again.[67]

If an offense against another person has been committed, the sinner can be forgiven by God only after appeasing the wronged party, in addition to acknowledging the sin, confessing it, feeling genuine remorse, and committing not to repeat it in the future. Appeasement may require financial compensation, in a case where financial or property interests have been damaged, as well as assuaging the feelings of the person who has been hurt.

Although it is customary to ask forgiveness of one's family and friends immediately prior to Yom Kippur, seeking forgiveness from other people should not wait until then. Human beings, as Aristotle pointed out and as Maimonides reiterated, are social animals. In order to keep their relations positive and constructive, people need to clear the air when necessary, and generally speaking, the sooner the better. The holiness code in Leviticus states this clearly:

> Do not hate your brother in your heart. You should rebuke your neighbor, and not carry his sin with you; do not take revenge or bear a grudge against the members of your people – you should love your neighbor as yourself, I am the EverPresent God. (Lev. 19:17–18)

There is actually a double obligation here – on the person who feels wronged to communicate the sense of hurt to the offender, and on the person who has wronged another to request forgiveness. While God forgives individuals who have sinned in a ritual matter, in Judaism

---

65. Laws of Repentance 1:1 ff.
66. Ibid., 2:5
67. Ibid., 2:1.

God does not have jurisdiction to forgive a person for having wronged another human being on an ethical matter. Only the wronged person can do that.[68]

Here too, there is an obligation on the person who has been hurt to act in a reasonable manner. Assuming that the offending person has materially righted the wrong and made three sincere requests to be forgiven, the tradition instructs the wronged person not to use his/her sense of victimhood to withhold forgiveness.[69]

The model for this noble forgiveness is Joseph in the Book of Genesis, a key figure in the saga of Yom Kippur.[70] While his brothers' enmity resulted in him being enslaved and imprisoned for thirteen years, once he was convinced that they had genuinely repented of their actions toward him,[71] Joseph wholeheartedly forgave his brothers and reframed their wrongdoing as part of a greater divine plan (Gen. 45:5–8; 50:19–21). In so doing, Joseph, who had rhetorically asked his brothers, "Am I a substitute for God?" (Gen. 50:19), foreshadowed the lesson of God's subsequent forgiveness of the Jewish people after their sin in worshiping the Golden Calf. In forgiving one another, we emulate God's ways of forgiveness, earlier embodied by Joseph in forgiving his brothers.

Repentance on the one hand, and granting forgiveness on the other, are the twin axis points around which a healthy Jewish community and social order revolve. When properly done, they permit people to get past their burdensome pasts, heal the frictions that often mar human interactions, and allow all parties to actualize their full, God-given potential.

---

68. A striking application of this principle in the aftermath of the Holocaust can be found in Simon Wiesenthal, *The Sunflower* (New York: Schocken Books, 1976).
69. Maimonides, *Mishneh Torah*, Laws of Repentance 2:9.
70. As per the section about the goat sent to *Azazel* in the biblical Temple service and the rabbis' reason for including the martyrology in the *Musaf* service of Yom Kippur, above.
71. As most clearly evidenced by Judah's willingness to enter into a lifetime of slavery to save his youngest brother Benjamin from that same fate. See Gen. 44:18–34. For further evidence of the brothers' recognition of their previous sin and their remorse, see Gen. 42:21, 22, 28 and 44:16.

Liturgical Echoes of Yom Kippur

The twin themes of repentance and forgiveness on Yom Kippur also overflow into our liturgy throughout the year.

In the fifth and sixth blessings of the daily silent devotional prayer, the *Amida*, which come right after we ask God for knowledge and understanding, we petition God for the following:

> Return us, our Father, to Your Torah, and bring us closer, our Sovereign, to Your service, and return us with complete repentance before You…. Forgive us, our Father, for we have transgressed, pardon us, our Sovereign, for we have sinned, for You pardon and forgive.

Throughout the year, God is addressed as He is during the Ten Days of Repentance and, repeatedly, on Yom Kippur, as our Father and Sovereign. We pray that God will empower us to return and repent and, in turn, forgive and pardon us – the twin themes of Yom Kippur.

After reciting these two blessings, thrice daily, standing upright, we double down on these requests in the morning and afternoon liturgies through the daily recitation of *Taḥanun*, supplications. These are recited seated; if there is a Torah scroll, representing the Divine Presence, in the room, the *Taḥanun* (also known as *nefilat apayim*, falling on the face) is recited in a bent-over, supplicating position. The prayer begins: "Compassionate and Gracious One, I have sinned before You, EverPresent God, full of compassion, have compassion on me and accept my pleas." In the version of the prayer service originating in Spain and North Africa, the *Taḥanun* prayer is preceded by the communal confessional recited in the *Seliḥot* prayers that is repeated ten times on Yom Kippur ("We are guilty, we have betrayed…"). In this way, the liturgy of Yom Kippur is literally carried over into the liturgy recited throughout the year. This provides a framework for each individual to begin the process of repentance on any given day, and even multiple times each day. Every day of the year presents an opportunity to begin the process of repentance and to trigger the possibility of receiving God's compassionate forgiveness in return.

Aside from these daily prayers for repentance and forgiveness, the *Musaf* service recited on the three pilgrimage festivals of Passover, Shavuot, and Sukkot contains a paragraph which begins: "Because of our sins we were exiled from our land and driven from our country." This prayer, in modified form, also appears in the *Musaf* service on Shabbat Rosh Ḥodesh.[72] Its purpose is not to engage in paralyzing self-blame, but on the contrary, to prod the community and its individual members toward self-improvement and *teshuva*.

The concept of *teshuva*, "return," one of the central pillars of Yom Kippur and of our liturgy throughout the year, is to instill within the Jewish people the fundamental conviction that, as individuals and as a community, we are responsible for and capable of taking charge of our own destiny. Taking responsibility for our lot in life and history, forthrightly admitting that we made mistakes and correcting them through *teshuva*, is the opposite of projecting blame onto others or meekly acquiescing to the erratic twists of fate. *Teshuva* affirms that through our own efforts, by going back to doing the "right thing," we can ultimately restore our good fortune. It says that no matter how far afield we may have strayed from the path of righteousness, we can always turn around, and get closer to God, to our fellow human beings, and to our own true selves. As such, it becomes one of the hallmarks of Jewish thinking, and one of the reasons that the Jewish people have been able, over the millennia, to bounce back from historic reversals to resume their mission of being a source of blessing to the world (Gen. 12:2–3).

---

72. When the beginning of the new lunar month coincides with Shabbat.

Chapter Five

Living With God: Sukkot, Shemini Atzeret, and Simḥat Torah

> *All Jewish citizens shall dwell in sukkot, in order that future generations will know that I had the Jewish people dwell in sukkot when I extracted them from Egypt, I, the EverPresent, your God.*
>
> (Lev. 23:42–43)

The festival of Sukkot begins on the fifteenth day of the Hebrew month of Tishrei – just four days after the conclusion of Yom Kippur. The festival is celebrated for eight days, making it the longest of the biblical festivals. Like Passover, it has two "sacred days," the first and the eighth, the latter of which is called Shemini Atzeret or the "Eighth Day of Assembly." In between are the intermediate days of the festival that include the ritual elements of the festival without the restrictions on work that mark the first and eighth days.

The most outstanding rituals of the first seven days are the dwelling in sukkot – portable, temporary huts that we erect and colorfully decorate prior to the festival – and the taking/waving of four species of the Land of Israel bound together: citron, palm branch, two willow branches, and three myrtle branches. The dominant emotional motif of the holiday is joy. In fact Sukkot, alone among all of the biblical holidays, includes in its biblical description in the Book of Deuteronomy two separate commands to be joyful.[1]

A host of other rituals developed in the rabbinic and medieval periods that further enhanced the joyful character of this eight-day festival. Some of the most familiar include the recitation of the *Ushpizin*, an invitation to the Jewish people's biblical patriarchs to join us in the sukka during the first seven days of the festival; the Simḥat Beit HaShoeva, the spirited water-drawing celebration during the intermediate days of the festival; the Hoshana Rabba (Great Hoshana) procession, marked by colorful pageantry, on the seventh day of the festival; the recitation of the special prayer for rain, *Tefillat Geshem*, on the eighth day; and the ecstatic celebration of the Torah, Simḥat Torah, on the last day of the festival. We will examine this joyful festival and its rituals to understand their underlying meaning.

LIVING WITH GOD IN THE DESERT: DWELLING IN SUKKOT

Why does Sukkot begin only four days after the conclusion of Yom Kippur? Is there a relationship between these two holidays? Why is the holiday eight days long,[2] and why are both the first and eighth day sacred?[3] What revelational events in the biblical narrative do these two sacred days commemorate?

When we left the biblical narrative at the end of Yom Kippur, Moses had just come down with the second set of tablets inscribed with

---

1. On other holidays, the command to be joyful is not repeated as it is for Sukkot, in Deut. 16:14, 15.
2. Passover, which commemorates the greatest event in the Jewish people's experience, is only seven days long. One would think that the greater event would be longer, not shorter.
3. On Passover, as on the Sabbath, it is the seventh day that is sacred.

the Ten Commandments. As mentioned in the previous chapter, almost the first thing that Moses did the following day[4] was to assemble the people and request voluntary contributions from them for the creation of a physical home for God, the Mishkan:

> Moses said to the whole community of the Jewish people: "This is what the EverPresent God has commanded: 'Collect gifts from among yourselves for the EverPresent God; everyone whose heart moves him shall bring them... gold, silver, and copper; blue, purple, and crimson yarns; fine linen and goat's hair, tanned ram skins, and acacia wood; oil for lighting, spices for the anointing oil and for the aromatic incense; lapis lazuli and other precious stones for the setting of the Ephod and the breastplate. And let all among you who are skilled come and make all that the EverPresent God has commanded.'" (Ex. 35:4–10)

The requested contributions for the Mishkan and its construction were a test. Would the people remain steadfast in their return to God? Would they devote their resources and themselves wholeheartedly to constructing a home for the Divine Presence, as they previously misdirected their efforts to worshiping an Egyptian idol? In fact, the people passed the test with flying colors, contributing more resources than requested (Ex. 36:3–7) and working for the next several months, six days a week (see Ex. 35:1–3), constructing the structure and furnishings of the Mishkan until its completion in the early spring. By assembling all of these precious gifts and using them to build a home for God, the people concluded the process of their repentance for worshiping the Golden Calf at the foot of Mount Sinai.

---

4. The first thing that Moses did the following day (the eleventh day of Tishrei) was to assemble the people to reiterate and reinforce the preeminence of Shabbat (Ex. 35:1–3). Its placement prior to the instructions concerning the construction of the Mishkan means that the observance of Shabbat, sacred time, trumps the importance of creating the Mishkan, sacred space. See *Sifra, Kedoshim* 7:7 and the chapter on Shabbat below for a fuller explication of this thesis.

God is pleased with their efforts, as the Torah makes clear at the end of the Book of Exodus, and the Divine Presence makes itself visible to all the Jewish people and fills the newly completed Mishkan:

> So Moses finished the work. Then the cloud covered the Tent of Meeting, and the glory of the EverPresent God filled the Mishkan. And Moses was not able to enter into the Tent of Meeting, because the cloud hovered above it, and the glory of the EverPresent God filled the Mishkan. And whenever the cloud rose up above the Mishkan, the Children of Israel would travel in all their journeys. But if the cloud did not rise, then they would not journey until the day that it rose. For the cloud of the EverPresent God was upon the Mishkan by day, and there was fire in it by night, in the sight of all the House of Israel, throughout all their journeys. (Ex. 40:34–38)

We build the sukka today to reenact the building of the Mishkan, and celebrate the first sacred day of Sukkot as a commemoration of the return of the Divine Presence among the Jewish people. God came down to dwell in the Mishkan where the Divine Presence could be visibly manifest to all the people, not at a distance, as after the Golden Calf (Ex. 33:9–10), but from within their very midst. Once present, God accompanied the people through all their desert journeys.

According to a penetrating reading of the biblical text by the eighteenth-century Lithuanian scholar the Gaon of Vilna, God's presence returned to the Jewish people even earlier, as soon as the people began the actual construction of the Mishkan. By the Vilna Gaon's reckoning, this was on the fifteenth day of Tishrei – four days after Moses came down from Mount Sinai with the second set of tablets. This explanation then accounts for why we begin the holiday of Sukkot on that day, just four days after the conclusion of Yom Kippur, rather than on the first day of Nisan when the Mishkan was actually completed.[5]

---

5. Rabbi Jacob ben Asher, in his *Tur Shulḥan Arukh, Oraḥ Ḥayim* 625, offers what has become the conventional explanation for why we celebrate the holiday in the autumn rather than in the spring immediately after the Exodus: Since people generally sit out in huts to cool off during the spring and summer months, their sitting in sukkot

It also explains the custom to begin building the sukka immediately after Yom Kippur, as the Jewish people in biblical times began to assemble the materials for building the Mishkan immediately after receiving atonement from the Golden Calf.[6]

Whether or not the Gaon of Vilna is correct that God's presence returned as soon as construction of the Mishkan began on the fifteenth day of Tishrei, or whether the Clouds of Glory, symbolizing the Divine Presence, only returned once the Mishkan was completed, as the plain reading of the text implies, Sukkot is the celebration of that return and a commemoration of that divine revelation in plain sight of all the Jewish people.

This enables us to understand the Torah's meaning in the words, cited at the head of this chapter, "All Jewish citizens shall dwell in sukkot, in order that future generations will know that I had the Jewish people dwell in sukkot when I extracted them from Egypt, I, the EverPresent, your God." We might certainly wonder what the Torah was referencing. It is true that immediately after leaving Egypt, the Jewish people's first stop was a place called Sukkot.[7] However, because they were fleeing Egypt, it is unlikely that the people stayed there more than one night before moving on to their next stop. As far as we know, nothing of consequence transpired at Sukkot, so this stop would hardly be worth commemorating.

A dispute in the Talmud makes clear that classical readers of the biblical text were also puzzled by this verse and had differing views on how to understand it. R. Akiva said that the sukkot to which the verse refers are the portable desert huts which the people inhabited. R. Eliezer said that the sukkot referred to by the Bible are "the Clouds of Glory"

---

huts during that period would not have been something of which people would take note. Mandating that it be celebrated in the fall, when the weather has already turned cooler, shows the special devotion of the Jewish people to heeding God's command of dwelling in sukkot. However, this does not explain the particular choice of the fifteenth day of Tishrei as the precise day on which to commence the holiday; the Vilna Gaon's explanation does this.

6. Ex. 36:3. See the Gaon of Vilna in the non-mystical section of his commentary on the Song of Songs, 1:4, in *Writings of the Gra* [Hebrew], p. 10. I am indebted to Dr. Neil Rothstein for supplying me with the text of the Gaon.

7. Ex. 12:37, 13:20; Num. 33:5, 6.

which guided and protected the people from the dangers of the desert in every direction (Sukka 11b).

When I was young, I found R. Akiva's explanation far more plausible as it resembled the world that I knew – one in which there were no visible magical clouds protecting us. Presumably, R. Akiva believed that the Jewish people's willingness to endure the difficult conditions of their desert journey in vulnerable huts was worthy of commendation and commemoration. That was an example of heroic self-sacrifice with which I could identify.

As I began studying the holidays, however, I realized that, more than celebrating our ancestors' heroic characteristics, they celebrate something extraordinary that God did for the Jewish people in their first year as a free nation – the Exodus from Egypt, the splitting of the sea, the raining down of the manna from heaven, the theophany at Mount Sinai, and the divine forgiveness for the sin of the Golden Calf. With that logic, Sukkot also needed to commemorate something extraordinary which God did for the people beginning in that first year, which would be worthy of recalling every year for millennia. Living in portable huts, while certainly commendable, did not represent such an extraordinary Godly action. Being guided for forty years in the vast desert and protected constantly from the elements by God's Clouds of Glory, however, would have been just such an extraordinary happening.

In the context of the reasons for all the other holidays, R. Eliezer made more sense.[8] This may be why Rashi cites R. Eliezer's opinion as the plain meaning of the verse.[9] It also makes Moses' review in Deuteronomy of the people's desert wanderings more understandable:

---

8. Cf. the commentary of Rabbi David Halevi Segal's (Poland, 1586–1667) *Turei Zahav* on Rabbi Joseph Karo's *Shulḥan Arukh, Oraḥ Ḥayim* 625, where he argues that according to R. Akiva, the purpose of the sukkot is not so much to recall the journey through the desert as to remember the miracle of the Exodus from Egypt and God's kindness in freeing us from Egyptian bondage. This commemoration at the onset of the fall-winter months is meant to parallel our commemoration of the Exodus on Passover at the onset of the spring-summer seasons.

9. See Rashi on Lev. 23:43. Rabbi Jacob ben Asher's Code of Jewish Law, the *Tur Shulḥan Arukh*, also takes it as a given that the sukkot to which the Torah refers are

Remember the long way that the EverPresent God made you travel in the desert these past forty years.... The clothes you wore did not wear out, nor did your feet swell these forty years ... beware, lest your heart grow haughty and you forget the Ever-Present God who freed you from the land of Egypt, the house of bondage; who led you through the great and terrible desert with its snakes and scorpions, a parched land with no water in it, who brought forth water for you from a flinty rock and who fed you manna in the desert. (Deut. 8:2–4, 14–15)

Moses was alluding to the special divine guidance and protection afforded to the people in the desert, from the provision of food and water to protection from snakes and scorpions, to preservation of their shoes and clothing. Such divine providence for forty years – the text twice emphasizes the forty-year period – would be worthy of recollection and reenactment for one week each year in the form of sukkot built for just this purpose.

Nor, as we have seen, was R. Eliezer wildly imaginative in his notion of the Clouds of Glory. The biblical text, describing God's revelation to the people at the completion of the Mishkan, twice mentions that the divine cloud rested upon the Mishkan and the glory of God filled the Mishkan. This cloud, which offered shade during the day and had a fire in it by night, guided and illuminated the Jewish people through

---

the Clouds of Glory under whose protection the Jewish people dwelled in the desert (*Oraḥ Ḥayim* 626, *Hilkhot Sukka*). In contrast, Rashi's grandson, Rabbi Samuel ben Meir, known as the Rashbam, in his commentary on the verse disagrees with his grandfather and bases himself on R. Akiva. For the Rashbam, one dwells in sukkot to remind the Jewish people of the ramshackle huts in which their ancestors lived in the desert in contrast to the comfortable homes they currently inhabit. This is to humble them so that their newfound wealth does not cause them to forget the divine cause of their success (see Deut. 8:2–18). While I concur with Rashbam's sentiment and quote these very verses from Deuteronomy in relationship to the Omer and Shavuot, I do not find them to be congruent with the exceptionally joyous spirit of Sukkot mandated by the Torah (Deut. 16:14, 15). Moreover, if "putting the people in their place" is the meaning of Sukkot, that would detract from the motivation to dwell in the sukka during the holiday and ultimately undermine its observance – the opposite of what the Torah intended in offering the rationale for its observance.

all their forty years of journeying in the desert. The description of the cloud's role in leading the people is reiterated in even greater length and detail in the Book of Numbers, after the Mishkan was set up and situated in the very center of the encampment:

> On the day that the Mishkan was set up, the cloud covered the Mishkan, the Tent of Meeting; and in the evening it rested over the Mishkan in the likeness of fire until morning. It was always so: the cloud covered it, appearing as fire by night. And whenever the cloud lifted from the Tent, the Jewish people would set out accordingly; and at the spot where the cloud settled, there the Jewish people would encamp. At the command of the EverPresent God, the Jewish people broke camp, and at the command of the EverPresent God they set up camp; they remained encamped so long as the cloud stayed over the Mishkan. (Num. 9:15–18)

R. Eliezer understood this cloud, which appeared over the Mishkan,[10] as radiating outward from the center of the camp where the Mishkan stood, and enveloping and protecting the entire encampment of the Jewish people.[11] This was not simply a magical cloud as I imagined in my youth, but a tangible, visible expression of God's presence among the people, made possible by the building of a home for God in the people's midst. Hence, according to R. Eliezer, the sukkot in the Bible were the divine clouds centered over the Mishkan, under which the people dwelled during their forty-year trek in the desert. We reenact the situation of living under that divine cloud by building and dwelling for one week in our sukkot today.

---

10. When it was completed, or, according to the Gaon of Vilna, when the Mishkan's construction was begun.

11. See Rashi on Num. 9:18, quoting the *Baraita Melekhet HaMishkan* 13 and 14: "When the Jewish people traveled, the pillar of cloud [above the Mishkan] would fold itself up like a beam above the tribe of Judah [who led the march through the desert] ... and when the Jewish people would encamp, the pillar of cloud would straighten back up and form a protective sukka above the tribe of Judah and envelop the Mishkan from outside and fill the Mishkan from within."

In addition to reenacting the Clouds of Glory, which hovered night and day over the Jewish people, the physical structure of our sukkot recalls the Mishkan in several ways.[12]

Etymologically, the word "sukka" is related to the word *skhakh*, which refers to the covering, or roof, above the sukka. The laws concerning the *skhakh*, as well as the dimensions of the sukka, parallel those of the Mishkan. Here is the beginning of the first mishna of Tractate Sukka: "A sukka which is above twenty cubits high is not valid…. One which is not ten handbreadths high, one which has not three walls, or which has more sun than shade is not valid."

As the talmudic discussion of the mishna makes clear, the law requires that the *skhakh* provide more shade than light during the day and yet permit one sitting in the sukka to see the larger stars at night.[13] This parallels the description of the manifestation of God's presence over the Mishkan that we saw earlier: "For the cloud of the EverPresent God was upon the Tabernacle during the day, and there was fire in there at night, in the sight of all the House of Israel, throughout all their journeys" (Ex. 40:38).

God's presence in the cloud hovered above the Mishkan, providing shade from the burning hot sun by day, while the fire enveloped within the cloud provided light in the dark wilderness at night.[14] Thus, the roof of the sukka, the *skhakh*, under which we dwell during Sukkot, reflects the cloud/fire of the Divine Presence over the Mishkan, God's home, and by extension over the entire encampment, during the journeys of the people in the desert.

The dimensions and number of walls of the sukka also mirror those of the Mishkan. At its highest point, the Mishkan reached twenty cubits. Therefore, a sukka cannot be taller than twenty cubits (somewhere between thirty and forty feet, depending on how one defines a

---

12. The King James Bible, in fact, translates the word "Mishkan" as the "Tabernacle" and the holiday of Sukkot as the "Feast of Tabernacles," clearly connecting the two.

13. See Maimonides, *Mishneh Torah*, Laws of Sukka 5:21.

14. The illuminating function of the nighttime fire is emphasized in Neh. 9:12, 19, which recounts God's graciousness to the generation that left Egypt. See also Ps. 105:39, which shares this interpretation and understands the cloud as providing protective shading for the people.

cubit). It also must not be shorter than ten handbreadths (somewhere around forty inches). The reason for the latter dimension is connected to the Ark containing the Ten Commandments, which is listed first among the vessels to be constructed for the Mishkan. The Ark was nine handbreadths high and the Ark cover (the *kaporet*, without the cherubs) was one handbreadth thick. Hence, as the Talmud points out, the sukka must be at least high enough to contain the covered Ark of the Mishkan – i.e., the seat of the divine throne from which God spoke and communicated with Moses.[15]

The Mishkan also had three walls, with the fourth side partitioned into three to form an entryway. A sukka, therefore, as per the Mishna, needs to have at least three walls.[16] In sum, the structure of the sukka is meant to telegraph its similarities to the structure of the Mishkan.

Aside from its basic structure, the colorful ornaments with which the sukka is decorated also reflect the ornamentation of the Mishkan, which included pictures woven into the curtains in a variety of rich hues. Thus, not only the building and structure, but the design of the sukka, reflects that of the Mishkan.

God was so gratified with the enormous effort and thoughtfulness[17] that the Jewish people invested into the Mishkan that God's presence settled there upon its completion. We construct the sukka, our own "portable Mishkan," to reenact that effort of our ancestors; we dwell in it to bask in the protective radiance of the Divine Presence that we pray will descend upon us as God's presence descended upon our ancestors.[18]

---

15. See Sukka 4b–5a.
16. The talmudic discussion on the mishna concludes that the third wall need only be seven handbreadths wide. Nevertheless, the mishna's stated requirement is significant. See also Y. Sukka 1:6, which derives from the curtain that separated the Holy from the Holy of Holies that the walls of the sukka (unlike its covering) need not be made from something that grows from the ground and are not capable of becoming ritually impure.
17. Ex. 31:2–6. The architect of the Mishkan, Bezalel, is described as being filled with God's spirit in wisdom, understanding, and knowledge to think thoughts regarding the work of gold, silver, copper, stone masonry, woodworking, etc. His craftsmen are similarly described as being instilled with God's wisdom.
18. The traditional meditation, based on the mystical text of the Zohar, recited as one enters the sukka, reads as follows: "May it be Your will, EverPresent God and God

After God's glory filled the Mishkan, the first thing that God did was to call to Moses from within the Mishkan, in essence, inviting him in to join Him.[19] Therefore, the first thing that is customarily done upon entering the sukka on each of the seven days of the Sukkot festival is to recite the prayer known as the *"Ushpizin."* In it, we invite Moses and six of the Jewish people's greatest patriarchs – Abraham, Isaac, Jacob, Joseph, Aaron, and David, one in the lead role for each night of Sukkot – to join us in our respective sukkot. These patriarchs were indispensable in founding and assuring the continuity of the Jewish people through the generations, and their efforts brought the Divine Presence into the lives of the nation. We therefore invite these seven illustrious guests of honor into our sukka/Mishkan, imitating God's invitation to Moses to be His guest in the Mishkan.

But why does the Torah command us to dwell in sukkot for precisely seven days? After inviting Moses to join Him in the newly completed Mishkan, God instructed him regarding the array of sacrificial offerings in the Mishkan. Afterward, Moses was told to dress Aaron and his sons in their full priestly attire, to consecrate them before all the people, and to train them for their priestly service. This training, which involved running through the sacrificial service with the priests-in-training, concluded with Moses charging the priests as follows:

> And you shall not go out from the entrance of the Tent of Meeting **seven days**, until the days of your training are completed for **He shall fill your hands for seven days.** As has been done this day, so the EverPresent God has commanded be done to make an atonement for you. And **at the entrance of the Tent of Meeting you shall dwell, day and night, seven days**, and keep the charge of the Ever-Present God…. And Aaron and his sons did all the things which the EverPresent God commanded through Moses. (Lev. 8:33–36)

---

of my ancestors, that You cause Your Divine Presence to rest among us and that You spread over us the tabernacle of Your peace, in the merit of the commandment of sukka which we are fulfilling…. May You surround it with the radiance of Your holy and pure glory, spread over their heads like an eagle…and from there may a rich flow of life stream down on Your servant."

19. Cf. Ex. 24:16. See also Nahmanides, Commentary on the Torah, Lev. 1:1.

The rabbis in the Talmud noted the linguistic parallels in the command to the priests in the newly minted Mishkan – "at the entrance of the Tent of Meeting you shall dwell, day and night, seven days" – and the commandment to all the Jewish people of "in sukkot you shall dwell for seven days" (Lev. 23:42). Through the second of R. Ishmael's thirteen hermeneutical principles[20] they derived from here similarities between the behaviors regarding the Mishkan and the sukka as well. Just as the priests were commanded to dwell both day and night at the entrance of the Mishkan, so too are the Jewish people commanded to dwell both during the day and during the night in their sukkot, sleeping in them in addition to eating and spending their waking hours within them (Sukka 43b). The rabbis were able to cross-reference these two commands because they recognized that the priests who were consecrated for the seven days prior to the inauguration of the Mishkan represented the Jewish people, who were consecrated by God at Mount Sinai as His "kingdom of priests" (Ex. 19:6).

This command to the priests to leave their permanent homes and dwell adjacent to the entrance to the Mishkan for seven days is why we leave our permanent homes and dwell in our sukkot for seven days. During the seven days that the priests dwelled at the Mishkan entrance, they trained to offer sacrifices on the altar by observing Moses conduct the model service in preparation for the consecration of the altar at the Mishkan's inauguration ceremony on the eighth day.[21] Moses describes this seven-day period as one in which the priests literally "filled their hands," practicing the sacrificial service (Lev. 8:14, 18, 22, 27) and eating the divinely permitted portions of the sacrificial offerings (Lev. 8:26, 31). As God's "kingdom of priests," we, likewise, dwell in the sukka for seven days, sitting around our table,

---

20. This principle is known as *"gezera shava"* – an inference drawn from identical wording in two separate biblical passages. The thirteen hermeneutic principles are found in the introduction to the *Sifra*, the halakhic commentary on the Book of Leviticus, and are recited at the end of the "sacrifice section" in the morning prayers.

21. As we will see shortly, the eighth day, on which the Altar was inaugurated, corresponds to Shemini Atzeret, the "Eighth Day of Assembly."

our makeshift altar, our hands filled with God's bounty in fulfillment of God's command.[22]

LIVING WITH GOD IN THE DESERT:
THE EIGHTH DAY OF ASSEMBLY

Why does the Torah mandate an Eighth Day of Assembly during which the focus of the holiday shifts from the sukkot outside of our homes to the indoor service in our synagogue sanctuaries? In telling us that the purpose of the priests' training was "to make atonement," the biblical text offers an important clue. These seven days were preparation for the atonement sacrifices by the High Priest that would inaugurate the altar on the eighth day. These sacrificial offerings were to be made before the entire, assembled community of Israel and were to be the pinnacle of the six-month effort of constructing and preparing the Mishkan for use (Lev. 9:5). On the eighth day, Aaron brought the sacrificial offerings on the altar to atone for his own sins and for the Jewish people's sins at the Golden Calf.[23] These sacrifices were visibly accepted by God in the presence of all the Jewish people.

> So Aaron approached the altar, and slaughtered the calf of the sin offering, which was for himself... and he took the goat of the sin offering which was for the people, and slaughtered it, and offered it.... And Aaron lifted up his hands toward the people, and blessed them... and the glory of the EverPresent God appeared to all the people. And fire came forth from before the EverPresent God and consumed upon the altar the burnt offering... and when all the people saw it, they shouted, and fell on their faces. (Lev. 9:1–24)

The acceptance by God of these atonement sacrifices and of Aaron's role in offering them was significant. It was one thing for God's presence to fill the Mishkan before all the people at the end of Exodus, and speak

---

22. In addition to fulfilling the command of dwelling in the sukka, the preferred custom is to recite the blessing over, as well as wave, the Four Species in the sukka, literally with our hands full, clutching our citron and palm, willow, and myrtle branches.
23. In the chapter on Yom Kippur we already decoded the meaning of the calf (or in the case of Yom Kippur, the bull, a mature calf) as a sin offering for the High Priest and the goat as a sin offering for the people.

from the Holy of Holies to Moses, as recorded at the very beginning of Leviticus. Moses had, after all, remained God's close friend despite the people's betrayal during the incident of the Golden Calf. God was willing to lead the people through Moses. However, the Jewish people still wondered whether God would truly accept them and their representative, Aaron, the High Priest, who had been instrumental in shaping the Golden Calf. Would God validate the priestly blessing that Aaron bestowed upon the people after offering the sacrifices and "shine His face" on them?[24] God's acceptance of the atonement offerings of the High Priest and the people by dramatically consuming their offerings in a burst of divine fire provided the exhilarating and awesome answer to these questions. In response, the people shouted out for joy and fell on their faces in front of the altar.[25]

The Eighth Day of Assembly thus commemorates the eighth day in which the entire assembled Jewish people witnessed God's acceptance of their offerings of atonement and of Aaron, their representative. The twin revelations of God's presence associated with the Mishkan – one, when the physical structure was completed and the Cloud of Glory filled it, and one as the fiery response to Aaron's offerings – are the reason that both the first and eighth day are sacred days. And this double manifestation of the Divine Presence and of divine acceptance explains our double joy in celebrating the eight-day holiday today.

Nevertheless, despite the joy associated with the eighth day, the immediate aftermath of God's revelatory fire singed the day with tragedy. Immediately after the people fell on their faces, as narrated in the Book of Leviticus, Aaron's two sons presented their fatal incense offering before the Holy of Holies:

> And Nadav and Avihu, the sons of Aaron, each took his censer, put fire in it, and laid incense on it, offering strange fire before

---

24. See Rashi ad loc. He interprets Aaron's blessings here as the priestly blessings found in Num. 6:24–27.
25. The service of the High Priest and the divine fire that remained lit continuously under the Sacrificial Altar were the Mishkan's components in sacred space that reminded the people of God's fiery revelation celebrated on the holiday of Shemini Atzeret.

the EverPresent God, which He had not commanded them. And there came forth fire from before the EverPresent God and devoured them…. And Aaron was silent…. And Moses said unto Aaron, and to Elazar and Ithamar his sons: "…Let your brothers, the whole house of Israel, bewail the conflagration which the EverPresent God has kindled." (Lev. 10:1–6)

Although Aaron and his sons, as ordained priests, could not exhibit public signs of mourning for the deaths of Nadav and Avihu, the rest of the biblical Jewish people could. This may be why on Shemini Atzeret, which our liturgy repeatedly describes as a day of joy,[26] the custom is to recite the somber *Yizkor* prayer – recited also on the other pilgrimage festivals – which recalls the loved ones among our family members and our people who have perished. Like the Jewish people who mourned the loss of these two promising young men on an otherwise joyous day, we too mourn the loss of our family members and our people on this joyous day in the Jewish calendar. Having acknowledged the loss of life and our own mortality, we then follow the *Yizkor* service by praying for life-giving rains during the upcoming winter months.[27]

As the Sacrificial Altar was the focal point of the eighth-day celebration in biblical times, its surrogate in our synagogues, the *bima*, the pulpit from which the cantor prays and upon which the Torah is read, becomes the focal point of the day's celebration (at least in Israel, where the *Hakafot* around the *bima* with the Torah scrolls take place on the eighth day).[28]

In sum, there is an intentional parallelism not only between the Mishkan and our sukkot but also between the events surrounding the inauguration of the Mishkan, the seven days of the festival, and the

---

26. In the Kiddush recited on the evening of Shemini Atzeret, the Eighth Day of Assembly, as well as in the silent devotional prayers (the *Amida*) recited during the day, the appellation "the time of our joy" is added to the name of the holiday just as it is added to holiday of Sukkot.

27. In the prayer for rain, the prayer leader emphatically proclaims that the rains should be constructive rather than destructive ones, "for life and not for death." The congregation then affirms this proclamation in unison with an equally emphatic "Amen."

28. Some communities in the Diaspora encircle the *bima* on Shemini Atzeret as well.

Eighth Day of Assembly as well. The building of the sukka parallels the beginning of the building of the Mishkan. The sacredness of the first day celebrates the filling of the Mishkan by the Divine Presence upon the completion of the construction. The leaving of our permanent homes to dwell in our sukkot for seven days as God's proverbial "kingdom of priests" parallels the priests' leaving their permanent homes and dwelling at the entrance of the newly constructed Mishkan, where they practiced performing their priestly duties at the altar for seven days.[29] And the sacredness of the Eighth Day of Assembly commemorates the fiery manifestation of the Divine Presence at the official inauguration of the altar on the eighth day before all of the assembled Jewish people.

Supporting this reading of the meaning of the sukka is the fact that several hundred years later, King Solomon chose to assemble all the people (as Moses and Aaron had done at the start of the seven-day installation period of the priests) and dedicate the First Temple in Jerusalem during the holiday of Sukkot.[30] As in the Mishkan, when the Temple was completed and the Ark was placed in the Holy of Holies, the cloud of the Divine Presence appeared, completely filled the Temple, and settled in to dwell among the Jewish people (I Kings 8:6–11). Solomon then blessed the people from the Temple on the eighth day before sending them home, as Aaron and Moses did on the eighth day from the Mishkan (I Kings 8:66).

LIVING WITH GOD IN THE LAND:
TAKING THE FOUR SPECIES

The above explication provides an understanding of the description of the holidays of Sukkot and Shemini Atzeret as first presented in Leviticus 23:

> On the fifteenth day of the seventh month, there shall be the Feast of Sukkot to the EverPresent God for seven days. The first day

---

29. See Sukka 45a, which equates the waving of the Four Species with the priestly service in the Mishkan: "Whoever takes his palm branch tied together [with the other three species] is considered by Scripture as if he built an altar and offered a sacrifice upon it."
30. Solomon extended the dedication ceremonies for fourteen days – seven days before Sukkot (including Yom Kippur), followed by the seven days of Sukkot and concluding with the blessing on the eighth day corresponding to Shemini Atzeret (I Kings 8:65).

shall be sacred, you shall not work at your occupations. Seven days you shall bring sacrificial offerings to the EverPresent God. The eighth day shall be sacred and you shall bring a sacrificial offering to the EverPresent God; it is [a day of] Assembly, on which you shall do no work at your occupations. (Lev. 23:34–36)

However, our explanation above does not account for the command, central to our observance of Sukkot, to take the Four Species – palm branch, citron, willow, and myrtle branches – and to rejoice with them before God. That command appears later in the text in Leviticus 23. There we encounter something unusual that all biblical commentators struggle to explain. The Torah appears to sum up all of the biblical holidays, of which Sukkot and Shemini Atzeret are the final ones:

These are the set times of the EverPresent God that you shall celebrate as sacred, bringing sacrificial offerings to the EverPresent God – burnt offerings, meal offerings, sacrifices, and libations, on each day what is appropriate for it – apart from the Sabbaths of the EverPresent God and apart from your gifts and from all your pledged offerings and from all your voluntary offerings that you give to the EverPresent God. (Lev. 23:37–38)

Then, rather abruptly, the Bible returns to the holiday of Sukkot and describes the holiday a second time in a different context – this time, from an agrarian perspective – and in a different tone of voice:

However, on the fifteenth day of the seventh month, when you have gathered in the yield of your land, you shall observe the festival of the EverPresent God [to last] seven days: a complete rest on the first day, and a complete rest on the eighth day. And you shall take on the first day the fruit of goodly trees, branches of palm trees, and boughs of thick trees, and willows of the brook, and you shall rejoice before the EverPresent, your God, seven days. You shall observe it as a festival of the EverPresent God for seven days in the year; you shall observe it in the seventh month as a law for all time, throughout the generations…. And Moses declared to the Children of Israel the appointed seasons of the EverPresent God. (Lev. 23:39–44)

Besides the abrupt switch from Mishkan-centered to land-centered worship of God – "when you gather in the yield of your land" – what immediately jumps out at the reader in this second description of the Sukkot holiday is the taking of the four plant species on the first day.

Two questions are thus raised by the biblical text. First, why does the text seem to sum up all the holidays, and then begin again with a second description of the holiday of Sukkot? Second, why does the Torah's command to take and wave the Four Species come only in the second description?

Closely reading the biblical text, contemporary rabbinic and literary Bible scholars have explained the separate descriptions of Sukkot as follows. The first description (Lev 23:33–36), which revolves around the sacrificial offerings in the Mishkan, was intended for the generation of the desert. In contrast, the second description of Sukkot is directed at future generations of Jews ("a law for all time throughout the generations"), commencing with entering the land. Hence, it states, "However… when you have gathered in the fruits of the land." The verse refers here not only to the season of the year in which Sukkot takes place (early autumn), but also to the historical and geographic setting – that is, the period following the Jewish people's settling in the Land of Israel.[31]

In this understanding, the sukka still represents the Divine Presence hovering in the protective Clouds of Glory above the Mishkan in the desert. However, when the people entered the Land of Israel, the Clouds of Glory that had guided them and protected them from the harsh conditions of the desert were no longer necessary. Like the manna which ceased once the people began to eat the yield of the land, the Clouds of Glory vanished into thin air once the people entered the more benign climes of Israel. These clouds did not reappear until King

---

31. See Elchanan Samet, basing himself on Rabbi David Zvi Hoffman (1843–1921, Germany) in "The Parasha of the Festivals: Its Structure and Significance," http://www.vbm-torah.org/parsha.63/31emor.htm.

Solomon inaugurated the First Temple, when they again came to dwell in its holy precincts.[32]

Anticipating this new reality of celebrating God's presence that resides with the Jewish people in the Land, the Torah puts forward a second Sukkot ritual for future generations: the taking of the Four Species. Maimonides, in his *Guide for the Perplexed*, explains that we take these four species because they are plentiful in the Land of Israel and exemplify the verdant, fragrant, fertile land to which God brought the Jewish people after their forty-year sojourn in the arid desert.[33] As Moses later reminds us in Deuteronomy, the fertility of the land is indicative of God's presence and providence in the land when the people keep God's commandments:

> But the land that you are about to cross into and possess … is a land looked after by the EverPresent God, your God, on which the EverPresent God always keeps His eyes focused, from year's beginning to year's end. If, then, you obey the commandments that I command you this day, loving the EverPresent God, your God, and serving Him with all your heart and soul, then I will grant you the rain for your land in its proper time, the early rain and the late rain. You shall gather in your new grain, your wine, and your oil; I will also provide grass in the fields for your cattle – and thus you will eat and be satisfied. (Deut. 11:10–15)

By taking the Four Species and blessing God through these fruits of the land, we acknowledge God's protective presence, not only during the forty-year journey in the desert, which we express through our dwelling in the sukka, but also after the arrival of the people in the Promised Land. Like the abundant trees and foliage in the Garden of Eden which Adam and Eve shared with God's presence,[34] the abundance of fruit and

---

32. There is no mention of a "cloud" or of "God's glory" until Solomon inaugurates the First Temple and the cloud and God's glory return (I Kings 8:11). Both literally vanish from the biblical text for the first couple hundred years that the Jewish people dwelled in the land.

33. Maimonides, *Guide for the Perplexed* III:43.

34. Gen. 3:8 and cf. Lev. 26:1–12.

foliage in the land reflect God's presence among, and providence over, the Jewish people.[35] As Moses later says to the people, in God's name: "The land in which you live … [is one] in which I Myself dwell, for I the EverPresent God dwell among the Jewish people" (Num. 35:34).

The commandment to take the Four Species may have also anticipated a crucial episode related to the Jewish people's connection to the Land of Israel: the story of the spies.[36] When Moses sent the spies out to scout the land, he instructed them to report on the quality of the land and its fruits and vegetation. Specifically he asked them to report whether there were **trees**, "*Hayesh ba etz*" and to **take** samples of the **fruit of the land**, "*ULekaḥtem mipri haaretz.*" Moses of course hoped that the spies' positive report about the fruit and foliage would generate enthusiasm among the Jewish people and encourage them to undertake the conquest of the land. Instead, the spies used their negative report about the land and the samples of fruits which they brought back to discourage the Jewish people from conquering the land. Rather than describe their luscious fruit samples as being ripe for consumption, the spies said the opposite: "We saw a land which consumes its inhabitants (Num. 13:32)." The spies, and the Jewish people who followed their lead, rejected God's land and shunned its wonderful fruit.

Anticipating the sin of the spies, and providing a vehicle for the Jewish people's complete repentance for all generations, the Torah text in the second description of Sukkot tells us to **take hold** of the beautiful **fruit** and **tree branches** of the land – "*ULekaḥtem … pri etz hadar, kapot temarim, anaf etz avot ve'arvei naḥal*" – and rejoice with God in

---

35. On the symbiotic relationship between the fertility of the Land of Israel and the Jewish people's dwelling in the land, see Ezek. 36:8 and R. Abba's comment on the verse in Sanhedrin 98a.

36. According to Rashi, commenting on Ex. 31:18, this parallels the way that the biblical text tells us of God's command to Moses to construct the Mishkan before the sin of the Golden Calf, even though Moses was really only told to construct the Mishkan after the sin of the Golden Calf and as a response to it. Following this reading, in both the sin of the Golden Calf and the sin of the spies, the biblical text prescribes a way of repentance even before the sins were committed. This accords with Rava's (and Resh Lakish's) opinion in the Talmud, that The Holy One, Blessed Be He, "creates a remedy for the Jewish people prior to afflicting them" (Megilla 13b).

thanks for this wonderful, fertile, and fruitful land with which God has blessed us.[37]

This is why Sukkot closely follows Yom Kippur (Lev. 23:27, 34), the day on which "all of the sins of the Jewish people" were meant to be atoned (Lev. 16:30, 34). As we pointed out in the chapter on Yom Kippur, the rabbis sought, through the rabbinic liturgy of *Kol Nidrei*, to effect atonement on Yom Kippur not only for the sin of the Golden Calf but also for the sin of the spies.[38] After they repented for the sin of the Golden Calf, the people built the Mishkan (and we today build a sukka). But to demonstrate their follow-through on their initial gestures of repentance, the people also needed to prove their persistence and dedication to complete repentance after the sin of the spies. They were able to do this through the taking of the Four Species. Today, by taking the Four Species on Sukkot and blessing God over these fruits and trees (branches) of the land, we reverse the ingratitude of the generation of the spies and add another link in repairing the people's relationship with God and God's blessed land.

For the same reason, when we wave the Four Species we do so in all six directions, showing that God was and is the true sovereign of the land. Unlike the spies, who saw the indigenous nations as being the indomitable masters of the land – from the south ("the Amalekites are sitting in the south") to the north ("the Hittites, Jebusites, and Amorites sit on the mountain") and from the west ("the Canaanites sit on the sea") to the east ("and on the banks of the Jordan river") – as well as above them ("they were giants") and below them ("we were like grasshoppers")[39] – we proclaim, through our waving of the Four Species in all directions, that God is the sovereign of the land, and indeed, of all the earth.[40]

If Passover celebrates God's taking us out of the house of bondage in the land of Egypt, Sukkot celebrates both our journey to, and our

---

37. Maimonides, *Guide for the Perplexed* III:43.
38. Hence the concluding verses of *Kol Nidrei*. See the chapter on Yom Kippur, above.
39. Num. 13:28–29, 31–33.
40. The dovetailing of God's presence in the desert and in the land explains why in the Jewish tradition, the preferred place to wave the Four Species in all six directions is in the sukka.

settling in, the Land of Israel, God's Promised Land. Being privileged to live with God both in the desert and in the Land of Israel is another reason why the Torah in Deuteronomy tells us twice that the holiday of Sukkot should be experienced with joy (Deut. 16:14, 15). Regardless of whether Jews are journeying through history toward the Land of Israel, or have arrived there, when they follow God's commands, they can merit the accompaniment of the Divine Presence.[41]

LIVING WITH GOD IN THE LAND: SIMḤAT BEIT HASHOEVA, HOSHANA RABBA, AND *TEFILLAT GESHEM*

Three important rabbinic traditions of the festival of Sukkot are organically related to God's protective providence in the Land of Israel. These traditions, although not written in the Bible, were already important in the time of the rabbis, who based their celebration of them on oral traditions dating back to Moses.[42] The rituals of Simḥat Beit HaShoeva during the intermediate days of Sukkot, Hoshana Rabba on the seventh day of the festival, and the prayer for rain – *Tefillat Geshem* – on the eighth day of Shemini Atzeret all reflect the central role of divinely sent rainwater in bringing forth the Land of Israel's vegetation and fruitfulness.

Once the Jewish people had built the Temple in Jerusalem, the festival of drawing water, Simḥat Beit HaShoeva, became one of the centerpieces of the holiday. The young priests drew water from the Shiloah Springs near the Temple and brought it to the High Priest, who poured it on the altar each morning as a special sacrificial offering during the days of Sukkot. Like the offerings of the Omer and the Two Breads on Shavuot, this offering reflected the principle of reciprocity. God watched over His people and His land, providing them with water from the sky, which sustained them all year long. The people, represented by the priests, poured water from the springs of the land on the altar as an offering to God, sending it up as evaporated vapor toward the sky for seven days.

---

41. This is what is meant by the Aramaic aphorism "*Shekhinta BeGaluta*" in the Zohar on *Parashat Shemot* 2a – when the Jewish people are in exile, God accompanies them there.
42. Taanit 2b–3a and Sukka 43b.

The timing for the water libations and for our rain prayer (*Tefillat Geshem*) on the eighth day was dictated by the rabbinic understanding in the Mishna that on Sukkot the world is judged regarding its rainfall for the coming year (see Mishna Rosh HaShana 1:2). This association of Sukkot with the year's quota of rainfall is alluded to in the Book of Zechariah, from which we read the prophetic portion on the first day of Sukkot. Zechariah prophesizes that in the end of days, those nations that fail to come up to Jerusalem to pay homage to God on the holiday of Sukkot will not merit rainfall that year (Zech. 14:16–17).

The pouring of the water on the altar for a period of seven days symbolized the covenantal relationship between the people and God and echoed the covenant of Shabbat, the seventh day of every week. It expressed the gratitude of the people to God for the water that He provides – something that might otherwise be taken for granted – and God's providential care for His people in their land, represented by that water. That it was offered in the Temple, the other symbol of God's abiding presence among his people, enhanced the meaning of this ritual and the joy to which it gave rise. Hence, the rabbinic sages themselves led the joyful celebrations for the water-drawing ceremony, highlighting the festive parade to the Temple with music, dancing, and fire juggling. So uninhibited was this ceremony that the Talmud states: "Whoever did not see this celebration never saw real celebration in his life" (Sukka 51a).

A similar set of reasons explains the unique traditions of Hoshana Rabba, "the Great Hoshana," another tradition reputed to have been transmitted orally from Moses at Mount Sinai. In Temple times, the priests would march around the altar each day of the holiday of Sukkot with their Four Species. On the seventh day, they would surround the altar with the branches of the spring willow. As the name implies, these spring willows grew near natural bodies of water and were an example of the verdant flora of the Land of Israel. The priests would arrange the willow branches so that the leaves would overhang the top of the altar, creating a protective canopy above it.

Like the *skhakh* that covers our sukka, also made of tree branches, this leafy canopy recalled the Clouds of Glory that protected the Jewish people in the desert. The priests would then march around the Temple altar seven times sounding the *tekia* and *terua* shofar sounds, praying for God to save and redeem His people.[43] The seven circles around the draped altar on the seventh day of Sukkot in the seventh month of the year – three sets of seven symbolizing the triple helix of covenantal connection between God and His people – brought to a climax the purpose of the holiday of Sukkot, the dramatic expression of God's intimate relationship with, and presence among, His people.[44]

After the destruction of the Temple, the custom of circling the altar once each day of Sukkot and seven times on the seventh day was democratized. Now, all the congregants in traditional synagogues – not just the priests in the Holy Temple in Jerusalem – circle their synagogue *bima* (pulpit, the contemporary surrogate for the altar) on the day that became known as Hoshana Rabba. At the pulpit, a member of the congregation holds a Torah scroll – the closest thing that we have today to God's presence – as the assembled congregation prays to God for spiritual deliverance and the material blessings of life-giving rainwater, with the very same words uttered in Temple times by the priests. They then beat a bunched set of five spring willows against the ground three times as if to draw forth its moisture.[45]

A different, possibly related, explanation for the rituals of Hoshana Rabba is offered in the Jerusalem Talmud, which views the priests' seven circles around the Temple altar as a reenactment of the conquest of Jericho, the first battle in conquering the Land of Israel.[46] There too, the people marched around the walled city of Jericho once a day for six days and then seven times on the seventh day, while the priests sounded the *tekia* shofar sound and the people shouted out the staccato sounds of the *terua*, causing the walls of the city to crumble (Josh. 6:2–20).

---

43. There is a difference of opinion in the Talmud as to whether on the seventh day the priests marched around holding the Four Species or just the willow branches. This disagreement, which continued into the geonic period, extends until present times in our synagogues on Hoshana Rabba.
44. The double helix holds the secret of DNA and of all life; the triple helix, binding together God and the Jewish people, holds the secret of Jewish life.
45. Reminiscent of God's instruction to Moses to strike the rock to draw forth its waters in the desert: see Ex. 17:6; cf. Num. 20:7–11.
46. Y. Sukka 4:3.

The resemblance between the seven-day circling ceremony on Sukkot in the Temple and the seven-day conquest of Jericho is uncanny. From the perspective of the Jerusalem Talmud, the holiday which celebrated God's protective presence of the people in the desert and divine providence in God's fertile land was suggested by God's miraculous providence over the people as soon as they began the conquest of that land. The inauguration of the Mishkan and the inaugural conquest of the land, both symbols of God's special relationship with His people, thereby overlapped within the seventh day of Sukkot – Hoshana Rabba – and became one. Once having conquered and taken possession of the land, instead of carrying stones, spears, arrows, and other accoutrements of battle as weapons to subdue their enemies, who resisted their taking possession of the land, the people were able to carry their citrons, palm willow, and myrtle branches around the altar in the Temple in celebration of the bounty of the land. The seven-day encirclements, which climaxed with seven circles on the seventh day, served to dramatically reenact the beginning of the conquest of this fruitful land and express gratitude for the divine providence that enabled the Jewish people to settle there.

LIVING WITH GOD THROUGH THE TORAH: SIMḤAT TORAH

The festival of Simḥat Torah, which celebrates the annual completion of the reading of the Torah, occurs in Israel as part of the celebration of the eighth day and in the Diaspora on the ninth day of the holiday of Sukkot.[47]

---

47. The reason the Diaspora celebrates a "ninth day" of what the Bible describes as an eight-day holiday has to do with how the dates of the holidays were set before the establishment of a fixed calendar. The first day of each month, and subsequently the precise dating of every biblical holiday in that month, was determined by two witnesses, who testified to the sighting of the new moon before the high court in Jerusalem. Since sighting of the new moon could vary between two given days, depending on astronomical and weather conditions, by the time word reached the Diaspora as to when the moon was sighted, the holiday might have been missed or celebrated prematurely. Therefore, the rabbis established the custom of celebrating two days in the Diaspora to mark every sacred day in the Torah. This insured that one of the two days would accord with the biblical command. The commemoration of all the biblical sacred days, with the exception of Yom Kippur (a day of fasting and therefore too difficult to observe two days in succession), was therefore "doubled"

The historical challenge faced by Diaspora Jewry was what to do with the second day of the holiday of Shemini Atzeret, that is, the ninth day from the beginning of Sukkot. The eighth day, as we saw earlier in this chapter, was meant to commemorate the inauguration of the altar in the Mishkan and, later on, the final day of celebration for the dedication of the First Temple in Jerusalem built by King Solomon. However, in the extended holiday period of the Hebrew month of Tishrei, already brimming with two days of Rosh HaShana, one day of Yom Kippur, seven days of Sukkot, and an Eighth Day of Assembly, having yet another sacred day which merely duplicated the commemoration of the previous day presented a challenge of meaningful observance for the Diaspora community.

Like the holidays of Shavuot and Rosh HaShana, which, because of historical exigencies, were reinterpreted by the sages to commemorate events with which they were not explicitly biblically associated, the ninth day was reinterpreted by later generations of Diaspora rabbinic leaders in an attempt to fill a void caused by history and circumstance.

After the destruction of the Temple and the exile from the Land of Israel, there was a vacuum in the relationship of the Jewish people with God. Without the land and the Temple, the study of Torah filled that vacuum and became the way in which to experience God's presence. The Torah became for the Jewish people, and especially the rabbinic leadership of the Diaspora, the main conduit to accessing God's will and love.[48] If the purpose of celebrating Sukkot and Shemini Atzeret was to experience the intimacy of the Divine Presence, then what better

---

in the Diaspora – there were, in effect, two days of commemoration to mark each biblical revelation. In all cases except for Simḥat Torah, the meaning of the sacred day was transferred to its "twin" as well (first and second, seventh and eighth days of Passover; Shavuot, two days; Rosh HaShana, two days; and first and second day of Sukkot).

Although this uncertainty regarding the precise date of the appearance of the new moon was dispelled once the fixed Jewish calendar was established, our ancestors' custom of keeping two days as sacred days was kept in place as a matter of privileging a long-held tradition (*"minhag avotenu beyadenu"*).

48. For example, the blessing said immediately before the *Shema* prayer, Judaism's credo, talks about God's great love for His people in bestowing the Torah upon them.

way for Jews in exile to do so than through the celebration of the Torah?[49] The celebration of God's intimacy on Shemini Atzeret, the eighth day, metamorphosed into the celebration of Simḥat Torah on the ninth day.

There are two other thematic continuums between the biblical Shemini Atzeret and the rabbinic Simḥat Torah, which make this transition between the eighth and ninth days more organic. The first one is the theme of taking leave. In the Talmud, the rabbis mandated that the Torah reading of the ninth day in the Diaspora should be the final chapters of the Torah, in which Moses blesses the Jewish people before taking leave of them (Megilla 31a). This follows the prophetic reading of the eighth day, in which King Solomon takes leave of the people by blessing them on the eighth and final day of the Temple inauguration celebrations before sending them back to their homes (I Kings 8:66). Both leave-taking episodes are captured by a well-known, touching midrash cited by Rashi as the reason underlying Shemini Atzeret:

> It is like a king who invited his children to a party for several days. When it came time for them to depart, the king said to them: "My children, please stay with me just one more day, because your leaving is so painful to me."[50]

---

49. As the preponderance of world Jewry lived in the Diaspora after the destruction of the Temple, the tradition that developed in the Diaspora to make the ninth day one of celebrating the concluding reading of the Torah was eventually adopted by communities in the Land of Israel as part of their celebrations of the eighth day – Shemini Atzeret – making that day in Israel a hybrid of the both the biblical Shemini Atzeret and the rabbinic Simḥat Torah celebrations. Historically, this occurred when the communities living in the Land of Israel were decimated by the Crusades in the late eleventh century, and the Jews who repopulated the country after the reconquest of the land by Saladin came from Europe (primarily France), where the custom that originated in Babylonia was to read through the entire Torah each year. The custom that had been prevalent in the Land of Israel then switched from a triennial reading of the Torah, which meant that the Torah was completed once every three or three and a half years, with each community finishing it on a different Shabbat, to the yearly reading of the entire Torah, where every congregation completed reading the Torah at the same time.

50. The talmudic source for this rabbinic midrash is found in Sukka 55b. Rashi's paraphrase is found in his commentaries on Lev. 23:36 and Num. 29:35.

Both Moses' and Solomon's taking leave of their respective generations of the Jewish people, and God's taking leave of us during the last days of the holiday, capture something of the separation anxiety and sweet sorrow that is felt at the conclusion of this festive holiday period. In that sense, Simḥat Torah follows through on the theme of leave-taking that marks Shemini Atzeret.

Second, Simḥat Torah – literally, the "Joy of the Torah," as its name implies – continues the joy that is present in Shemini Atzeret – the reenactment of the people's joy at having experienced the revelation of God's presence and their leaders' blessings at the inauguration of the Mishkan and the First Temple – and carries it forward to the joy of embracing the Torah.

There is a dimension, however, to that expression of joyfulness on Simḥat Torah that appears to break new ground, going well beyond the solemn joy of Shemini Atzeret. That added element is reflected in the seven circles (*Hakafot*) around the pulpit with Torah scrolls, often accompanied by boisterous singing and dancing; the *aliyot* given to everyone, including children who are not ordinarily called to the Torah; the special calls to the Torah for the "Groom of the Torah" and the "Groom of Genesis"; the communal Kiddush prior to *Musaf*; and finally the custom, in the Diaspora, to have the priests bless the congregation during the morning service rather than in the *Musaf* service. Where does this array of boundary-breaking customs and practices come from?

Although these unusual customs appear to come out of nowhere, several of the customs of Simḥat Torah can be traced back to three practices that took place in the Temple during the holiday of Sukkot: *Hak'hel*, Simḥat Beit HaShoeva, and *Hakafat HaMizbe'aḥ* (circling the Altar). These celebrations from the Temple were then telescoped over the centuries into Simḥat Torah, the final day of the festival. This metamorphosis of Temple-era customs from Sukkot and Shemini Atzeret into the celebration of Simḥat Torah maintained the memory of the Temple and of the Divine Presence and permeated the hearts and minds of the Jewish people scattered throughout the four corners of the Diaspora for millennia. But it did more than maintain those nostalgic memories – it also transferred the accompanying feelings of awe and joy from the Temple onto the Torah.

Hak'hel (lit., assemblage) took place in Temple times on the holiday of Sukkot-Shemini Atzeret that concluded the Sabbatical year.[51] During the *Hak'hel* ceremony, the entire nation – men, women, and even infant children – assembled, and the king, standing on an imposing, raised platform in the Temple courtyard, read from the Book of Deuteronomy. In so doing, he completed, over the holiday of Sukkot, what may have been, according to a source brought by Abrabanel,[52] a seven-year cycle of reading the Torah. *Hak'hel* functioned, every seven years, as a reenactment of the revelation of the Torah before all of the assembled people at Mount Sinai.[53] Therefore, on Simḥat Torah we complete the annual Torah cycle by reading from Deuteronomy. We award the final *aliya* to the "Groom of the Torah," a respected member

---

51. Deut. 31:11 and Mishna Sota 7:8. There is a difference of opinion between the Jerusalem Talmud, which understands the mishna to mean that *Hak'hel* took place on Shemini Atzeret, and the Babylonian Talmud, which understands that it took place on the evening following the first day of Sukkot. Maimonides in *Mishneh Torah*, Laws of the Holiday Sacrifice 3:3, follows the Babylonian Talmud. For an exhaustive discussion of the disagreement, see Dr. David Hanshakah, "When Was the Time of *Hak'hel* in the Tannaitic Period?" [Hebrew], *Tarbiz* 61 (1992): 177–192 [Hebrew].

52. I am following the suggestion of Abrabanel in his commentary on the Torah of the command of *Hak'hel* found in Deut. 31:10–13. Although Rav Avraham Yaari in his comprehensive work on Simḥat Torah, *Toledot Ḥag Simḥat Torah* [Hebrew] (Mossad HaRav Kook, 1964), 353–357, minimizes the impact of *Hak'hel* on the development of Simḥat Torah, I have found no more compelling evidence for concluding the Torah on the last day of the *ḥag* in his book or elsewhere than this biblical command. Even Yaari, who takes exception to Abrabanel's claim, grudgingly admits that the eased-up separation between men and women and the inclusion of the children in the Simḥat Torah rituals may indeed be rooted in the *Hak'hel* ceremony.

53. Cf. Deut. 31:12–13 to Deut. 4:10–11 where Moses uses the word "*Hak'hel*" to describe the gathering of the people at Mount Sinai. In both the description of the Sinai revelation and of the *Hak'hel* ceremony, the purpose is to instill a sense of awe in its participants. In Deuteronomy, recalling the Sinai revelation, Moses quotes God as saying: "Gather the people so that I may cause them to hear My words so that they learn to be in awe of Me all the days that they live on this land and teach the same to their children" (Deut. 4:10). Paralleling this, in commanding the *Hak'hel* ceremony at the end of Deuteronomy, Moses says: "Gather the people to me … so that they will listen and learn to be in awe of the EverPresent your God … and their children … will listen and learn to be in awe of the EverPresent your God all the days that you live on this land" (Deut. 31:2–13). See also Maimonides, ibid. 3:6, in which he explicitly associates the *Hak'hel* ceremony with the day of the revelation of the Torah at Sinai.

of the congregation who acts as the surrogate for the king. In fact, the custom in some congregations during medieval times was to crown the Groom of the Torah to recall the king of Israel.

Hak'hel brought together men, women, and children who crowded in the Temple courtyard to hear the king read. From this mixed assemblage in close quarters may have come the eased-up separation between men and women even in Orthodox synagogues during the *Hakafot* on Simḥat Torah.

We also have some evidence that at *Hak'hel*, the men would bring their own copies of the Torah with them to read along with the king. From there may derive the traditional custom for every man to be given an *aliya* to the Torah on Simḥat Torah. Even small children are called to the Torah in a special *aliya* known as *Kol HaNe'arim*, literally, "all of the children." It reminds us of the unique experience of *Hak'hel*, where even the smallest children were brought to the king's reading of the Torah, to instill in them a feeling of awe and fealty to God's word. During the blessings of the Torah, recited with the accompanying adults, we create a canopy over all the children to remind us of the midrash which says that God held the mountain of Sinai above the heads of the Jewish people when He gave them the Torah.[54]

The joyous water-drawing ceremony of Simḥat Beit HaShoeva and the music, dancing, and fire juggling celebrations surrounding the water libations that took place on the intermediate days of Sukkot during Temple times may be the source of the singing, dancing, and wild antics that often accompany the *Hakafot* that take place in synagogues prior to the reading of the Torah. The joyous spirit of the Temple ritual rooted in the Land of Israel was thereby diffused to each and every synagogue on Simḥat Torah, whether in Israel or across the Diaspora.

The *Hakafat HaMizbe'aḥ*, in which the priests circled the altar in the Temple during Sukkot with lulav and etrog, culminating in the seven circles around the altar on the seventh day of the holiday, was telescoped into dancing seven times around the synagogue pulpit on Simḥat Torah with all of the Torahs in the synagogue. Each dance

---

54. Shabbat 88a commenting on Ex. 19:17: "And they stood at the foot of (lit., under) the mountain."

circuit around the synagogue on Simḥat Torah begins with the leader of the procession chanting, "Please God, save us; please God, help us be successful," the same prayer recited during the altar circuits in the Temple. Thus, these three Sukkot celebrations from the Temple – *Hak'hel*, Simḥat Beit HaShoeva, and the *Hakafat HaMizbe'aḥ* – were brought together in creative synergy on the last day of the festival to celebrate the Torah.

Two remaining customs on Simḥat Torah, the rabbinic final day of the festival, may be linked to the event which, I have argued earlier in this chapter, underlies Shemini Atzeret, the biblical final day of the festival. The first is for each man, after receiving an *aliya*, to make Kiddush and to partake of refreshments as part of a *Kiddusha Rabba*, an especially expansive Kiddush. This custom has reverberations from the biblical celebration of the first animal sacrifices offered on the altar, God's table as it were, on the eighth day, the day of the altar's inauguration in the Mishkan. Part of those sacrifices were supposed to be eaten by the priests,[55] who represented the people at God's table.

The custom in the Diaspora for the priests to bless the congregation during the morning prayers, and not during the *Musaf* prayer, as is customary, is usually linked to this early Kiddush custom. It was prompted by a concern that the priests may have partaken of alcohol during the Kiddush, and thus become ineligible to conduct the priestly service. The law that prohibits the priests from performing their duties if they have imbibed alcohol was promulgated in the immediate aftermath of the inauguration of the altar in the Mishkan. Aaron's two sons offered incense not authorized by God, and were consumed by divine fire on that eighth day:

> And the EverPresent God spoke to Aaron, saying: "Drink no wine nor strong drink, neither you nor your sons so that you do not die when you go into the Tent of Meeting; this shall be a statute forever throughout your generations. That you may separate between the holy and the common, and between the unclean and the clean; and that you may teach the Children of

---

55. See Lev. 10:12–15.

Israel all the statutes which the EverPresent God has spoken to them through Moses." (Lev. 10:8–10)

Thus, both the customs of the early Kiddush and of the early priestly blessing may have their roots in the original story upon which the Eighth Day of Assembly is based and which was merged into the peculiar mélange of customs that together comprise Simḥat Torah.

Simḥat Torah thereby intertwined pieces of the Sukkot festival that preceded it with its own distinct customs, bringing the array of biblical holidays beginning on Sukkot and concluding with Shemini Atzeret to a joyous conclusion. But it did more than that. It made the scroll of the Torah the new focal point of the Jewish community, signaling the rabbinic shift from a Temple-centered Judaism to a Torah-centered Judaism.

SUKKOT LESSONS FOR JEWISH LIFE

The impact of the twin divine revelations commemorated by Sukkot and Shemini Atzeret was so powerful that it reverberated in the ethics, rituals, and liturgy of Jewish life throughout the year.

Living with Our Fellow "Images of God": Jewish Ethics

The first ethical responsibility that is grounded in the holiday of Sukkot is to share the bounty that God has granted us with those who are less fortunate than we. In the Book of Deuteronomy, the Torah begins its description of the holiday of Sukkot as follows:

> You shall keep the feast of Sukkot seven days, when you gather [the fruits] of your threshing floor and winepress. And you shall rejoice in your feast, you, and your son, and your daughter, and your male servant, and your female servant, and the Levite, and the stranger, and the orphan, and the widow who resides within your gates. (Deut. 16:13–14)

In the Torah, celebrating Sukkot involved sharing one's good fortune not only with one's family and employees, but with those community members who were disadvantaged in one way or another. This included the Levite and the stranger, who were not landowners according to biblical law, and the orphan and widow, who most likely also did not own land.[56] In an agricultural society, these residents could not benefit directly from the bountiful harvests.

Regarding the duty to help the disenfranchised and include them within one's celebration, Maimonides writes:

> When a person sacrifices festive and celebratory peace offerings, he should not eat alone, together with his children and his wife, and think he is performing a perfect mitzva. Instead, he is obligated to bring joy to the poor and unfortunate. As the Torah states: "the Levite, the stranger, the orphan, and the widow." One should grant them food and drink according to his wealth. If one ate of his sacrifices and did not bring joy to these together with him, to him are applied the words of censure (Hos. 9:4): "Their sacrifices will be like the bread of those defiled by the dead, of which all who eat of it become impure."[57]

The holiday of Sukkot commemorates the protective shelter provided by God for the collective Jewish people in the desert and then later in the Land of Israel. It seems to me, then, that beyond the explicit biblical mandate to share our good fortune with the disadvantaged, we are ethically obligated to provide decent housing for the homeless in our communities[58] and provide loans so those who temporarily lack the resources can keep up their mortgage payments rather than lose their homes. The commands to care for the vulnerable members of the community, issued in the Book of Deuteronomy in the framework of the Sukkot holiday, clearly spill over into one's duties toward these individuals during the rest of the year as well.

A second ethical principle that is grounded in the holiday of Sukkot is the welcoming of guests. Here too, this ethical value emerges

---

56. See for instance the story of Ruth, where Elimelekh's field must be redeemed by his relative Boaz in order for Elimelekh's widow and widowed daughter-in-law to have a home of their own.
57. Maimonides, *Mishneh Torah*, Laws of the Festive Offerings 2:14.
58. See Is. 58:7, read as the prophetic portion on the morning of Yom Kippur.

organically from the Jewish people's experience in the desert and in God's land. The desert is often referred to as "no-man's-land." The Jewish people in the desert were therefore God's guests. Like guests in all of the ancient Near East, they came under the protection of their host, God. In the Land of Israel, the Jewish people continue to understand that we are God's guests: "The land should not be sold in perpetuity for the whole land is Mine; you are resident aliens with Me" (Lev. 25:23).

In both the desert and the Land of Israel, we were welcomed as God's guests and protected by God's Clouds of Glory. God also modeled the gesture of inviting guests by inviting Moses into the completed Mishkan immediately after the Divine Presence settled in. It is therefore not surprising that, as mentioned previously, the first thing that traditional Jews customarily do upon entering the sukka is to invite "guests," the patriarchs of the Jewish people – one each night – to "join" their families in celebrating Sukkot. This fanciful invitation to our ancestors is meant to be complemented by an actual invitation to one's neighbors – especially those who may not have the ability, means, or space to build their own sukkot. Sukkot therefore becomes a natural holiday on which to fulfill the commandment of "welcoming guests" – what the tradition calls *hakhnasat orḥim*.

Sitting in the sukka symbolizes sitting in the shade of the Divine Presence. But the rabbinic sages teach that "greater is the welcoming of guests than the welcoming of the Divine Presence" (Shabbat 127a). This aphorism is learned, appropriately enough, from our patriarch Abraham, the "imaginary" guest invited to join us on the opening night of Sukkot. According to one interpretation of the biblical text, Abraham left God's presence to feed and care for three angels disguised as desert travelers whom he sighted from the doorway of his tent.[59] This welcoming of guests extends not only to one's sukka on Sukkot, but to one's home throughout the year, as emulation of our biblical patriarch and of God, who hosted us both in the desert and once we reached the Promised Land.

---

59. See Rashi on Gen. 18:3, *"Davar aḥer."*

Living with God: Jewish Rituals

The holidays of Sukkot and Shemini Atzeret celebrate, at least in part, the completion and inauguration of a biblical sacred space – represented by the Mishkan – where the Jewish people could both address God through the priestly service and be addressed by God from the Holy of Holies. Today, when we no longer have a Mishkan, a High Priest who can perform the service therein, or prophets who can hear the divine word directly, we have the closest thing to a replacement in the synagogue sanctuary.

After the destruction of the Temple, the synagogue became the surrogate for the Mishkan, with its two main functions – communicating with God through the sacrifices and being communicated to by God through the prophets – channeled into the synagogue service. Instead of the priests bringing sacrifices to communicate with God on our behalf, all of us are empowered to express our thoughts and feelings through our individual and collective prayers directly to God.[60] The cantor, or as referred to traditionally, the *sheliaḥ tzibbur* (lit., the representative of the community), plays the role in the synagogue that the priest played in the Mishkan. Instead of the prophet directly hearing God's word, all of us are able to hear God's word, at least indirectly, through the reading of the Torah in the synagogue service. The Torah reader and the rabbi who offers the weekly sermon on the Torah portion play the role, as it were, occupied by Moses in the Mishkan.

It is also no accident that the synagogue mirrors many of the furnishings in the Mishkan: an ark holding the Torah, a pulpit that represents the altar, an eternal light to represent the eternal light of the altar, and occasionally a menora to replicate the Menora in the Mishkan. Many synagogues even situate a special sink right outside the synagogue sanctuary for the ritual laving of the hands before entering, reminiscent of the washing stand that stood outside the Mishkan and Temple for the priests. In these ways, the rabbinic tradition sought to maintain the continuity between the Mishkan and the synagogue.

---

60. See Hos. 14:3, which the rabbis interpreted in this way in Numbers Rabba 18:21. In every Orthodox prayer book, after the morning blessings and before the "Verses of Song," traditional Jews recite the sacrificial service based on the notion that reading of the sacrifices is the modern equivalent of offering them (see Taanit 27b).

In addition, the prayer shawl, the *tallit*, that is traditionally wrapped around the body during prayer services, can be understood as symbolizing the Divine Presence enveloping the person addressing God. Like the Tent of Meeting, which served as the place of rendezvous between the Jewish people and God, the *tallit* forms a protective tent and enables the supplicant to commune with the Divine Presence without distractions. The opening verse from Psalm 104 recited as a meditation before putting on the *tallit* captures its tent-like quality: "My soul blesses the EverPresent God: 'My God, You are very great, clothed in majesty and splendor, wrapped in a garment of light, spreading out the heavens like a tent.'" If the basis of prayer, as I will soon argue, is to be conscious of standing in the presence of God, wearing a *tallit* helps one to tangibly sense the immanence of the Divine Presence.[61]

Even the Kiddush which often follows prayer services in the synagogue echoes the practices of the Mishkan. In the latter, many of the sacrificial offerings were consumed in part by the priests, representing the people, or by the person and his/her family and friends who brought the offering. The proverbial "breaking of bread" of the people with God, a symbol of the domestic intimacy and familiarity made possible by the construction of the Mishkan, continued in King Solomon's Temple and continues into our synagogue Kiddush celebrations today.

In sum, the centrality of the synagogue and its associated practices which help make God present in Jewish life has its roots in the sacred space of the Mishkan and Temple of biblical times, whose "grand opening" and "housewarming" we celebrate during the holidays of Sukkot and Shemini Atzeret.

---

61. It is noteworthy that the wearing of *tefillin*, phylacteries, is associated with the Exodus for which we celebrate Passover, the first pilgrimage festival of the Jewish year; and the *tallit* is associated with the enveloping Divine Presence in the Mishkan, for which we celebrate Sukkot, the final pilgrimage festival of the Jewish year. These two ritual objects, traditionally worn together during daily prayer services, wrap one simultaneously in the strength of God who extracted the Jewish people from Egyptian bondage and the gentleness of God who came to dwell with the people during their desert journey.

Talking with God: Jewish Liturgy

There are at least two ways that the holidays of Sukkot and Shemini Atzeret overflow into our yearlong liturgy. First, in the blessing prior to the evening *Amida* every day and three times on every Shabbat and holiday, the sukka is used liturgically to reflect God's protective presence. The prayer before Shabbat and holidays reads:

> Lay us down, our EverPresent God, peacefully, and raise us up, our King, to life, and spread over us Your sukka of peace.... Guard our going out and our coming in for life and for peace, from now and forever, and spread over us Your sukka of peace. Blessed are You, EverPresent God, who spreads a sukka of peace over us, over all His people, Israel, and over Jerusalem.

Thus, the sukka became a liturgical symbol of the "Clouds of Glory" that protected the Jewish people in their desert wanderings and that we pray will continue to protect each of us and our collective people in all of our life journeys.

Second, the special prayer for rain recited on Shemini Atzeret as part of the *Musaf* silent devotional prayer also overflows into our liturgy the remainder of the year. In the second blessing of every *Amida* prayer from Shemini Atzeret until the first day of Passover, we add the line "*Mashiv haruaḥ umorid hageshem,*" praying that God bring back the winds and bring down the rains in the Land of Israel. So important is this prayer for requesting life-giving water to the inhabitants of the Land of Israel that tradition teaches that if one fails to mention it, the silent devotional prayer should be repeated in its entirety.

In addition, shortly after the conclusion of Sukkot, as the rainy season is scheduled to begin, another prayer for rain is inserted in the ninth blessing of the *Amida*: "Bless this year for us, our EverPresent God, and all its types of produce for good, and grant dew and rain as a blessing on the face of the earth."

These short passages leave distinctive marks from Sukkot and Shemini Atzeret on our liturgy throughout the year, and connect us, however briefly, to the Land of Israel and the fate of its inhabitants.

Looked at more broadly, all of our liturgy – its structure and timetable – is based, according to one important source in the Talmud, on the sacrificial order in the Temple.[62] If, in the times of the Bible, communication with God was through the demonstrative, symbolic actions of the sacrificial offerings, in contemporary times we communicate with God through our words offered in a state of *kavana*, or mindful intentionality.[63] Both are ways of responding to the awareness of being in the Divine Presence.[64]

This awareness of living in God's presence, which is at the heart of the holidays of Sukkot and of Shemini Atzeret, has been weakened for many in our fragmented, post-modern age. When properly understood and internalized, these holidays can act as a healthy corrective to our post-modern, secular tendencies and bring that awareness of God's presence back to our thoughts and prayers throughout the year. It can enable us to experience our own rendezvous with God.

Finally, there is the overflow of Simḥat Torah. Within the rabbinic tradition, the Torah scroll, rather than the Temple, emerged as the most sacred symbol of Jewish civilization, while the study of Torah became the paramount Jewish activity.[65] This was so because, in a world in which God's presence in history was and is often hidden, the Torah represents God's tangible love letters to His people. With God's saving presence in history sometimes indiscernible, the Torah becomes God's precious legacy that the Jewish people can access and review over and over again in order to derive God's will. The Torah scroll becomes the one tangible embodiment of the Divine that every Jewish person can embrace, kiss, and passionately love. Indeed, on Simḥat Torah, the Jewish

---

62. R. Yehoshua b. Levi, cited in Berakhot 26b.
63. As the sages interpreted the words of Hos. 14:3: "Instead of bulls we will pay with the offering of our lips." See *Midrash Tanḥuma, Parashat Tzav 6*.
64. This notion, which is rooted in the thought of the medieval rabbis stretching from Rashi, through Maimonides and Nahmanides, was one of the central themes of prayer taught to me by my teacher, Rabbi Joseph B. Soloveitchik. See, for instance, *The Lonely Man of Faith* (Doubleday, 2006), 53–54.
65. In the morning liturgy, immediately after reciting the blessings for the study of Torah, one reads the first mishna in Pe'ah, which lists many of the mitzvot. It then concludes "and the study of Torah is equivalent to all of them."

people dance with the Torah scrolls as lovers do with one another. The reverence and love accorded to the Torah is the closest that Judaism comes to making God incarnate.

This love of the Torah as the embodiment of the Divine Presence is what sustained the Jewish people through two millennia of exile. It is this love that, we pray, will keep us bound to God as covenantal mate, whether in Israel or in the Diaspora, until the end of time.

Chapter Six

The Sacred Space-Time Continuum[1]

> *And you will make Me a Sanctuary (Mishkan), and I will dwell amongst you. According to all that I show you, the design of the Mishkan and the design of all its furnishings, so shall you make it.*
>
> (Ex. 25:8–9)

The biblical holidays represent the sacred times when the Divine Presence rendezvoused with the collective Jewish people. They are called in the Bible *"Mo'adei Hashem,"* the meetings or rendezvous times with

---

1. I am using this term made popular by Albert Einstein to suggest the interwoven nature of sacred space and sacred time to help us understand and reenact our biblical rendezvous with God. Like Einstein's term which helped scientists understand how the universe works on the macro level (e.g., galaxies) and micro level (atoms), understanding the single purpose of sacred space and time in the Bible to encounter God helps us to understand both the larger institutions of the holidays and the Mishkan as well as their myriad ritual particulars.

God. But even before these sacred meeting times were so designated, the Bible had already designated a sacred space, the Mishkan, a three-dimensional space in which the Jewish people or their representatives could continually meet with God and encounter the Divine Presence. The Bible referred to the enclosed area of this sacred[2] space in the Mishkan as the *"Ohel Moed"* – the Tent of Meeting or, as I prefer, the tent of rendezvous.[3]

The cosmic importance of this sacred meeting space between the people and God is expressed in a number of classical biblical commentaries. The *Midrash Rabba*, for example, a medieval midrashic compilation, comments on a verse in the Book of Numbers describing the "first day" gifts brought for the newly completed Mishkan:

> R. Samuel the son of Abba said: "What was meant by the words on the 'first day'? From the first day that The Holy One, Blessed Be He, created the world, He desired to dwell with His creatures in the terrestrial regions. See how it is stated on the first day of creation (Gen. 1:5), 'and it was evening and it was morning, one day.' It does not say the 'first day', it says 'one day'.... Why does it say 'one day'? Because so long as The Holy One, Blessed Be He, was the one and only one in His world, He desired to dwell with His creatures in the terrestrial regions; however, He did not do so until the Mishkan was erected and The Holy One, Blessed Be He, instilled His presence. When the princes came to present their offerings, The Holy One, Blessed Be He,

---

2. The enclosed area of the Mishkan consisted of the area of the Holy (*Kodesh*) in which were housed the Menora, Show Table, and Incense Altar, and the Holy of Holies (*Kodesh HaKodashim*) which housed the Ark covered by the cherubs.

3. The basis for this appellation is found in Ex. 25:22: "I will meet/rendezvous with you there, and speak to you from above the Ark cover." Moses stood in the area of the Holy and God spoke to him from the Holy of Holies. The first use of the term "Tent of Meeting" is found in Ex. 27:21. Everett Fox, in his biblical translation *The Five Books of Moses* (New York: Schocken Books, 1995), 413, notes that Roland Devaux refers to this enclosed area as the "Tent of Rendezvous."

said: 'Let it be written that on this day the world was created' [i.e., this was the 'first day' because this was the first day in which God's desire in creation to dwell with His creatures was fulfilled]." (Numbers Rabba 13:6)

This midrash attempts to answer what is perhaps Judaism's most important theological question: Why was the world created, and what is the role of the Jewish people in the world? The answer, a bold one that is perhaps at first difficult to accept, is that God desired to dwell in the "terrestrial world" with human beings out of God's aloneness.[4] Human beings, however, from Adam and Eve onward, did not cooperate and were continuously disobedient to God's will. It was not until Abraham came along and his descendants built a sacred space on earth in which God could dwell that God's original desired purpose for creation was actualized.

Nahmanides suggests a similar approach. On the verse from Exodus, "And they will know that I am the Lord their God who took them out of Egypt that I may dwell in their midst" (Ex. 29:46), he writes:

Read the verse as stating that I only took them out of Egypt so that I will be able to dwell among them.... And if this is correct then there is a great secret revealed in this matter, because according to the plain meaning of the verse, the dwelling of God's presence was to fulfill a human need [i.e., so that the people would get to know the God who took them out of Egypt] and not a need from on high [but now, we understand the verse to mean that the indwelling of the Divine Presence in the Mishkan was a divine need – God rescued the Jewish people from Egypt to fulfill this purpose of dwelling with them on earth].

---

4. See the interpretation of Moshe Aryeh Merkin on this midrash in his commentary on Numbers Rabba [Hebrew] (Tel Aviv: Yavneh Press, 1974), 58.

For both the Midrash and for Nahmanides, God's dwelling among the Jewish people in the sacred space of the Tent of Meeting and then later, in the Temple in the Land of Israel, was the apogee of all creation and the very purpose of Jewish chosenness.[5]

Many contemporary scholars, too, have noticed the linguistic parallels between the story of creation in Genesis 1 and the narrative describing the construction of the Mishkan in Exodus 25–40.[6] We can read these parallels as arguing for a parallel in meaning between the creation of the universe and the construction of the Mishkan – between God creating a home for human beings created in God's image to dwell with God, and the Jewish people reciprocating God's beneficence by constructing a home for God, their Creator and Redeemer,

---

5. It is not only those influenced by the mystical Jewish tradition such as the medieval kabbalist Nahmanides who adopted this interpretive lens. As sober a scholar as Rav Aharon Lichtenstein, *z"l*, former head of Yeshivat Har Etzion, in a commentary on this verse published online (http://etzion.org.il/en/i-might-dwell-their-midst), cited both the midrash in Numbers and Nahmanides' interpretation of this verse in Exodus to extrapolate this meaning:

   > If we combine the above teaching of *Ḥazal* [the sages] with the verse from the *parasha*, we arrive at the full picture. God desires to live in the world generally, but He wants to dwell in one place more than in all others: among *Am Yisrael* [the Jewish people], in *Eretz Yisrael* [the Land of Israel], in the Temple. The verse explains that owing to this desire on God's part, there was a need to redeem Benei Yisrael from Egypt, for God could not dwell in their midst so long as they were still enslaved and mired in the forty-ninth level of impurity.

6. These scholars include Martin Buber (*On the Bible*), Umberto Cassuto (*Commentary on the Book of Exodus*), Nahum Sarna (*Exploring Exodus*), and Nehama Leibowitz (*Studies in Shemot*, vol. II, 474–486, 696–698). The parallels include the use of the word "making" (seven times in the story of creation, over two hundred times in the building of the Mishkan); the prominent positioning of the Sabbath in both stories; a review of the work, which is found to be good or properly executed; and both God and Moses offering their blessings upon the completion of the work using the term "*melakha*" to denote the work both of creating the universe and constructing the Mishkan. Of course, in the Bible, both the universe and the Mishkan – including all the furnishings of each (e.g., sun, moon, and stars in the universe; large altar, small altar, and lights of the Menora in the Mishkan) – were designed exclusively by the same divine architect, which explains the artistic similarities between them.

to dwell with them. This mutual interdependency, as it were, between human beings and God, is depicted by the exquisite literary symmetry in the Bible.

It is no wonder then, with the story of creation serving as backdrop, that the Torah devotes so much attention to God's "sacred space," the Mishkan, in the books of Exodus, Leviticus, and Numbers. The dwelling of the Divine Presence in the Mishkan among the Jewish people brought full circle the entire narrative of the Bible beginning with the story of the world's creation. As in the Garden of Eden, God, in the Tent of Meeting, rendezvoused with the creatures made in His image, with whom God chose to be in relation.

Given the centrality of the Jewish people and the Mishkan in the biblical narrative, it is also not surprising to find that the multiple furnishings of the Mishkan were designed, not merely to bring to culmination the story of creation in the Book of Genesis, but to embody and give expression to the stories of God's seven rendezvous with the Jewish people in the books of Exodus and Leviticus. To understand how this is so, let us briefly return to our commemoration of Passover, the holiday that celebrates the first rendezvous, the Exodus from Egypt.

In chapter 2 above, we saw how the Passover Seder included three overlapping ways of telling the story of the Book of Exodus – verbally, through the narrative of *Maggid*; kinesthetically, through the actions of the Seder ritual; and visually, through the representations on the Seder plate. How did the rabbis come up with this three-pronged approach for telling their foundational narrative? The Passover Seder was modeled by the rabbis of the early Common Era on the Bible, which used the three mediums of sacred narrative, sacred time, and sacred space (in Hebrew, *"mikra," "moed,"* and "Mishkan") to tell the story of God's redemptive relationship with the Jewish people.

As in the Passover Haggada (the centerpiece of which is *Maggid*, the "Telling"), the Bible's sacred narrative is the anchor, the basis for all that follows. The order of the biblical story determines the order of the holidays which, like the Passover Seder, reenacts those stories. The Mishkan, like the Seder plate, through the use of dramatic, visual art, symbolically embodies the stories of redemption that the holidays celebrate and reenact. All three primary human faculties – hearing/ speaking, doing/acting, and visualizing/seeing – are thereby employed by the Bible to communicate the redemptive relationship between God and the Jewish people.

Like the biblical Jewish people who saw the Mishkan in the center of their encampment, we need to visualize the Mishkan to extract its meaning. The Mishkan comprised three sections: an outer courtyard into which ordinary people could come to participate in sacrifices; an inner courtyard designated as "the Holy" and accessible only to priests; and an innermost chamber, the Holy of Holies, into which the High Priest alone entered only once a year on Yom Kippur. Each section had specific dividers and covers and very specific furnishings. These furnishings told the story of God's redemptive revelations to the Jewish people in their first year of freedom.

THE COURTYARD

The large **Copper Sacrificial Altar** stood in the outer courtyard of the Mishkan. The term for sacrifice in Hebrew is "*korban,*" best translated as "closeness offering." The function of the *korban* was to forge a closer relationship between the person bringing the offering and God, in two separate ways. First, the life of the animal offering served as a surrogate for the life of the person or the family offering it.[7] Second, it acted as a gift, giving expression to the thoughts and feelings that the person bringing the offering wished to communicate to God. Depending on the type of sacrifice brought, the donor might then eat from the roasted animal, sharing a meal from the Altar, God's table.[8]

---

7. This was the meaning of the "*semikha*" which took place prior to each closeness offering in which the donor would place his/her hands on the head of the animal and symbolically transfer his life essence to the animal so that it would in effect serve as a sacrificial surrogate for the person bringing the animal.

8. Maimonides, in his *Book of the Commandments*, positive commandment 20, understands the bringing of sacrifices as the first and primary purpose of the biblical Sanctuary.

The Jewish people were commanded to bring their first closeness offering on the night of the Exodus, the first night of Passover. They were commanded to slaughter a lamb, take some of the blood of the lamb, and smear it on the doorposts and the lintel above the doorway before roasting and eating the lamb during the evening. The Torah tells us what would happen when God would then cross through the land of Egypt and slay all the Egyptian firstborns:

> And the blood will be a sign for you on the houses in which you are staying, and I will see the blood and I will pass over you, so that there will not be any plague among you when I strike Egypt. And this day will be a day of remembrance to you, and you will celebrate it as a festival to God, an eternal festival. (Ex. 12:12–14)

By smearing the blood on the doorposts and lintels of their homes in Egypt, the people in effect made their homes into symbolic altars on the night of Passover. The blood on the four corners of their doorways served as a surrogate for their own blood and spared their lives. It also expressed thanks to God for sparing them and freeing them from Egyptian servitude.

The smearing of the blood of the Passover sacrifice on the four corners of the doorways in Egypt presaged the rite in the Mishkan of spraying the sacrificial blood on the four corners of the courtyard's altar. Thus, the Copper Sacrificial Altar in the outermost portion of the Mishkan embodied the first revelation of God to the Jewish people on the night of Passover. From then on, every year that a Jewish person approached the Mishkan's Altar to offer the Passover sacrifice, he would recall that he owed his life and that of his family to God who spared all of them when they left Egypt. This engendered a sense of deep humility and gratitude.

The **Pitcher and Basin** stood at the portal connecting the outer courtyard to the Tent of Meeting. As the priests prepared to move from the outer courtyard into the holiness of the Tent of Meeting, they poured water from the Pitcher over the Basin set up for that purpose on their hands and feet (right side first, followed by left). This ritual action was reminiscent of the second revelation of the Divine Presence to the Jewish people at the splitting of the sea, for which we celebrate the seventh day of Passover as a sacred day. There, God made sheets of water stand erect to the right and left of the Jewish people as they passed through the dry seabed, and then poured the water back into the sea basin over the Egyptian legions after the people reached the safety of the shore.[9] The Bible commemorated the splitting of the sea and the "pouring" of water into the sea basin both materially, through the Pitcher and Basin in the Mishkan's courtyard, and ritually, through the designation of the seventh day of Passover as a sacred day. Later on in the Temple, the Pitcher and Basin were combined into one sink-like unit, named appropriately the "Sea."

Both the waters of the sea and the waters of the Pitcher and Basin served as a transitional station from one domain to another. At the sea, from an area still in the military orbit of Egypt, to the desert, symbolic of God's sovereign domain; in the Mishkan, from the outer courtyard with the altar which recalled the Passover sacrifice in Egypt, to the area of the Holy, God's exclusive domain for the priests.

THE HOLY

The Holy area of the Tent of Meeting contained three objects: the Table laden with twelve loaves of display bread; the Altar of Incense producing a misty cloud of aromatic fragrance; and the Menora burning with seven lights.

The **Table** with the twelve breads of display reminded the Jewish people of the manna – the bread from heaven – which God served to them every morning in the desert on a "table" of moist dew (Ex. 16:14). One loaf of bread was offered on this table for each of the twelve tribes

---

9. Ex. 14:22, 29. It was this double pouring, from the left and right, that, I conjectured in my book *Leading the Passover Journey* (138–141), the Haggada imagines Moses praying for at the shores of the sea, in the paragraph that begins: "Pour out Your wrath on the nations that do not know You ... pour out Your anger upon them."

as a token of appreciation for God's nurturing sustenance of the tribes as they trekked through the desert.[10]

The table consisted of six golden shelves, one shelf for each day of the week on which the manna fell (manna did not fall on Shabbat). Each of the six shelves held two breads, each weighing two omers, serving to remind the people of the double omer of manna that fell on the sixth day to enable the observance of Shabbat (Ex. 16:13–14). In the Jewish calendar cycle, the bringing and counting of the Omer and the bringing of the Two Breads offering on Shavuot was the way that the Jewish people commemorated this revelation in which God nurtured the Jewish people for forty years as they wandered in the desert.

The **Golden Altar** of Incense produced a cloud of sweet-smelling vapor every day of the year and was especially crucial to the High Priest's service in the Mishkan on Yom Kippur. Without the cloud of incense, the High Priest would have been unable to perform the annual special atonement service in the Holy of Holies. In fact, in the instructions to construct the Golden Altar of Incense (Ex. 30:1–10), as well as in the Mishkan service prescribed in the Bible for the Day of Atonement (Lev. 16:2, 12–13), the Torah connects the significance of this altar to the Temple service on Yom Kippur.[11]

Throughout the year, the burning of sweet-smelling incense was designed to attenuate the pungent smells of the animal sacrifices and create a more pleasant ambience in the Holy section.[12] On Yom Kippur, however, the cloud of smoke produced by the incense was essential for veiling the Divine Presence from the eyes of the High Priest when he entered the Holy of Holies. Moses' mask, when he returned on Yom Kippur from his third encounter with God on Mount Sinai, served a similar function, blunting the intensity of the divine radiance so that

---

10. As added testimony to the miracle of the manna, a jug with one omer of manna was placed for safekeeping in the Holy of Holies.
11. Yom Kippur was the only time in the year when sacrificial blood was sprayed on the Golden Altar.
12. See Maimonides, *Guide for the Perplexed* III:45.

the priest and other people could stand in close proximity to the Divine Presence.

In the context of the Yom Kippur Temple service, the cloud of incense produced above the altar mimicked the cloud of the Divine Presence which descended over Moses' Tent of Meeting[13] after God pardoned the people for the sin of the Golden Calf.[14] This cloud-like revelation of the Divine Presence is the very reason that we commemorate Yom Kippur. This cloud later filled the completed Mishkan and symbolized God's complete reconciliation and indwelling with the Jewish people (Ex. 40:34–38).

The **Golden Menora** was meant to recall the revelation of the pillar of cloud and fire over the completed Mishkan, for which reason we celebrate Sukkot. This pillar of cloud and fire, which would rest and rise over the Mishkan, illuminated and guided the Jewish people – God's "kingdom of priests" – always (*tamid*), both during the day and night in the desert.[15] Similarly, a light on the western side of the Menora was always lit,[16] day and night, to provide light and guide the priest in his service in the otherwise darkened, enclosed Holy section of the Mishkan.[17] Like the pillars of cloud and fire, the eternal light (*Ner Tamid*) radiating from the Menora symbolized God's eternal presence guiding His people (Shabbat 22b).

The Bible, in an interesting linguistic parallel, seems to connect the revelation of the pillars of cloud and fire over the Mishkan with the kindling of the flames of the Menora. In relating the revelation of the pillars of cloud and fire over the just-completed Mishkan, the text three times uses the root A-L-H to describe the rising of the cloud/fire to guide the people (Ex. 40:36–37). In the three places that the lighting of

---

13. Ex. 33:9–10. Moses' Tent of Meeting was a temporary structure that Moses erected outside the Jewish people's encampment before the Mishkan was built. At that time, since God was still estranged from the Jewish people because of the sin of the Golden Calf, Moses needed a place at some distance from the people to keep open the lines of communication with God.

14. See the chapter on Yom Kippur, above.

15. See Num. 9:16; Neh. 9:11, 19.

16. Ex. 27:20 as per the *Sifra, Emor* 13:7.

17. Ex. 25:37; Num. 8:2.

the Menora is commanded, the same root word is consistently used to describe the rising or kindling of the flames of the Menora,[18] though this word choice to denote kindling is unusual.[19]

The Menora's design itself also hints at the deeper meaning behind the celebration of Sukkot. The stylized tree shape, with its flowery and fruit-like motifs, was an embodiment of the fruitfulness of the Land of Israel. The latter was an expression of God's special providence over His people in the land, the second reason that we joyously celebrate Sukkot as a holy day.[20] Thus, the kindling of the oil of the Menora by the priest in the Mishkan represented, in sacred space, what the command to take the Four Species on the holiday of Sukkot by God's "nation of priests" symbolized in sacred time: an anticipation of the fertility of God's providential land. Strengthening this interpretation is the use of olive oil, one of the seven species through which the Land of Israel is abundantly blessed, to fuel the seven wicks of the Menora (Deut. 8:8). The oil from the olive tree and the seven "tree branches" of the Menora symbolize the seven blessed species of the land, celebrated on the seven days of Sukkot in a triple intertwining helix of the covenantal number[21] seven.[22]

---

18. Ex. 27:20; Lev. 24:2; Num. 8:2–3.
19. The more regularly used Hebrew root word for kindling, the one we still use today when we light the Shabbat or Ḥanukka candles, is D-L-K. This forces almost all biblical commentators who are puzzled by this term to explain the meaning of the A-L-H term as being synonymous with kindling. When understood to reflect the rising of the Divine Presence over the Mishkan, their puzzlement as to the use of this unusual term to denote the kindling of the Menora falls away.
20. See chapter 6, above.
21. In Ex. 31:16–17, the Shabbat, the seventh day, is described as the symbol of the covenant between God and the Jewish people. Later on, in Leviticus 26, the violation of the Sabbatical year, the seventh year, is the only specific violation cited for the extensive punishments with which God threatens the Jewish people for breaking the covenant. Umberto Cassuto has persuasively shown in his biblical commentaries how the number seven is used literarily as the organizing numeral of the Torah, which can plausibly be described as the Book of the Covenant. See for example, Umberto Cassuto, *From Adam to Noah* (Magnes Press, Hebrew University, 1972).
22. It is worth noting that the bringing of the first fruits of the land, which began on the holiday of Shavuot, concluded during the holiday period of Sukkot, the time that the olive harvest was reaching its apex.

Along with the Menora, the walls and draperies of the Mishkan conveyed the revelation of the eternal Divine Presence upon the completed physical structure. The Tent of Meeting in the Tabernacle was surrounded and partitioned into its three sections[23] by modular walls covered with precious metals and the woven, ornamental draperies of the Mishkan. As we saw in the chapter about Sukkot above, the number and height of these walls were echoed in the biblical and rabbinic rules for constructing the walls of the sukka. The colorful embroidery in the curtains and the glitter of the gold, silver, and bronze appurtenances of the Mishkan were also reflected in the custom of decorating the sukka with colorful ornaments. Thus the walls and draperies of the Mishkan along with the Menora conveyed the revelation of the eternal Divine Presence upon the completed physical structure of the Mishkan.

THE HOLY OF HOLIES

The **Holy Ark, cherubs,** and **Torah Scroll** were all contained in the Holy of Holies, the innermost chamber of the Tent of Meeting. The Holy Ark held the Ten Commandments, both the shattered fragments

---

The strong connection in the tenth chapter of II Maccabees between the holiday of Sukkot and the festival of Ḥanukka as a substitute for Sukkot, as well as the miracle of the Menora's oil as the central reason in rabbinic literature for the celebration of the Ḥanukka festival (Shabbat 21a), would lend additional credence to this interpretation of the Menora representing the holiday of Sukkot. As the eternal light of the Menora testified to God's eternal presence among the Jewish people in the desert, the miracle of the Menora staying lit continually in the Second Temple for eight days on only one day's oil testified to the return of the Divine Presence to the Jewish people as a result of the Maccabean revolt. This may be why the *haftara* portion read in synagogue on the first Shabbat of Ḥanukka includes Zechariah 4:2–7, with its strong imagery connecting the branches of the olive tree and the Temple's Menora.

Finally, the use of the Menora as the central symbol of the modern State of Israel echoes both its role in the Tabernacle representing the blessed fruitfulness of the land in biblical times and in the Temple as the symbol of restored Jewish sovereignty over the Land of Israel during the Hasmonean era.

23. The three sections consisted of the Outer Courtyard, the Holy, and the Holy of Holies.

of the first set of tablets as well as the second set of tablets.[24] Next to the Ark lay the scroll of the Torah that Moses completed shortly before his death (Deut. 31:24–26). Upon the cover of the Ark stood two angel-like cherubs facing each other, eyes cast downward, with their wings outstretched. These cherubs formed a throne for the invisible Divine Presence, with the Ark beneath it serving as the divine footstool. From the space between the cherubs emanated the divine voice that communicated with Moses.[25] Altogether, the furnishings in the Holy of Holies were meant to embody God's kingship and the revelation of the covenant and the book of the covenant – the Ten Commandments and the Torah – at Mount Sinai. The commemoration of this revelation, accompanied, as it were, by the threefold soundings of the shofar proclaiming the coronation of God as king, is the main reason that we celebrate Rosh HaShana.[26]

Finally, the service of the High Priest, in all the glory and grandeur of his priestly regalia,[27] and the eternal flame that burned continuously on the outer courtyard's Sacrificial Altar (*esh tamid*) symbolized the seventh and final revelation before all the people in their first year as a nation: when the divine flame burst forth on the eighth day and consumed the sacrificial offerings brought by Aaron on behalf of the assembled people.[28] The role of the High Priest was to carry all the

---

24. The opinion of R. Yosef in Bava Batra 14b.
25. Num. 7:89. God's communication to Moses from the Holy of Holies which he then passed to the people, along with the people's sacrifices and the priest's service, were the two essential purposes of the Mishkan. Through the sacrifices and the priestly service the people demonstrated their worship of and devotion to God and through the divine communication, God demonstrated His providence and devotion to the people.
26. See chapter 3 of this volume.
27. Ex. 28:2. The priestly clothing, a uniform as it were, was essential to the service of the priest as the people's representative. Without wearing the priestly garb, he could not function in his priestly role. See Zevaḥim 17b and Maimonides, *Mishneh Torah*, Laws of the Furnishings in the Holy Sanctuary 10:4. Like the furnishings in the Mishkan, the priests were consecrated through anointment (Ex. 29:7).
28. It is possible that the outer altar and the sacrifices offered on it therefore represented not only the first divine revelation on the night of the Exodus but also the seventh

Jewish people, metaphorically, on his shoulders and close to his heart. When he performed his service in the Mishkan, the High Priest wore an apron with the names of the tribes inscribed on twelve precious gemstones covering his heart (Ex. 28:29–30), as well as on the two stones that he carried on his shoulders (Ex. 28:11–12). At the same time, he wore a golden band on his forehead inscribed with the words "Holy to God" (Ex. 28:36–38). Together, these vestments symbolized the High Priest's role and responsibility as the representative of the collective Jewish people in their devoted service to God.

The divine fire, in turn, eternally lit under the outer altar, represented God's acceptance of the High Priest's – and by extension, the people's – service and sacrificial offering. Without the High Priest's service, which began officially on the eighth day, and the divine fire which burst forth to consume the sacrifices offered from that day forward, the Mishkan, no matter how beautifully furnished, would have been a cold, empty house. The priests' service and the divine fire turned it into a warm, living, vital home – a home in which the Jewish people dwelled with the Divine Presence, who passionately embraced their

---

and final revelation on the day the Mishkan's altar was inaugurated. The sacrifices brought before these two divine revelations were different, however, and represent two different dimensions of the sacrificial system. The Passover sacrifice offered in Egypt by the people on their "home altars" was a personal thanksgiving sacrifice offered by the head of each family without a priestly representative; in contrast, the sacrifices offered on the Mishkan's altar on the eighth day were communal sacrifices and sin offerings offered by the High Priest as the designated representative of the collective community of Israel.

These different dimensions of the sacrificial offerings are also evident in the early chapters of Leviticus: chapters 1–5 focus on the individuals, bringing and offering their voluntary and mandatory sacrifices to the Mishkan with the priest's assistance; chapters 6–9 focus on the priests' proper preparation and offering of the sacrifices on the people's behalf. For the latter, the eternal flame under the altar is emphasized over and over again in the biblical text (Lev. 6:1–6). The fire that consumed the offerings of the priest on behalf of the people represents the eternal Divine Presence accepting the people's offerings and dwelling among them (see Ex. 29 and especially vv. 44–45). The altar thus served to bring together both the individual and priestly dimensions of the sacrificial system and both the first and last divine revelations to the people in their honeymoon year with God as a covenanted couple.

service. The revelation of the fiery Divine Presence to consume the priestly offering is why the Eighth Day of Assembly, immediately following the seven days of Sukkot, is a sacred day.

The furnishings, the walls, and the High Priest's service in the Mishkan reflected the seven revelations of the Divine Presence before all the Jewish people. In each furnishing, as in each revelation, the people caught a glimpse, as it were, of the Divine, and continued to reexperience the awe and glory of God's seven rendezvous with His people.

Visualizing God's Hidden Face

Beyond the individual furnishings of the Mishkan, we can study the composite picture of the Mishkan in its entirety to reveal an extraordinary sight: God's concealed face.[29]

The Psalmist in fact teaches, "On Your behalf, my heart says, 'Seek My face!' Your face, EverPresent God, I will seek" (Ps. 27:8). To best apprehend the divine face embedded in its design, it is useful to view the Mishkan this time from the inside out, beginning with the innermost Holy of Holies, and then moving to the Holy and the outer courtyard.[30]

If we imagine the uncovered Mishkan from a bird's-eye view, we will see at the top of the image the Ark and Ark cover, a rectangular box with the cherubs reaching upward, placed north to south in the very center of the Holy of Holies. The contents of the Ark and the space immediately above it between the cherubs contained, as it were, the "divine mind" which was communicated from the Holy of Holies to Moses (Ex. 25:22). God's mind is represented by the Holy of Holies, at

---

29. On the secret of God's concealment in the Mishkan, see Nahmanides, Commentary on the Torah (Ex. 25:1). I first came across this idea of God's hidden face, writ large, although not in all its details, in a book entitled *Ohel Yehoshua*, Homily 1: section 26–28, originally published in 1882 by Rabbi Aharon Heller. The author was the head of the *beit din* in the city of Telz and toward the end of his life, a spiritual leader in the city of Vilna. I am indebted to Rabbi Eliyahu Millen, head of Yeshivat Meor HaTorah in Chicago, Illinois, who sent me a reprinted copy of this book as a gift many years ago.

30. See table and illustration entitled "The Hidden Face of God" at the end of this chapter, pp. 222–223.

the top of our image, the way the human mind would be represented at the top of the human face, by the forehead.[31]

Separating the Ark in the Holy of Holies from the section of the Holy was a curtain embroidered with the picture of the two cherubs, representing, if you will, the brows above each eye. In front of the curtain, in the Holy, stood two objects equidistant from the center, the Menora on the south side and the Table on the north side. From the Menora emanated light that enabled the priest to see in the enclosed

---

31. There is an intriguing parallelism between the placement of the Ark and design of the Ark cover in the "divine face" of the Mishkan, and the placement and design of the head *tefillin* on the human face. The Torah instructs that the head *tefillin* be placed as "*totafot*" between the eyes. The meaning of "*totafot*" is not clear, as it is a unique biblical word. The firm halakhic tradition is to place the head *tefillin* above the hairline (*Shulḥan Arukh, Oraḥ Ḥayim* 27:9). Still, there are many people whose custom is to wear the *tefillin* a bit lower than the hairline, more or less on the center of the forehead over what is sometimes called "the third eye." Nevertheless, all agree that the *tefillin* are placed precisely in the center of the head, between and above the eyes.

The placement of the Ark in the Holy of Holies of the Mishkan appears to parallel where the head *tefillin* are placed on the human body. The head *tefillin* are designed so that on either side of the head *tefillin* box there is a protruding Hebrew letter "*shin*." On one side, the *shin* is normal, consisting of a base from which rise three prongs; on the other side, the *shin* is unique, having a base with four prongs rising upward. The prongs of the two *shin* letters total seven, the number of the covenant as noted before (also reflected in the seven windings around the arm of the hand *tefillin*). If one looks at them carefully, one notices that the *shin* letters are also designed so that if the two were brought together, they would be able to interlace with one another.

These two *shin* letters placed above the human face may have represented the two winged cherubs that protruded from the cover of the Ark, on the "forehead" of the "divine face." The Talmud teaches that when God was pleased with the conduct of the Jewish people, the two winged cherubs would not merely face each other but interlace with one another (Yoma 54a).

This parallelism between the placement and design of the Ark and its cover on the one hand, and the head *tefillin* on the other, sheds new light on the passage in the Talmud that claims that God too wears *tefillin*, and especially, as R. Eliezer the Great says, head *tefillin* (Berakhot 6a). While our human *tefillin* contain four passages praising God, God's *tefillin* praise the Jewish people with whom God is wed in covenant.

Holy section; on the Table stood the breads of display[32] that were, as their name implies, seen but not consumed by God. Both of these furnishings are thus related to sight and represent the eyes of God.

Continuing down from west to east, precisely between and below the Menora and Table stood the Altar of Incense.[33] The purpose of the incense every day of the year, other than Yom Kippur, was to produce a pleasing scent.[34] The placement of the altar on which it was offered corresponds to the placement of the bridge of the nose, the organ of smell, on a human face.

Still moving eastward, we move from the Holy into the outer courtyard, where we would come across the Pitcher and Basin. On the image of the "divine face" that we are here developing, these small vessels standing next to each other are found in the place that would correspond to the nostrils on a human face.[35]

---

32. In Hebrew "*Lehem HaPanim*," which the King James Bible translates as "shewbread."
33. Despite the plain meaning of Exodus 30:6 which implies that the Altar of Incense stood just in front of the curtain separating the Holy from the Holy of Holies, the Talmud in Yoma 32b asserts that the Incense Altar was placed below rather than above the Menora and Table – that is, facing the dividing curtain but not sitting directly in front of it. Our description of the "Hidden Face of God" follows the Talmud's opinion.
34. See Deut. 33:10.
35. We argued above that the pitcher of water and wash basin represented the revelation at the splitting of the sea. Both the congealing of the sea and its dissolving to drown the Egyptian legions were caused by gale force winds brought by God. The Song of the Sea sung by Moses and the Jewish people after they had witnessed what may have been the greatest single miraculous spectacle in Jewish history ("What a handmaiden saw at the sea, even the priest [and prophet] Ezekiel the son of Buzi did not see"; Midrash, *Yalkut Shimoni, Beshallah* 247) gives poetic expression to these gale force winds with the following metaphor (Ex. 15:8–10): "At the inhalation of your nostrils the waters towered, flowing waters stood still like a wall, the depths congealed in the heart of the Sea …. You exhaled Your breath and the sea covered them, they sank like lead in the mighty waters." The translation of "*apekha*" (plural) as "nostrils" in Exodus 15:8 follows Rashi (ad loc.) and is found in Everett Fox's literary translation of the Bible, *The Five Books of Moses*, 337. To the minds of the Jewish people at the sea, God's nostrils, inhaling and exhaling, brought about the miracles that they witnessed and were soon after embodied in the Mishkan.

Finally, in front of the Pitcher and Basin stood the Sacrificial Altar, lit by the divine fire upon which the priests, as representatives of the Jewish people, offered the various sacrifices and libations. Leading to the altar was a long ramp. Together with the altar, which consumed the food offered to the Divine, it created an image that corresponds to the mouth on a human face.

What then is the composite picture that emerges from the placement of the Mishkan's furnishings? That of a human face, with the Holy of Holies corresponding to the forehead; the Holy corresponding to the eyes and nose; and the outer courtyard corresponding to the nostrils and mouth.

Of course, the people were unable to look directly at this representation of the divine face, first, because the Holy and Holy of Holies were enclosed by walls into which they could not enter and veiled from above with multiple coverings. Second, God had told Moses that no human being could gaze upon the divine face and live (Ex. 33:20). Still, from having meticulously constructed every item in the Mishkan and moving it and its furnishings from place to place in the desert, the people knew about the other features of the divine face and could imagine them, as we can today in reading about them, as constituting the divine visage.[36]

Though the people could not look directly at God's face, they understood that from the Mishkan, God's face was looking at them. Therefore, when the biblical text talks of the people coming on the festival pilgrimages to the Mishkan, or receiving the priestly blessings

---

36. See Yoma 54a, which states that in the period of the First Temple, during the pilgrimage festivals, the curtains to the Holy of Holies would be rolled up and the people could see the cherubs above the Ark interlocking like lovers. *A fortiori*, it is plausible that with the curtains rolled up the pilgrims could also see the vessels in the Holy section of the Temple. This implies that at least in that historical period, the people could see the otherwise veiled face of God when they came on pilgrimage to the Temple. This may also explain the law found in Mishna Ḥagiga 1:1, that a blind person was exempt from going on pilgrimage to Jerusalem on the three pilgrimage festivals. Maimonides explains the rationale for the exemption as follows: "Just as the people come to be seen by God, so they also come to see the glory of His Sanctuary and the house of the Divine Presence; this exempts a blind person who cannot see" (*Mishneh Torah*, Laws of the Festivals 2:1).

there, it explicitly mentions God's face, which is present to take notice and to bless them. The first time that the pilgrimage festivals are commanded, the Torah says, "They shall not appear before My face empty-handed...three times during the year, appear before the face of your Lord, God."[37]

The priestly blessing, which was first recited at the inauguration of the Mishkan, and which was bestowed upon the people when they made a pilgrimage to the Mishkan, is even more explicit: "May God bless you and protect you; may God's face shine upon you and be gracious toward you; may God raise His face to you and grant you peace" (Num. 6:24–26). For the biblical Jewish people, "God's face" was no mere metaphor for God's attention, as we understand it, but rather pointed to the physical reality of God's visible presence in their midst.

In sum, not only did each major furnishing in the Mishkan symbolize and recall at least one of the seven revelations of the Divine Presence to the Jewish people, but the Mishkan as a whole revealed, as it were, the face of God's presence to them. God's partially concealed face along with the Clouds of Glory that enveloped the Mishkan and the surrounding camp made God's continuous presence palpable to the people. When God spoke to Moses from within the precincts of the Holy of Holies, His commanding voice was made accessible to them through Moses' teachings. Each time the people gazed upon the cloud-covered Mishkan in the center of their encampment, they imagined the golden furnishings within and were reminded of their founding narrative, the story of their unique relationship with God in their first year as a people, which shaped who they were as a nation. This is why the Mishkan, the Bible's sacred space, plays such a prominent role in the biblical books that narrate the Jewish people's sacred story.

By retelling that story, celebrating the biblical holidays, and imagining the sacred space of the Jewish people, we rendezvous with God and surround ourselves with the Divine Presence just as the biblical Jewish people in the desert were enveloped by God's protective presence. Throughout the Jewish year, we imagine ourselves intimately

---

37. Ex. 23:15–17 and 34:23; Deut. 16:16 and 31:11.

reliving our honeymoon year with God, a year in which we followed God into the desert, in a land that was unsown. The prophet Jeremiah says that the memory of that period of time, and of the loving-kindness of our youth and our love as God's bride, is sacred to God (Jer. 2:2–3). So too is the Torah's recollection of that period of time and of God's revelations to our people sacred to us, who yearn to feel the divine embrace in our secular age.

The Hidden Face of God: Key

1. Forehead – Holy of Holies (*Kodesh Kodashim*)
2. Mind – Holy Ark and Cover (*Aron* and *Kaporet*)
3. Left & Right Eyebrows – Curtain separating the Holy from the Holy of Holies (*Parokhet*)
4. Left Eye – Menora
5. Right Eye – Display Table (*Shulkhan HaPanim*)
6. Bridge of the Nose – Incense Altar (*Mizbe'aḥ HaKetoret/HaZahav*)
7. Nostrils – Pitcher and Basin (*Kiyor* and *Kano*)
8. Mouth – Sacrificial Altar (*Mizbe'aḥ HaNeḥoshet*)

The Hidden Face of God

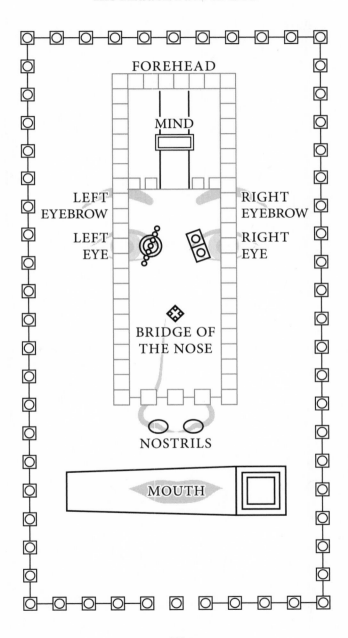

FOREHEAD

MIND

LEFT EYEBROW

RIGHT EYEBROW

LEFT EYE

RIGHT EYE

BRIDGE OF THE NOSE

NOSTRILS

MOUTH

Chapter Seven

Shabbat: The Purpose of Creating Heaven and Earth

*You made the seventh day sacred for Your name's sake,
the purpose of the creation of heaven and earth, and
You blessed it from among all the days and made it
sacred from among all the times.*

(Friday evening *Amida* prayer)

Shabbat is the sacred day of biblically prescribed cessation from work that occurs on the seventh day of every week of every year for as long as one lives. In the biblical text in Leviticus, Shabbat is listed first among the sacred days,[1] and it is thus named the "first of the sacred days" in the Kiddush that ushers in the day. While Shabbat, like all the other

---

1. "These are the meeting times with the EverPresent God that you shall proclaim as sacred holidays. The following are My meeting times: Six days you shall do your work but on the seventh day there is a Sabbath of Sabbaths, a sacred holiday when you shall do no work. Wherever you may live, it is a Sabbath to the EverPresent God" (Lev. 23:2–3).

biblical "sacred days," is a reminder of the Exodus from Egypt, and the freedom from labor that the Exodus made possible, it also has a universal dimension – a reminder of God's creation of the world.

This double meaning for Shabbat is purposeful. God's purpose in creating the world and especially man and woman, as well as liberating the Jewish people from slave labor, was the same: to create the opportunity for a meaningful relationship between God and the human beings created by God in His own image. Just as God's presence rendezvoused with the Jewish people seven times in their first year as a free nation, God's presence rendezvoused with Adam and Eve in the Garden of Eden on the seventh day of creation, the Shabbat.[2] The possibility of that weekly encounter with God's presence continues to exist for every human being who recognizes the sacredness of the Sabbath.

On the Sabbath, the idea of meeting God in sacred time, which we have explored throughout most of this volume, dovetails with meeting God in sacred space, the idea we developed in the previous chapter. So it is only now, after understanding the coming together of sacred time and sacred space in the biblical narrative, that we can fully appreciate today the meaning and observance of Shabbat, the first of the sacred days in the Bible.

SHABBAT AND CREATION

The Kiddush blessing over wine on Friday evenings telegraphs to us the three key features of Shabbat, a "commemoration of the act of creation," a "reminder of the Exodus from Egypt," and the "first of the sacred festivals":

> Blessed are You, EverPresent God, our God, King of the universe, who made us sacred with the commandments and desired us, and with love and will invested us with the sacred Sabbath, as a

---

2. I am indebted to my colleague Dr. Daniel Polisar, Provost of Shalem College, who first formulated this insight for me in November 2004. It is worth noting that this triple helix of creation, revelation, and the special, intimate relationship of the Jewish people with God, are the intertwining themes of the evening, morning, and late afternoon silent devotional prayers in the traditional liturgy of Shabbat.

commemoration to the act of creation. It is the first among the sacred festivals, reminding us of the Exodus from Egypt. For You chose us, and made us sacred from all the nations, and with love and will You invested us with Your Holy Sabbath. **Blessed are You, EverPresent God, who makes the Sabbath sacred.**

How does the commemoration of the twin events of creation and the Exodus find expression in the observances of Shabbat? Indeed, newcomers to Judaism are often puzzled by the myriad of rituals that are performed on Shabbat and the seemingly innumerable prohibitions of the day. While they may be charmed by the former – candlelit dinner, sumptuous meals replete with freshly baked *ḥallot*, wine, song, and warm fellowship – they tend to be overwhelmed by the latter – a long list of activities that are prohibited on Shabbat.

Asking why those activities are prohibited on the Shabbat, they are often told that they were included in the thirty-nine categories of work, or their derivatives, that were performed in the Mishkan. Whether they articulate and voice their puzzlement or not, they then often wonder what the work done in the Mishkan has to do with commemorating the creation of the universe and the Exodus from Egyptian servitude, as stated in the Kiddush. Furthermore, they are flummoxed as to why the work done in the Mishkan over three thousand years ago has such a strong bearing on what is permitted on Shabbat in the twenty-first century. For instance, they wonder what the relationship might be between the strenuous manual labor done to construct the Mishkan and turning on an electric light, a computer, or a car on Shabbat, conveniences of modern life that certainly did not exist three millennia ago. Studying the biblical texts that link Shabbat first to creation and then to the Exodus from Egypt helps us discover the answers to these challenges.

At the conclusion of the story of creation in the Book of Genesis, we are told that God created the world in six days and rested on the seventh:

> On the seventh day God finished the work that He had been doing and He desisted on the seventh day from all the work that He had done. And God blessed the seventh day and made it sacred,

because on that day He desisted from all the work of creation that God had set out to do. (Gen. 2:2–3)

God "rested" on the seventh day and made it sacred. Not only was Shabbat the first sacred time, it was also the only sacred time in which God alone sanctified the day, with human beings playing no ancillary role. According to rabbinic tradition,[3] in all other sacred times, the declaration of the sacredness of the "holiday" was dependent on the authority of the Jewish court. Witnesses testified to the sighting of the new moon and the court then declared when the month was to begin and when the holidays in a particular month would occur. Even if the court erred in fixing the correct date, by rabbinic law their authority reigned supreme.[4] But, as recorded in the Book of Genesis, from the seventh day of creation onward, God alone designated every seventh day as *kadosh*, sacred. Unlike the other seasonal holidays in which the Kiddush concludes with "Blessed are You, EverPresent God, who sanctifies the Jewish people and the times" – giving the people a role in the designation of the times as sacred – the Shabbat Kiddush concludes with "Blessed are You, EverPresent God, who sanctifies the Shabbat," where God alone is the sanctifier of the day. With or without a Jewish court, anyone who can keep track of the setting and rising of the sun can know on which day to observe the Sabbath.[5]

Twice in the Book of Exodus, Moses draws on the creation rationale as the reason the Jewish people are commanded to keep the Sabbath. The first is in the Bible's first iteration of the Ten Commandments:

---

3. Interpreting Lev. 23:2, "Speak to the Jewish people and tell them: 'The meeting times of the EverPresent God, **which you shall proclaim** as sacred,'" the rabbis understood the power to proclaim and therefore to fix the date of the holidays as one given to the High Court, representing the collective Jewish people.

4. See the sixteenth-century biblical commentary of Rabbi Ovadiah ben Jacob Seforno on Lev. 23:4, citing Rosh HaShana 25a, which distinguishes between Shabbat, whose time was set by God at creation, and the other holidays, which were wholly dependent on the High Court in Jerusalem.

5. In fact, the sanctification of the Shabbat is the only time that we find the root word K-D-SH used to denote holiness in all the Book of Genesis.

Remember the Sabbath day to make it sacred. Six days you shall labor and do all your work, but the seventh day is a Sabbath of the EverPresent God your God: you shall not do any work – you, your son or daughter, your male or female slave, your cattle... and the stranger who is within your settlements. **For in six days the EverPresent God made the heaven and the earth and the sea, and all that is in them, and rested on the seventh day; therefore the EverPresent God blessed the Sabbath day and made it sacred.** (Ex. 20:8–11)

The second time in Exodus that Shabbat is linked to creation is at the conclusion of God's instructions to Moses to build the Mishkan. Coming where they do, after describing the "work" (Hebrew: *melakha*) that needs to be done, these verses should be read as saying that notwithstanding the command to engage in the work of building a sacred space for God, observing the sacred time of Shabbat takes priority.[6] And the reason has to do with creation:

> And God spoke to Moses saying, "You should speak to the Children of Israel saying: 'Notwithstanding [all that I have commanded], My Sabbaths you shall keep. Because it is a sign between Me and you for all generations, to make known that I am the EverPresent God who sanctifies you. And you should keep the Sabbath because it is sacred for you.... Six days you will do work and the seventh day shall be a Sabbath of Sabbaths, sacred to the EverPresent God.... The Israelite people shall keep the Sabbath, observing the Sabbath throughout the ages as a covenant for all time. It shall be a sign for all time between Me and the people of Israel. **For in six days the EverPresent God made heaven and earth, and on the seventh day He ceased from work and was refreshed.**'" (Ex. 31:12–17)

---

6. Almost all classic medieval commentators understand it this way including Rashi, Nahmanides, Ibn Ezra, Rashbam, Seforno, and Abrabanel. See also Ex. 35:1–3 and Nahmanides' commentary on 35:1.

In both of these paragraphs, the Torah is saying that like God, the Jewish people, who as human beings are created in the image of God, should act creatively and productively for six days and rest on the seventh. More than any other of the 613 commandments, the Sabbath drives home the truth that all human beings are created in God's image. Unlike the reigning ideology of the ancient world that assumed that only kings were created in the image of the Divine, the Bible posited a revolutionary thesis: All human beings are created in the divine image.[7]

In fact, the command for all members of ancient Jewish society – freemen as well as indentured servants – to rest on the Sabbath because God rested on the Sabbath only makes logical sense if we believe, as the Bible states, that all human beings are created in God's image. The injunction to the Jewish people to keep the Sabbath was also the "sign" (*ot*) that the Jewish people were chosen to carry this truth to the world.

There are two important aspects to the relationship between the Sabbath and creation that emphasize the idea that human beings were created in God's image. The first, often forgotten or ignored, is that like God, human beings are bidden to be creative and productive for six days each week. Part of believing in the God of the Bible is believing in our duty to continue God's work of creation through our own creativity and productivity.[8] In fact, Maimonides is very critical of certain able-bodied segments of the Jewish community that choose to subsist entirely through the work of others while they engage in ostensibly loftier spiritual pursuits.[9] Indeed, the kabbalistic tradition also interprets this way of life pejoratively by designating those who live off someone else's beneficence as living with the "bread of shame."[10] Those who do not heed God's command to Adam in the Garden of Eden, to "work it and to protect/preserve it," and who choose not to contribute to society when they could, fail to maintain the world in which God seeks to dwell

---

7. In this regard, see Joshua A. Berman's landmark book, *Created Equal: How the Bible Broke with Ancient Political Thought* (New York: Oxford University Press, 2008).

8. See Rabbi Joseph B. Soloveitchik, part I of the *The Lonely Man of Faith* (Jerusalem: Maggid Books, 2012).

9. See for instance, Maimonides, *Mishneh Torah*, Laws of Torah Study 3:1; Commentary on the Mishna, *Ethics of the Fathers* 4:5.

10. Known in Aramaic as *"naama dekhisufa."* See also Y. Orla 1:3.

in the condition that God desires. This is not merely a case of benign neglect but a gross dereliction of duty and a violation of our fiduciary responsibility. God endowed us with a creative capacity that mirrors His, and entrusted us with the physical world. It is our duty to guard it and develop it to its fullest potential.[11]

The second aspect is God's resting on the seventh day. While God's days during creation were not equivalent to our days (the sun and moon, by which human beings measure day and night, were not created until day four), the point of the biblical story is to understand the seven days of creation, not literally, but as a metaphor for a unit of time. God rested on His seventh unit of time.[12]

Why did God do so? The Torah does not tell us. However, we might conjecture that God wished to set aside a period of time with which to enjoy His creation[13] and particularly the relationship with the beings created in God's own image. After all, why create a God-like human being with whom to share the world, if not to set aside quality time with that being? God's resting from the work of creation and the reason for doing so are meant to serve as models for human beings. After imitating God in being creative and productive for six days, we are expected to desist from our work on our seventh day and set aside our productive activities in order to enjoy an intimate relationship with God and with other "images of God" in our world. Our creative work, like God's during the six days of the week, is to enable us to fully actualize our relationships, with God and with other images of God, on the seventh day.

Moreover, Shabbat and the relationships that it makes possible are part and parcel of God's created order for the universe. This is why

---

11. This is a plausible interpretation of Gen. 2:3 – "for on this day God desisted from all of His work which He created for [us] to do" – that is, God limited creation, so that human beings would have a role in further developing God's created world. On this view, see Joseph B. Soloveitchik, "Majesty and Humility," in *Confrontation and Other Essays* (Jerusalem: Maggid Books, 2015), p. 25.

12. See Saul J. Berman, "The Extended Notion of the Sabbath," *Judaism*, vol. 22, no. 3 (Summer 1973): 342–52.

13. Hence, on the cusp of the Shabbat, "God saw all that God had done and behold it was very good" (Gen. 1:31).

the Kiddush designates it as a "commemoration of the act of creation" and not as a period of divine rest following creation. By linking Shabbat to the act of creating heaven and earth, the Torah teaches us that for both God and human beings resting from everyday work and reserving the Shabbat to relate to others is the apogee of creation and part of the very fabric of the created universe.

SHABBAT AND THE EXODUS

In the second iteration of the Ten Commandments, found in the Book of Deuteronomy, Moses cites a different rationale for keeping the Sabbath. There, the sacred day of Shabbat is a reminder of God's redeeming the Jewish people from slave labor in Egypt:

> Guard the Sabbath day and keep it holy…the seventh day is a Sabbath of the EverPresent God your God; you shall not do any work – you, your son and your daughter, your male and female slave…or the stranger in your settlements, **so that your male and female slave may rest as you do. Remember that you were a slave in the land of Egypt and the EverPresent God your God freed you from there with a mighty hand and an outstretched arm; therefore the EverPresent God, your God, has commanded you to observe the Sabbath day.** (Deut. 5:12–15)

Here the day of rest is commanded not to imitate the Creator God but the Redeemer God. For the generation of Jews who had personally experienced Egyptian servitude, there was no need to explicitly link the experience of slavery in Egypt and redemption from it to the duty to give their male and female servants, and strangers, a chance to rest. The relationship of the two was self-evident. All that was necessary was to reiterate that all members of society – including the most vulnerable – were to be granted rest, as stated in the first iteration of the Ten Commandments.[14] However, to the next generation, who had grown

---

14. Part of this rationale for observing the Shabbat, minus the mention of Egyptian servitude and liberation, was already mentioned in Exodus 23:12 shortly after God's revelation at Mount Sinai. It was apparently part of the "Book of the Covenant" that

up in freedom and who would themselves be masters and proud citizens rather than slaves and strangers in the land that they were about to conquer, the duty to free one's subordinates from work on Shabbat had to be explicitly linked back to the experience of servitude in, and exodus from, Egypt.

The second and subsequent generations addressed in Deuteronomy had no actual memories of being enslaved; the command to remember meant to conjure up in their imagination what it felt like, emotionally, to be a slave seven days a week, and to acknowledge and emulate God's freeing of the people from slavery.[15] In the second iteration of the Ten Commandments, as in the first, there was a recognition and an emulation of the Divine in the people's conduct. As God freed the people from servitude in Egypt so were the Jewish people to free their slaves from work for one seventh of their period of servitude. As God's chosen mate in history (Ex. 19:4–6), the people were to act as God did, and emulate God in their values and actions. In this way, they would fulfill their God-like potential so God could live with them in harmony.

Indeed, the Exodus from Egypt was so fundamental to the entire experience and identity of the Jewish people that in Jewish liturgy, if not in the Bible, all of the sacred days – from Shabbat through Shemini Atzeret – are said to be in commemoration of the Exodus from Egypt. This is so because the commemoration of all the sacred times in Judaism are premised on the Jewish people being free. God was not interested in a relationship with automatons. Human beings were created in God's image and endowed with free will so that they would freely choose to live in relationship with God. The Exodus enabled the Jewish people to freely choose to be "mates" of God in history. And central to this role was spending sacred time in relationship with God, as well as with other images of God who themselves would be free to live in

Moses read to the people before they proclaimed, "We will do and we will listen" to the covenant with God: "Six days shall you do your doings, but on the seventh day you shall desist, in order that your ox and donkey will rest and your handmaiden and stranger will be refreshed."

15. See chapter 1, "Passover – Leaving Egypt": The Timeless Ethical Values of the Exodus, pp. 29–32.

relationship with God and each other. Both the weekly Shabbat and the seasonal holidays were the sacred times in which the Jewish people could and would rendezvous with God.

SHABBAT AND THE OTHER BIBLICAL HOLIDAYS

The order of the holy days in the Book of Leviticus follows the chronological order of the events they commemorate. Thus Shabbat, which commemorates both creation and the Exodus, is the first of the sacred times listed in Leviticus 23, the biblical chapter of the holidays. Passover, which commemorates only the Exodus, follows. The Omer and Shavuot follow that, etc. Separating the verses about Shabbat from the verses about Passover is a separate introduction to Passover and the other seasonal holidays, to signify that unlike Shabbat, which occurs every week, the seasonal holidays occur only once each year. Therefore, in relationship to God's revelation in the Exodus, Shabbat commemorates weekly what Passover commemorates annually.

However, Shabbat was not merely the first sacred day chronologically; rather, all the seasonal holidays, beginning with Passover, contain echoes of Shabbat in one way or another and all of them reinforce the primacy of its commemoration by ceasing work.

On the first day of Passover we remember the Exodus and on the seventh day we celebrate the splitting of the sea. On both, no work is permitted. The seven-day cycle of Passover implicitly also recalls and reinforces the notion of the "seventh day" being sacred – whether it is the seventh day that completed the creation of the universe, Shabbat, or the seventh day that completed the liberation of the Jews from Egyptian bondage. As noted earlier, the number "seven" is the symbol of the covenantal bond between God and the Jewish people and the organizing numeral of all the biblical holidays.

The second biblical holiday, Shavuot, is also integrally related to Shabbat and to its affirmation of the human being created in God's image. In chapter 2, on Shavuot, we showed how the easy access to the manna, its relative abundance compared to the scarcity of food in Egypt, and the ability to take the seventh day off from gathering it, helped to restore the human dignity of the former Jewish slaves as true images of God.

Moreover, as a practical matter, the rhythm of the falling of the manna trained the Jewish people to cease their work of gathering their sustenance on the Shabbat. Jews became habituated to counting time, not as the mere passing of individual days, but as the passing of seven-day blocs, punctuated by a day of rest.[16] The double amount of manna on the sixth day prepared the Jewish people to rest on the seventh day and created the experience of "observing Shabbat" among the first generation of Jews who were freed by the Exodus.[17] For later generations,

---

16. As we noted previously in chapter 2, weeks were ten days long in Egypt and did not conclude with a Sabbath, a biblical invention.
17. In thinking about the relationship of the Shabbat and the manna, what was the nature of the Shabbat that the Jews learned to keep from the rhythm of the falling manna? For most of the first year that manna began to fall, there was as yet no Mishkan, so there were no thirty-nine categories of "work" (*melakha*) from which to desist on Shabbat. However, it appears that there were at least three elements of work from which they were asked to refrain: first, gathering; second, cooking and baking; and third, traveling more than two thousand cubits in uninhabited regions. First, since gathering their portion of manna in the larger encampment was their main pre-occupation in the desert, the people were commanded to desist from doing so on the seventh day. Instead, they were told, a double portion would fall on the sixth day. This was preparation not only for how they would learn to keep Shabbat in the future, but also for how the Jews would be able to learn to keep a different Shabbat, the Shabbat of years – that is, the Sabbatical year – once they got to the Land of Israel (Lev. 25:1–7, 20–22). For the latter too, God promised to provide sufficient food to them in the sixth year to carry them over until their new crops bore fruit at the end of the eighth year. Second, they were told to do their cooking and baking on the sixth day and to eat the leftovers on the seventh day – implying that cooking and baking were not allowed on the seventh day. Third, since what the Jewish people were doing was traveling – journeying through the desert toward Mount Sinai – they were told, rather cryptically: "Every person should remain in his designated place. One may not leave his place on the seventh day."
   The rabbinic sages understood from this that the Jewish people were forbidden to walk more than two thousand cubits from the camp on Shabbat (Eruvin 51a; see also Maimonides, *Mishneh Torah*, Laws of Shabbat 27:1). Presumably then, the people desisted from their travels on the seventh day of each week. In addition, there is a possible fourth element that was taught through the rhythm of the falling of the manna. The great Spanish twelfth-century biblical exegete Ibn Ezra linked this instruction in Exodus to the verse in Isaiah which encouraged the Jews to refrain from trampling the spirit of Shabbat by engaging in trade and commerce (Is. 58:13). Rabbi Yaakov Medan, a contemporary scholar, has pointed out that the people, who had despoiled Egypt of silver, gold, and fine clothing before the Exodus, may have engaged in trading their wares with

the counting of the Omer and the scheduling of Shavuot at the completion of "seven full Shabbats" (Lev. 23:15) reinforced the idea of Shabbat
as the organizing principle of time for the Jewish people. Finally, just
as Shabbat served to cap the completion of the seven-day week, so did
Shavuot – with its name that contains the word "Shabbat" – serve to
cap the completion of seven seven-day weeks, doubly reinforcing the
sacredness of the number seven.

If Passover incorporated the significance of the number seven in
its seven days of observance, and Shavuot did so in culminating the passage of seven weeks, the remaining biblical holidays all did so by taking
place in the seventh month, the Hebrew month of Tishrei.[18]

Rosh HaShana, which commemorates the acceptance at Sinai
of God's kingship and covenant embodied in the Ten Commandments,
suggests two connections to Shabbat. The first, on the simplest level,
is the fourth of the Ten Commandments that begins, as we saw above,
with the admonition to "Remember the Sabbath day."[19]

Second, the purpose of the Ten Commandments, and indeed all
of the Torah's 613 commandments that comprise the covenant that we
celebrate on Rosh HaShana, is to develop the covenantal relationship
between God and the Jewish people. That is why, in the preamble to the
verbal revelation of the Ten Commandments, God used metaphors of
relationship and intimacy to explain the meaning of the covenant with
the Jewish people, God's soon-to-be betrothed:

> You saw what I did to Egypt, and I carried you on eagle's wings
> and I brought you to Me. And now, if you listen to My voice,

---

each other and with trade caravans that came through the desert from the surrounding region (Yaakov Medan, "The Wanderings of Bnei Yisrael in the Desert," http://
www.hatanakh.com/sites/herzog/files/herzog/medan%204.pdf). Hence, aside from
desisting from gathering, cooking/baking, and traveling, the "work" on Shabbat from
which they learned to refrain may have been related to conducting commerce.

18. The follow-through of the number seven in delineating sacred time continues in
the seventh year (the Sabbatical year) and in the culminating of seven times seven
years – the Jubilee. Both the Sabbatical and the Jubilee commence in the seventh
month of their respective years.

19. In rabbinic tradition, the Ten Commandments were spoken by God to the Jewish
people on Shabbat: see Shabbat 86b.

and keep My covenant, then you will be treasured to Me from amongst all the nations, even though the whole earth is Mine. And you will be to Me a kingdom of priests and a holy people. (Ex. 19:4–6)

Like Shabbat which is a sign of the covenant (Ex. 31:16–17), the holiday of Rosh HaShana that commemorates the Jewish people's acceptance and proclamation of God's kingship and the obligations of the covenant created the solid foundation on which to sustain that intimate relationship with the Divine Presence.

The second holiday of the seventh month, Yom Kippur, is the only seasonal holiday that, like Shabbat, is called "*Shabbat Shabbaton*,"[20] "a Sabbath of Sabbaths," and on which, in addition to all other forms of work, the use of fire to prepare food is also prohibited. Immediately following the Golden Calf debacle for which the Jewish people required atonement, we find the explicit prohibition by the Torah of the use of fire on Shabbat, only one of the thirty-nine categories of work prohibited on the Sabbath. As we pointed out in the chapter on Yom Kippur,[21] it is plausible that the mention of the specific prohibition to kindle fire on Shabbat at this point in the narrative is linked to the role that fire played in the commission of the sin of the Golden Calf.

The final holidays of the seventh month, Sukkot and Shemini Atzeret, which commemorate the building of the Mishkan and the indwelling of the Divine Presence within its precincts, are also inextricably intertwined with the observance of Shabbat. It is no wonder that the commandment to observe Shabbat is restated in conjunction with the command to build the Mishkan (Ex. 31:12–17 and 35:1–3). The purpose of the Mishkan in sacred space, and the seven-day holiday of Sukkot in sacred time, was to allow the Jewish people to dwell literally and symbolically with the Divine Presence. It was truly the Jewish people's reciprocation for creation: Just as God created the universe, the beautifully furnished Garden of Eden, and the Shabbat for human beings to dwell intimately with the Divine Presence, the Jewish people built and

---

20. Cf. Lev. 23:3 and 23:32.
21. See the chapter on Yom Kippur, pp. 119–120.

beautifully furnished the Mishkan – a home for God's presence to dwell in intimacy with them.[22] And like God who ceased His work of creation, on Shabbat the Jewish people ceased their work of creation in building the Mishkan too.

SHABBAT AND MISHKAN

After the destruction of the Temple, the rabbis telescoped both the categories of work used to build the Mishkan and therefore prohibited on Shabbat and the rituals of the priestly service in the Mishkan into the very paradigm of how we observe and celebrate Shabbat today. The creation of the world, the construction of the Mishkan, and all the sacred times beginning with Shabbat and ending with Shemini Atzeret converged in one common purpose: to carve out frameworks in both space and time in which God and human beings could dwell together in a covenantal, harmonious relationship. All Jewish free persons – and even those who were not yet free – would stop their creative, productive work, as God had, on the seventh day. This was the case even for God's work (building the Mishkan) that the people were commanded to do.

The Jewish tradition categorized all of the work involved in building and preparing the Mishkan for operation, including the clothing and feeding of the priests in preparation for the divine service, as "work" that was to be done during the six days of the week, but not on the seventh day. Broadly speaking, the categories of work relating to the Mishkan that were prohibited were those related to food production – plowing, sowing, reaping, up till and including the cooking/baking of food; those related to preparing garments – everything from shearing, laundering, and dyeing to sewing and tearing; those related to preparing leather goods – everything from trapping and slaughtering animals to scoring and cutting the leather; and finally, those related to construction – everything from

---

22. In this regard, see Joshua Berman, *The Temple: Its Symbolism and Meaning Then and Now* (Northvale, N.J.: Jason Aronson, 1995), 21–34. For further parallels between the Garden of Eden and the Mishkan, see also Lifsa Schachter, "The Garden of Eden as God's First Sanctuary," *Jewish Bible Quarterly*, vol. 41, no. 2 (2013): 73–77.

writing, building, and demolition to igniting or extinguishing a fire and transferring materials between private and public domains.[23]

In short, much of the work that produced human civilization at the time also enabled the construction and preparation of a home for God. These activities were prohibited by the Bible to the Jewish people on Shabbat.[24] They became the very definition of what constituted "work." In addition, the rabbinic sages throughout the generations and into the modern age derived other restrictions that fell into these categories, including the use of electric lights, electric appliances, and automobiles. These modern conveniences are the very stuff of which contemporary civilization is constructed; therefore, like the activities prohibited in the Bible that constituted work in that era, whether or not they were strenuous to perform, activating these appliances today is traditionally prohibited as well.

Why do these categories of work involved in building the Mishkan define what we do or do not do today on Shabbat? Theologically, for the same reason that we observe all the seasonal holidays: they help us reenact the first year of our people's existence and relationship with God. Just as the Jewish people in building the Mishkan rested on Shabbat, in commemoration of God's resting on the seventh day of creation, so do we today desist from our work on Shabbat. By aligning themselves with God's work/rest rhythm, the Jewish people who left Egypt endeared themselves to God. We continue their traditions to remain God's beloved mate today. By causing the Divine Presence to dwell in the midst of the people when the Mishkan was completed, God rewarded our ancestors for both their construction of the Mishkan and desisting from that construction by honoring Shabbat as God had commanded. Today, by working on six days of the week and desisting from that work on the seventh, we too yearn to have God's presence dwell amongst us

---

23. With the availability of the Internet, a comprehensive list of the thirty-nine categories of work and the explanations for each can be easily accessed by googling "thirty-nine *melakhot*."

24. The engagement in commerce and perhaps several other Shabbat prohibitions were already prohibited at the time of the falling of the manna, according to the persuasive interpretation of Rabbi Yaakov Medan (see footnote 17, p. 235–6).

each and every Shabbat in our homes and synagogues, the miniature sanctuaries which we inhabit today.

Socially, observing Shabbat in a way that connects us to the practices of our ancestors unites generations of Jews into one shared community. Even when people are spread out all over the globe, observing Shabbat allows us to experience a sense of commonality of purpose with the people with whom we share a house, neighborhood, town, or city. This real live community reminds us that we are part of an even greater living entity called "*Kenesset Yisrael*" – the eternal community of the Jewish people that covers the planet and stretches from the earliest days of our people to the end of time.

Philosophically, the work that is forbidden on Shabbat is what Martin Buber, in his most famous philosophic work, *I and Thou*, characterizes as "I-It" relationships – relationships whose primary purpose is utilitarian, relationships in which we maintain control over things and use other people in our environment to serve our own selfish interests. The manipulation of nature and control over other creatures – human or animal – encapsulated in the thirty-nine categories of work used to construct the Mishkan is forbidden on Shabbat. By forbidding "I-It" activities, the Bible freed human beings to develop an "I-Thou" attitude toward God, other images of God, and nature itself. On Shabbat, instead of plucking and mowing, we, in effect, honor the flowers and the grass as fellow creatures in God's world; by withdrawing from the thirty-nine categories of work that are prohibited by Jewish tradition, we can stop and "smell the roses" instead of uprooting them for our own use.

As to other images of God, instead of focusing on producing, consuming, and on controlling others, on Shabbat we are freed from the slavery of the six days of the week, to just "be" and to allow others to "be."[25] Shabbat is meant to remind us to relate to others as equals

---

25. See in this regard the incisive essay by my teacher, Rabbi Saul Berman, "The Extended Notion of the Sabbath," *Judaism*, vol. 22, no.3 (Summer 1973): 342–52. See also Erich Fromm, *To Have Or to Be?* (Bloomsbury Academic Press, 2013). My understanding of Shabbat has been heavily influenced by Rabbi Berman's analysis.

before God. For one seventh of every week we are bidden not to evaluate others by their professions, their possessions, or their political or economic power and to view them instead as fellow travelers in God's universe. This change of attitude is designed to free us from the otherwise constant anxiety that we feel in our fast-paced society to perpetually advance ourselves and our interests, accumulate possessions, and judge others by those utilitarian standards as well. Instead of competing with others, we are freed on Shabbat to share ourselves – with our family, our friends, our neighbors, and our community.

SHABBAT RITUALS THAT REENACT
THE MISHKAN SERVICE

The "I-Thou" relationship with God is expressed on Shabbat not only by refraining from particular categories of work but also through engaging in rituals that dramatically reenact the acts of "I-Thou" service performed in the Mishkan by the priests and Levites. These acts of service were the ways that the priests in biblical times and that we today, as members of God's "kingdom of priests," connect with God and with each other.[26]

As pointed out in the previous chapter on sacred space, the Mishkan's furnishings each symbolized one of the divine revelations in the desert. The acts of priestly service performed using these furnishings expressed the people's gratitude for the seven rendezvous of God with them in their honeymoon year.

After the destruction of the Second Temple, the rabbinic leadership of the Jewish people, in effect, democratized the priestly service that had previously been performed solely in the Mishkan and Temple and made its rituals available as a means of expressing gratitude and relationship to God by all Jews everywhere. The priestly rituals were transfigured into the rituals that demarcated the Bible's first and most paradigmatic sacred time, the Shabbat. Every Jewish home became a "mini Mishkan" on Shabbat, in effect creating the ambience in which

---

26. Analogous to the "bids for connection" that, according to one prominent psychologist, mark successful marital relationships. See John M. Gottman, *The Relationship Cure* (New York: Three Rivers Press, 2011).

God could dwell among us. Many of our traditional Shabbat rituals and customs, described below, meaningfully recall elements of the priestly service and some of the foundational, revelatory events on which they are based:

1. In order not to kindle a flame on Shabbat (Ex. 35:3), prior to its onset, traditional Jews set up an electric Shabbat hot plate, or a Shabbat *blech* that covers a small flame which remains lit on the stovetop all of Shabbat. This Shabbat *blech* may be thought of as representing the perpetual flame, the "*esh tamid,*" that the priests took care to keep lit under the altar in the Mishkan. This eternal flame was ignited by the seventh divine revelation on the inauguration day of the outer Sacrificial Altar, for which reason we celebrate Shemini Atzeret.

2. The lighting of the Shabbat candles to begin Shabbat reenacts the lighting of the Menora in the Mishkan. The lit candles are a commemoration of the "eternal light" which the Menora provided and the pillar of cloud and fire that first appeared upon the completion of the Mishkan and accompanied the Jewish people in all their journeys, for which reason we celebrate the holiday of Sukkot. The tree-like shape and appurtenances of the Menora which our kindling of Shabbat candles evokes also remind us of the Garden of Eden and the story of the world's creation, which culminated in the designation of Shabbat.

3. Welcoming God's angels through the singing of "*Shalom Aleikhem*" to begin the Friday evening meal reminds us of the angelic cherubs that adorned the curtains of the Mishkan and the cover of the Ark in the Holy of Holies. In the song, God's angels sent by the King of kings, like the cherubs, whose outstretched wings formed a divine throne, remind us of the kingship of God accepted by the Jewish people at Mount Sinai, for which reason we celebrate Rosh HaShana.

4. The song "Woman of Valor" which follows *Shalom Aleikhem* certainly addresses and praises the person in the family who readies the home and hearth for Shabbat. But it also metaphorically praises the role of the Jewish people, "*Kenesset*

Yisrael," who are, as the kabbalists conceptualized it, God's loyal and valiant mate since the biblical covenant forged at Mount Sinai.[27]

5. The blessing of the children before reciting the Friday evening Kiddush is a channeling of the priestly blessing in the Mishkan for the Children of Israel toward one's own children (Num. 6:23). It is also reminiscent of the priestly blessing recited by Aaron right before the seventh revelation of the Divine Presence at the inauguration of the Mishkan's altar, for which reason we celebrate Shemini Atzeret.

6. At the culmination of creation, God sanctified and demarcated the Shabbat day with words (Gen. 2:3). We do the same through the recitation of Kiddush and Havdala.[28] The wine we use recalls the pouring of wine libations upon the altar together with the sacrifices. These wine libations and food sacrifices were a symbolic sharing of food and drink with God from God's table, the large Sacrificial Altar, by the priests and the Jewish people. Our tables become symbolic altars themselves, on which we eat our Shabbat meals, as it were, with God.

7. The ritual washing of the hands prior to eating the *ḥallot* recalls the laving of the hands by the priests using the Pitcher and wash Basin that was stationed in the outer courtyard, at the entrance to the inner Mishkan, prior to performing their sacred service. This pouring of water is reminiscent of God's second revelation to the Jewish people at the splitting of the sea, for which reason we celebrate the seventh day of Passover.[29]

---

27. The special role of the Jewish people as God's "one and only" is similarly expressed through the prescribed liturgy of the Saturday afternoon *Minḥa* prayer: "You are One, and Your name is One, and who is like Your people, Israel, one nation in the world." There is also a custom to recite the entire Song of Songs in the synagogue, prior to welcoming the Shabbat, as an allegory to the passionate love affair between the Divine Presence and the Jewish people. In many traditional prayer books, the Song of Songs appears right before the commencement of *Kabbalat Shabbat*.

28. Maimonides, *Mishneh Torah*, Laws of Shabbat 29:1.

29. See the section on the Pitcher and Basin in the previous chapter, "The Sacred Space-Time Continuum."

8. The blessing over two special *hallot* recalls the special display breads in the Mishkan that were arranged on six shelves of two breads each. The double breads were a symbol of the double portion of manna bread that fell on Fridays so that the people would not have to work to gather their bread on Shabbat. Like the special portion of manna bread that fell each Friday, the display breads were prepared on Fridays. Our twin *hallot*, *"lehem mishneh"* (Ex. 16:22), are reminiscent of the third revelation to the Jewish people in the desert, heralding the divine provision of the manna for which reason we count the Omer and celebrate Shavuot.

9. The salt sprinkled on the bread reminds us of the salt that was offered on all sacrifices brought on the altar in the Temple. The salt, which never spoils and which from time immemorial has acted as a preservative, was a fitting symbol of the everlasting covenant between God and the Jewish people (Lev. 2:13; Num. 18:19) encapsulated in the Shabbat (Ex. 31:16–17).

10. The traditional eating of meat with additional delicacies on Shabbat recalls the meat sacrifices consumed on the Sacrificial Altar along with the meal offerings that accompanied them. This practice is reminiscent of the Passover lamb, the first sacrificial offering of the Jewish people on the night of the Exodus from Egypt, which was also accompanied by matza and herbs.

11. The three separate meals we eat on Shabbat reflect the *"Musaf,"* the supplemental sacrificial offering that was brought to God on the altar on Shabbat, in addition to the two daily offerings brought morning and afternoon in the Mishkan (Num. 28:9–10).

12. The singing of special Shabbat songs, or *zemirot*, at all three meals recalls the Levites singing in the Mishkan and later, the Temple. This singing of songs of praise to God echoes the Jewish people's Song of the Sea after God's second revelation to the Jewish people.

13. The recitation of *divrei* Torah at the Shabbat table – interpretations of the weekly Torah portion read during the morning synagogue service – recalls the scroll of the Torah that was placed in the Holy of Holies adjacent to the Holy Ark. By association, it reminds us of God's fourth rendezvous with the Jewish people: the revelation of the Torah at Mount Sinai. In addition, it recalls the pivotal role

of the Levites and priests who were blessed by Moses, "to teach Your law to Jacob, and Your Torah to Israel" (Deut. 33:10).

14. Among Jews from the Middle East and North Africa there is the custom of sniffing sweet-smelling branches or flora before Shabbat in commemoration of the incense offered on the Golden Altar in the Mishkan. Like the Incense Altar, which played such a crucial role on Yom Kippur in bringing about the reconciliation between God and the Jewish people, Shabbat is a time for the coming together with family, with God, and with one's self. The sweet scent of these floras enhances the welcoming atmosphere of our own homes and is reminiscent of the sweet scent of incense that enabled the Mishkan to be a welcoming home for the Divine Presence.

15. All traditional Jews, both those from European and North African/Middle Eastern ancestry, conclude each Shabbat with the smelling of sweet spices to remember the incense offered on the Incense Altar. We also end the Shabbat on Saturday night with a blessing recited over a candle with at least two intertwining wicks, or two candles whose wicks are joined to constitute a flame (*esh*), reminding us of the *esh tamid*, the eternal flame under the altar, lit by God at the seventh and final revelation.

In sum, the Jewish people, over the course of generations, brilliantly wove together a set of rituals for all of Shabbat which reenacted the rituals of the priesthood in the Mishkan and Temple. Many of these Temple rituals were themselves reminiscent of the seven foundational revelations in the Jewish people's honeymoon year with God. By enacting these rituals every Shabbat, Jews relive those revelational events and rendezvous again with God, fulfilling the ultimate purpose of creation as God's mates in history.

THE OVERFLOW OF SHABBAT INTO THE WEEK

Unlike the seasonal holidays which occur only once a year, Shabbat occurs every seventh day throughout the year. Thus, it already permeates our consciousness all year long. Nevertheless, the key themes of Shabbat meaningfully permeate the remaining days of the week through our ethics, rituals, and liturgy.

Ethically, the twin themes of creation and the Exodus that underlie Shabbat emphasize the insight that people are "like" God. The duty to remember the act of creation includes the duty to remember that God created all human beings in His image. This notion has far greater repercussions than just how we treat our employees or subordinates on Shabbat. It shapes our worldview regarding the way we value all people – affirming their ultimate worth, fundamental equality, and absolute uniqueness every hour of every day.[30]

No human life is readily "expendable." Each person has a spark of the divine within that needs to be recognized and honored. While Judaism is mostly focused on human obligations and responsibilities, the concept of human rights which is the buzzword of the modern and post-modern political world is rooted in the biblical axiom that each and every human being is created in God's image. This is the working premise underlying Jewish ethics.[31]

Ritually, much of the work that was prohibited on Shabbat proper was converted by the rabbis into rituals that help us prepare for Shabbat during the week.[32] The purchase and preparation of food, bathing, laundering and preparation of one's better clothing, the preparation of one's shoes,[33] and whatever other activity is necessary to prepare ourselves and our homes for Shabbat, were brought under the category of

---

30. I am indebted to my teacher Rabbi Yitz (Irving) Greenberg for his teaching of the centrality of the "image of God" in understanding Judaism. See Shalom Freedman and Irving Greenberg, *Living in the Image of God* (Northvale, N.J.: Jason Aronson, 1998), 31ff.

31. However, despite this working assumption, one can forfeit the protections which come from being an image of God. When one intentionally murders other human beings, whether out of secular or avowedly religious motivations, the protective presumption of the intentional murderer as an "image of God" is suspended. The Torah itself condones capital punishment, not despite, but precisely because human beings are created in the image of God (Gen. 9:6).

32. An interpretation of Isaiah 58:13–14 recited in the prophetic reading of the morning of Yom Kippur: "If you will call My Shabbat a delight, and to God's holy day, honored ... then you can seek the favor of the EverPresent God."

33. Although this is not listed in the Talmud among the activities one should engage in before Shabbat, it was the custom in my family to have the male children polish the family's shoes in preparation for Shabbat.

"honoring Shabbat."[34] The custom of wearing freshly laundered, white clothing on Shabbat, which is prevalent among centrist and ultra-Orthodox men, has its source in the priestly clothing worn during the Mishkan service. Many of these mundane preparatory activities, which were normally outsourced to others, were performed by the sages themselves to personally honor the Shabbat.[35] They are, if you will, the ways that we symbolically build and prepare the "Mishkan" of our bodies and family homes each week to perform the divine service on Shabbat. Our bodies and homes are thus made ready to be potential dwelling places for the Divine Presence.

Liturgically, every morning, toward the conclusion of the morning prayer service, traditional Jews recite the daily psalm which begins, "Today is the (first/second...sixth) day of the Shabbat on which the Levites would recite in the Temple." This one-line introduction to the daily psalm keeps traditional Jews conscious the entire week of the centrality of Shabbat in their individual and collective lives.

RECALIBRATING THE INDIVIDUAL AND COMMUNITY

Shabbat points to one further phenomenon: the balance between the community and each individual in the community in the drama of reenacting our rendezvous with God. The entire saga of sacred time and sacred space in the Bible was collective. Indeed, the two great institutions of building community in the biblical narrative were the observance of Shabbat, which united the Jewish community in a common set of beliefs and behaviors, and the construction of the Mishkan, which united the Jewish people in purposeful, productive action (Ex. 35). Although individuals played prominent roles (Ex. 31:1–6) and were held accountable for their actions in the biblical drama,[36] the primary focus of these two sacred components in the biblical narrative was not the individual but the community of Israel.

In general, focusing on the collective is a healthy corrective for our generation. We live in an age, and have lived so not only in the

---

34. Maimonides, *Mishneh Torah*, Laws of Shabbat 30:1–6.
35. Shabbat 119a; Kiddushin 41a.
36. See for example, Num. 15:32–36.

post-modern era but also in the modern era, in which the increasing focus of our society and culture is on the individual. It is no coincidence that in today's world one owns an "I-pad" or an "I-phone" or takes a picture called a "selfie." Our world is obsessed with individual fulfillment and achievement. Popular music is fixated on the one individual falling helplessly in love with another individual; in contrast, songs about family, community, nation, or God are rarely heard on popular American or West European airwaves. We lionize the individuals who embody individual excellence, whether they be sports heroes, entertainment icons, political stars, or business entrepreneurs.

This intense focus on the individual as opposed to the collective that empowers the individual to shine carries a steep price. The cost is the sense of aloneness, isolation, and solipsistic alienation that many individuals feel, simply because everyone else is "other" than "I."[37] The twentieth-century French existentialist Jean-Paul Sartre, in his play *No Exit*, wrote: "Hell is other people."[38] For people who experience life in this way, the very point of living is sometimes called into question.

Whether we are always willing to acknowledge it or not, human beings are, as Aristotle posited some two and a half millennia ago, social animals. Deep down in our hearts we know that nothing of sustained value can be built in this world without the synergetic cooperation of others. We are as much interdependent as independent beings. Indeed, paradoxically, the most famous individuals are often leaders who are able to build a sense of community and purpose among their followers. Abraham and Sarah built a community around themselves.[39] Moses and Miriam led and educated the generation of the Exodus and their descendants who were later able to settle the Promised Land. Without

---

37. See in this regard, Robert N. Bellah, et al., *Habits of the Heart* (University of California Press, 1985); Robert D. Putnam, *Bowling Alone* (New York: Touchstone Press, 2000).

38. Jean Paul Sartre, *No Exit and Three Other Plays* (Vintage Press, 1989).

39. See Rashi, citing the Midrash in Genesis Rabba, interpreting Genesis 12:5 – "and the people that they made in Haran." Based on Abraham and Sarah's example, Maimonides, when explicating the "duty to love God" in his *Book of Commandments* (commandment 3), moves from the deeply personal obligation to love God to the obligation to reach out to others and persuade them to love God as well.

a community that passionately shares one's spiritual aspirations and vision, it is far more difficult to actualize one's self and one's values even intermittently; with a community, it is far more likely to occur. Shabbat, perhaps more than any other Jewish ritual, builds that sense of community and purpose. It is the true antidote to the less savory aspects of modern civilization.

Still, just as no individual can accomplish anything of significance totally alone, so too no group can accomplish anything of significance without highly motivated individuals and their outstanding contributions to the group. God's purpose in creating the world and choosing the Jewish people to be His mate in history was to be in relationship with each person created in God's image, not only to the collective group but to the multitude of individuals in that group. As individuals, each of us can help achieve God's dream at creation by carving out sacred times and sacred space in our own lives to be in authentic, deep relationship with God and with other images of God.

So, in the end, there needs to be a balance between the immense, supportive value of the collective, the primary thrust of the Bible's sacred times, and the abiding importance of the individual, which is the pervasive spirit of our age. When individuals in the community remember their shared past, reenacting and recalling God's revelations to the Jewish people in our shared foundational story of the Torah, they emerge with strengthened individual and collective identities, feeling proud of themselves and of being part of the larger Jewish nation. Proud individuals celebrating the Shabbat together in a supportive community can accomplish great things – perhaps even bring this world a little closer to God's dream at creation and to our own redemption.

Chapter Eight

The Hiddenness of God: Rabbinic and Modern Holidays

And I said, "I will hide My face from them;
I will see what their future holds."
(Deut. 32:20)

THE RABBINIC FESTIVALS OF ḤANUKKA AND PURIM

Every time God's presence became manifest to them in their first biblical year of existence, the Jewish people commemorated the divine revelation with a holiday. They literally made those days holy, that is, sacred, and set aside those days to reexperience the extraordinary events and what they represented for all generations.

When it comes to the rabbinically ordained festivals of Ḥanukka and Purim, the paradigm is more nuanced. In 167 BCE, when the Maccabees prevailed over the Greek Seleucid forces, who sought to assimilate the Jews into Hellenism, God did not show up to save them in an obvious, explicit fashion. Nor did God appear in an obvious way in the victory of Esther and Mordekhai over Haman and his Persian allies, who sought to physically annihilate the Jewish people in the fourth or fifth century BCE. Rather, in the Ḥanukka story, the people **sensed** the Divine Presence. First, there was the unlikely military victory of the outnumbered Maccabees against the Greek Seleucid armies. Then there was the discovery of a flask of oil, which burned for eight straight days in the Temple Menora, though it appeared to be sufficient for one day only. Similarly, in the Purim story, the people **sensed** the Divine Presence in the synchronicity and confluence of political events described in the Book of Esther, which led to salvation for the Jewish people and the annihilation of their enemies.

Still, because God did not show up in an overt fashion, neither festival could be made sacred – that is, into holy days on which "work" would be firmly prohibited.[1] If these festivals lacked the divine revelation that is the most important component of the biblical holidays, why then did the rabbinic sages establish Ḥanukka and Purim as joyous Jewish festivals to be observed throughout the generations?

The stories of Ḥanukka and Purim embody two trans-generational challenges, one spiritual and one physical, that were latent, but unexpressed, in the first five books of the Bible. The first was the challenge of building a permanent, physical home for God; the second was the challenge posed by the forces of radical evil to the Jewish people throughout their history. In addition, based on the Book of Deuteronomy, both of these rabbinic festive periods embody a more sophisticated understanding of God's presence in history.

Ḥanukka

In the Bible, the idea of building a permanent home for God in the Land of Israel did not begin with King David and King Solomon. Already in the Book of Genesis, Jacob/Israel – the Jewish people's third patriarch, after whom the Children of Israel are named – had this idea. Following his first encounter with the Divine at Beth-El, he vowed to build a home

---

1. See Megilla 5b. Although work was not prohibited on Purim, the Jewish tradition strongly discouraged it.

for God if he was privileged to return to his ancestral home from his imminent exile to the home of Laban in Haran (today, northwestern Iraq).[2] Jacob never fulfilled his vow in a literal sense, although he did so in a metaphoric sense, building an altar at Beth-El when he returned to the Land of Israel after establishing a family in exile – the "House of Israel" that became the Jewish nation.[3]

Later on, after the splitting of the sea, when they celebrated their rescue from the pursuing Egyptian legions, Moses and the Jewish people included in the codicil to the Song of the Sea mention of the establishment of a permanent Temple on the Mountain of God. So real was this vision, as part of the larger vision of their inheriting and living in the Promised Land, that the text describing what would transpire in the future was framed the past tense as if it had already occurred:

> Until You brought over Your people, O EverPresent God, until You brought over the people that You fashioned. You planted them on the mountain of Your heritage, the foundation of Your throne, which You prepared, O EverPresent God, the Temple of the Lord, founded by Your hands. The EverPresent God will reign forever and ever! (Ex. 15:16–18)

Further still, in the Book of Deuteronomy, Moses, as part of his final farewell to the Jewish people, emphasized over and over again that once the people enter the land, God is to be ritually worshiped only at "the place" with which God will choose to associate His name.[4] While this

---

2. The name Beth-El literally means the "house of God." The rabbis, because of the use of the language "the place" in this encounter, connect this place not to the city later known as Beth-El, but to the mountain of Moriah, where Jacob's father Isaac was offered up as a sacrifice by his grandfather Abraham. There too, the Torah refers to the mountain as "the place." See Hullin 91b and Rashi on Gen. 28:13.
3. See Gen. 35:1–7. Interestingly, in Gen. 34:30 and 35:2, Jacob's family is referred to as his "house" and the collective Jewish people are also referred to by the Bible as the "House of Israel" upon the completion of the Mishkan, the first (albeit, portable) house of God (Ex. 40:38).
4. See for example, Deut. 12:5–18; 16:1–12.

centralization of divine worship at a specific place does not explicitly call for the building of a Temple dedicated to God, its centrality as "the place" implies a permanent home for God where God would be enthroned.

We have seen that the Torah's description of Sukkot celebrates the building and inauguration of the portable Sanctuary, the Mishkan, and, after the people came to the land, the settling in God's fruitful land. King Solomon, when inaugurating the First Temple, overlapped its inauguration ceremonies with the holidays of Sukkot and Shemini Atzeret, presumably to associate the permanent Temple that he built in the Land of Israel with the portable Sanctuary built hundreds of years earlier by the Children of Israel in the desert. Both the temporary Mishkan and the permanent Temple were constructed to cause God's presence to dwell among the people. Still, the main celebration of Sukkot and of Shemini Atzeret was focused on the completed portable Sanctuary.

The festival of Ḥanukka, according to the Second Book of Maccabees, was established as a type of "*Sukkot Sheni*" – that is, as a "make-up" for the Jews who could not celebrate Sukkot that year because they were preoccupied with fighting the war against the Greeks.[5] When the victorious Maccabees retook the Second Temple, they celebrated their victory in an eight-day festival, meant to thank God for giving them the strength and resources to achieve their victory. They also celebrated the rededication of God's home and reinaugurated the Temple altar (I Maccabees 4:38–59).

Ḥanukka was thus the first festival solely dedicated to the (re)inauguration of the Temple, God's permanent home in Jerusalem.[6] Building and living in a permanent home, as opposed to a temporary, portable home, is no small matter. In contemporary terms, it is akin to the difference between living in a trailer and building one's own house. Achieving the latter is a cause for gratitude and joy.

---

5. See II Maccabees 10:6–7. The notion of a "make-up" holiday is based on the biblical *Pesaḥ Sheni*, described in Num. 9:6–14.
6. This was the rationale in Scripture for David and Solomon wanting to build "God's house": "It is not right for us to live in a palace of cedar while God dwells in a tent," II Sam. 7:2; I Kings 8:13.

Hanukka also reflected the rabbinic sages' religious sophistication in their understanding of how God operates in history.[7] Based on their reading of the Book of Deuteronomy, they did not attribute the Maccabees' success in battle to their military prowess alone. Rather, the sages recognized the hand of God behind the Maccabees' military exploits even though there were no overt miracles of the biblical variety to account for their success. The miracle of the Menora, which burned for eight days – a miracle cited by the Talmud, but not by other historical sources as the reason for the festival (Shabbat 21a) – occurred after the fact, and was witnessed only by the priests who performed the service in the Temple.

In comparison to the public manifestation of the Divine Presence to all the Jewish people at the splitting of the sea, for which we celebrate the seventh day of Passover, or at the inauguration of the Sanctuary, for which we celebrate Shemini Atzeret, this would seem to be a much-diminished miracle. Nor could the people of the Maccabees' generation afford to follow Moses' instruction to his people prior to the splitting of the sea: "Stand still, and see the redemption of the EverPresent God ... the EverPresent God will fight on your behalf and you be still" (Ex. 14:13–14). The Maccabees and their followers had to stand up and fight with all their might and cunning, even on the Sabbath (I Maccabees 2:41), to defeat the Seleucid Greek armies. Still, the rabbis established Hanukka as a festival for all generations because it reflected the more subtle rabbinic understanding of how God manifests the Divine Presence in history. They recognized the miracles implicit in the victory of the Jews against all odds, which resulted in the renewal of God's house, even though there were no public, overt miracles performed by God.[8]

---

7. Deut. 8:18. I am indebted to my colleague Dr. Micha Goodman for the insightful interpretation of Deuteronomy in his book, *The Last Speech of Moses* [Hebrew] (Dvir Publishing, 2014).
8. The *Al HaNissim* prayer, which is added to the *Amida* and the Grace After Meals during Hanukka, puts forward the rabbinic understanding:
   "And You, in Your great compassion, stood up for them in the time of their distress. You championed their cause, executed judgment, and avenged their wrong.

The rabbis gave the Jewish people the role and responsibility of publicizing both the miracle of the Maccabean victory and of the more "private" manifestation of the Divine Presence in the Temple through the miracle of the single flask of pure oil that burned for eight days. In fact, the rabbis emphasize that the central commandment of Ḥanukka, the lighting of the menora, should be done in full public view. They also mandated that, like the biblical holiday of Sukkot, for which it was a surrogate, Ḥanukka should be celebrated with the recitation of the thanksgiving psalms known as the "full Hallel" for all eight days of the holiday. In addition, the rabbis inserted a special prayer of thanksgiving – *Al HaNissim* – in the *Amida* prayer and the Grace After Meals to reinforce the public consciousness of the divine force behind the Maccabees' victory.[9] The Jewish people became, as it were, the public relations agents for the more hidden God, operating behind the scenes of history.

Purim

The manifestation of the Divine Presence was even more concealed from human view in the case of Purim. Indeed, the almost cosmic battle of good versus evil, of the Jewish people against Amalek – which has as its roots the struggles of our ancestor Jacob with his brother Esau, the ancestor of Amalek[10] – was one in which God's presence was veiled.[11] This is true also in the attack of Amalek on the Jewish people, Jacob's descendants, shortly after the Exodus. There, standing atop the mountain, staff held aloft like a military banner, Moses inspired the Jewish people

---

You delivered the strong into the hands of the weak, the many in the hands of the few... the wicked into the hands of the righteous... and for Your people, Israel, You performed a great salvation and redemption as of this very day."

9. Arakhin 10a; Maimonides, *Mishneh Torah*, Laws of Ḥanukka 3:5.
10. Gen. 25:22–26; 36:13.
11. Jacob's struggles with the mysterious "man" who attacks him prior to his encounter with Esau after returning to the Land of Israel also takes place in the deep of the night when Jacob cannot see the man who will determine his fate. Not coincidentally, the sages referred to the "man" as the angel of Esau. See Genesis Rabba 77 and Rashi on Gen. 32:25.

to do battle[12] while Joshua led a victorious military campaign below, seemingly without God's explicit, miraculous intervention.[13]

The Book of Esther, the biblical book describing the events of the period of Mordekhai and Esther in which the evil Haman sought to annihilate the entire Jewish people, does not mention God's name even once. In fact, the Book of Esther is the only narrative book in the Bible in which God's name is absent. The message underlying the story is that in the face of unprovoked, unexplained, diabolical evil, the face of God is hidden.

Yet here too, the rabbis derived God's hidden presence behind the scenes from the very absence of His name and face, a concept we first encounter in the Book of Deuteronomy (Deut. 31:17–18). Indeed, they associate the name of the heroine Esther with "*hester panim,*" the hiding of the manifest Divine Presence during periods of manifest evil.[14] To be sure, the human actors in the Purim tale – Esther and Mordekhai – play a decisive role in shaping events to the Jewish people's advantage. Still, the rabbis strongly believed that in the string of coincidences that occurred over a period of many years, God, though hidden, was very much present. Working together with Esther and Mordekhai's very human efforts, God ever so subtly manipulated events to achieve a redemptive outcome.[15] God, as it were, wore the mask of the heroine and hero of the Jewish people, Esther and Mordekhai, to manifest His will in the world.

---

12. This follows the naturalistic interpretation of the event by the twelfth-century biblical commentary of Rashbam on Ex. 17:11, and the thirteenth-century biblical commentary of Ḥizkuni, Rabbi Hezekiah ben Manoah, on Ex. 17:9. Moses may have been alluding to God's staff that he held aloft during the battle when he said, "The EverPresent God is my banner" (Ex. 17:9, 15).

13. Joshua's heroic role in the first battle against Amalek may be the reason that the walled cities which celebrate Shushan Purim are those that were walled from the days of Joshua Bin Nun and not, as one might expect, during the days of Mordekhai and Esther. It is not only the Land of Israel, whose conquest was led by Joshua, that is thereby given honor, but Joshua himself for his role in battling unprovoked evil and later establishing Jewish sovereignty in the land. Cf. Y. Megilla 1:1.

14. Ḥullin 139b and Rashi ad loc.

15. For an incisive and comprehensive analysis of the Book of Esther which concludes with this theological insight, see Jonathan Grossman, *Esther: The Outer Narrative and the Hidden Reading* (Winona Lake, Ind.: Eisenbrauns, 2011), 243–6.

The Jewish people's perpetual battle against the forces of radical evil, embodied in Amalek, is one which the rabbis decided needed to be given expression in the Jewish calendar. The survival of this tiny people thanks to the hidden presence of God, in the face of overwhelmingly superior forces of unabashed evil, needed to be acknowledged and celebrated annually. As the Jewish people's battle against evil continues from one generation to the next,[16] so the festival of Purim needs to be celebrated year after year. Hence, as on Ḥanukka, where a special prayer of thanksgiving (*Al HaNissim*) was inserted in the *Amida* prayer, so too on Purim, a variation of this prayer of thanksgiving was inserted by the rabbinic sages. For both Ḥanukka and Purim, the prayer begins: "(We thank You) for the miracles, the redemption, the mighty deeds, and the victories in battle which You performed for our ancestors in those days at this time."

Moreover, although there was initially resistance to doing so, the rabbis decided to insert the tale of this "masked miracle," the Book of Esther, into the biblical canon and to mandate its public reading on the night and day of Purim (Megilla 7a).

As with Ḥanukka, the rabbinic understanding of how God manifested the redemptive Divine Presence in history in a concealed manner led the rabbis to designate Purim as a festival – a joyous day on which we, like God, mask our faces as we acknowledge and celebrate our people's victory against the forces of incorrigible evil.

MODERN HOLIDAYS: YOM HASHOA, YOM HAZIKARON, YOM HAATZMA'UT, AND YOM YERUSHALAYIM

If the rabbinic festivals acknowledged and celebrated God's hidden presence in the events of the Second Temple period, the modern days of commemoration and celebration do so in an even more pronounced fashion. These commemorative days, still relatively new, are less universally observed than the ones that have come down to us through the

---

16. As articulated in the *Maggid* section of the Haggada on the holiday of Passover: "God's covenantal promise has stood the test of time for our ancestors and for us. For in every generation there are those who arise to destroy us, but The Holy One, Blessed Be He, saves us from their hands."

centuries. But their modern creators, and the large part of the Jewish community, especially in Israel, that observes them as religious events, experiences them as part of the ongoing tradition of seeing God's hidden presence in our history.

Yom HaShoa falls on the twenty-seventh day of the Hebrew month of Nisan. At first blush, it would seem well-nigh impossible to detect God's presence – even hidden – in the horrific events of the Holocaust, commemorated by this day. However, there are those, including my teacher Rabbi Yitzchak Greenberg, who have argued that God was indeed present, though entirely concealed to human perception, and suffering in agony with His people.[17]

God's identification with the suffering of the Jewish people is not a new concept. At the burning bush, God explains to Moses that the Jewish people will be redeemed from bondage in Egypt after hundreds of years because of God's awareness of and empathy with the suffering of the Jewish people.[18] As the Psalmist later says, speaking in God's voice: "I am with him in his suffering" (Ps. 91:15). The early hasidic master Rabbi Nachman of Breslov echoes this sentiment. Commenting on the verse, "I shall hide, utterly hide, My face on that day" (Deut. 31:18), he explains:

> Even in the hiddenness that is in the midst of the hiddenness, God the blessed one is certainly present. [God says]: "Even behind the difficult things that are passing over you, I stand, I stand, I stand."[19]

In this interpretation, on Yom HaShoa we stand in silent commemoration with God to mourn the suffering and annihilation of six million

17. Rabbi Irving Greenberg, *The Jewish Way: Living the Holidays* (New York: Simon and Schuster, 1988), 320–321.
18. See Ex. 2:23–25; 3:1–10. The presence of God's angel in the flames of the burning bush and God's voice emerging from the bush can be interpreted as God's presence in the very midst of His suffering people. See *Sifrei Zuta* 10, commenting on the words, "And it was." See also *Pirkei DeRabbi Eliezer* 39.
19. The comment from *Likutei Moharan* on this verse in *Parashat Haazinu* was made into a popular Hebrew song, *"VeAfilu BeHastara,"* by Yoeli Klein during Israel's summer 2014 military campaign in Gaza.

Jews, one third of the Jewish people, during the years of the Holocaust, 1933–1945.[20]

At the same time, Rabbi Greenberg argues, the horrific events of that period speak in a commanding voice to the Jewish people to take upon themselves an even greater role and responsibility in making God's saving presence felt in the world. Such is the meaning of the founding of the State of Israel and the Israel Defense Forces. As God's presence has become ever more hidden in the world, the challenge of the Jewish people is to imitate God's acts of redemption in the Bible and do all in our power to redeem our people from the forces of radical evil that wish to destroy us.

The establishment of the Jewish state, celebrated on the holiday of Yom HaAtzma'ut, and the heroic sacrifices of Israel's soldiers, somberly commemorated on Yom HaZikaron, are concrete expressions of the Jewish people's acceptance of that awesome responsibility to return God's redemptive presence to history.[21] Facing odds even greater than those experienced by the Maccabees, the Jewish people, after being decimated by the Holocaust of European Jewry, rose from the ashes. Only three years after the conclusion of World War II, they successfully established the State of Israel and defended themselves and their fledgling country.

Yom HaZikaron, Israel's Memorial Day, and Yom HaAtzma'ut, Israel's Independence Day, which occur only a week after Yom HaShoa, strengthen the will of Israel's citizens and of Israel-identifying Jews everywhere to continue to carry the burden of protecting the Jewish people's safety and well-being and to celebrate this generation's privilege of being able to do so. Through these modern days of commemoration and celebration, the Jewish people stand, as it were, shoulder to shoulder with God, not only in mourning, but in assuming the yoke of our national survival and flourishing.

For truly religiously minded Jews, the success of the Jewish state does not stem from triumphalism, hubris, or self-congratulation.

---

20. In the State of Israel at 10:00 a.m. on Yom HaShoa, air raid sirens blare for two minutes; the citizens of the state halt whatever they are doing and stand at attention in honor of those who perished.
21. Greenberg, *The Jewish Way*, 320–321 and 373ff.

Rather, it emerges from a humble recognition that it is God's hidden but ever-present redemptive spirit, bequeathed to the Jewish nation, that encourages and empowers us in the noble endeavor of sheltering and protecting the young Jewish State of Israel and individual Jews wherever they may be.[22] In recognition of God's hidden role in the establishment and continued existence of the Jewish state, national-religious Jews recite the Hallel or thanksgiving psalms on Yom HaAtzma'ut.[23]

That custom of reciting Hallel is also prevalent among national-religious Jews on Yom Yerushalayim, "Jerusalem Day," the twenty-eighth day of the Hebrew month of Iyar (three weeks after Yom HaAtzma'ut). This day celebrates the reunification of Jerusalem during the Six-Day War. This defensive war against the three threatening armies of Egypt, Syria, and Jordan, who massed on Israel's borders in the spring of 1967, was won decisively by Israel in only six days. In the annals of military history, it was indeed nothing short of a modern miracle, worthy of gratitude and abundant praise.

Nevertheless, forty-nine years later, the celebration is tempered and the victory is incomplete, fraught as it is with religious and political controversy. Jews may not pray on Jerusalem's Temple Mount, the focal point of God's presence in the Jewish tradition and the location of both the First and Second Temples. And most of Israel's political allies do not yet recognize Jerusalem as the capital of Israel. The mishnaic *Ethics of Our Fathers* teaches: "It is not incumbent upon you to complete the work, but neither are you free to desist from it."[24] The task of firmly establishing the Jewish people's sovereignty over its historic capital and spiritual center while accommodating the worship on the Temple Mount of Israel's Muslim citizens and residents remains the challenge of the Jewish state and of this and future generations of the Jewish people.

---

22. For example, the daring rescue of the passengers from the hijacked jet in Entebbe airport, Uganda, on July 4, 1976.
23. Based on Pesaḥim 117a.
24. *Ethics of Our Fathers* 2:21.

Chapter Nine
God, Torah, and the Holidays

A threefold cord is not readily broken.
(Eccl. 4:12)

W e are nearing the end of our journey. We have shown how the biblical holidays represent a cohesive, chronological account of the Jewish people's encounters with the Divine Presence some 3,200 years ago. Those holidays capture the peak experiences that marked our people's first year as a free people, during their honeymoon year with God, who liberated them from Egypt and took them to be His covenantal mate in history. The rituals and liturgy attached to those holidays dramatically reenact and retell those revelatory experiences that forever changed the identity and destiny of the Jewish people. The rabbinic festivals and modern days of commemoration and celebration reflect our tradition's continued commitment to helping us sense God's presence in history even when on the surface, the Divine Presence is hidden from our immediate perception.

But why does any of this matter? Why should we, living in the Western world in the first quarter of the twenty-first century, invest so much of our time and creative imagination reliving that honeymoon year of our ancestors in the desert over three millennia ago? What does such a robust engagement with our collective past do for us in the here and now? How do God's revelations so long ago break through the constraints of history and address us where we find ourselves today?

There are three ways in which the holidays continue to speak to us: through our belief in God, through our Torah's stories of redemption, and through the values that emerge from the Jewish holidays commemorating those stories.

We live in a period that few of us expected to witness in our lifetimes. From the horrific events of September 11, 2001, which challenged the Western world order and initiated the clash of civilizations between the West and radical Islam; to the financial debacle of 2008, which came close to collapsing the entire world economy; to the tsunami of anti-Semitism that is again engulfing Israel and parts of European Jewry only seventy years after the Holocaust – the world that we live in has become increasingly unstable and in some countries downright dangerous. In times like this, when truths that seem reliable one day are undermined the very next, we need a modicum of stability that will anchor us to solid ground. Our belief in the EverPresent God, our reliving of our foundational stories, and the celebration of our holidays are three such anchors.

The Jewish people throughout its history – but particularly over the past two millennia as a minority in the Diaspora – have lived on shaky ground. To be Jewish, to be part of a tiny people on a planet inhabited by billions of other human beings who do not share many of the stories and values that our people have come to cherish, is no small challenge. Facing such powerful forces, sometimes indifferent, sometimes actively arrayed against us, how did we remain true to ourselves and to our people's historical experience? How did we remain steadfast in the face of the buffeting winds of enmity that often threatened to sweep our miniscule people off the stage of history?

In the morning prayers, immediately after reciting the *Shema*, Judaism's credo, that proclaims God's kingship, covenant, and redemption from Egypt, we say the following:

True and firm, established and enduring, right, faithful ... awesome, mighty, perfect ... is this faith for us forever. True is the Eternal God, our king, rock of Jacob, shield of our salvation. He exists and His name exists through all generations. His throne is established, His kingship and faithfulness endure forever. His words live and persist, faithful and desirable forever and for all time.

From our earliest recorded thoughts as a people, the Jews posited the existence of a Creator God, concerned about human beings, who redeemed the Jewish people from bondage and who developed a covenantal relationship with all generations. To be a member of the Jewish people meant to root oneself in these beliefs and to embrace them as we would the most beloved person in our lives. We held on through two millennia of exile by reinforcing these truths every day through prayer and study; every week through the rituals of the Shabbat; and each and every year by commemorating and celebrating the Jewish holidays. On each holiday, we immersed ourselves in the drama of the Jewish people's collective story where we witnessed God's presence revealed. For brief periods of time each year, these immersion experiences of the holidays transformed the stories of our people's past into our lived present. We believed that not only our ancestors, but also we, were freed from the bonds of slavery in Egypt; were saved at the sea from the clutches of pursuing enemies; were given rich, physical sustenance from the heavens; stood in awe at Sinai and accepted the divine laws of morality and mutual responsibility; repented for our mistakes and were forgiven for our misdeeds; and constructed a sacred space in which we and God could live together in virtual intimacy.

The cycle of the holidays, encapsulating our foundational stories, gave form and substance to our own identities. They did not simply describe the past. They shaped our present and became our lodestars for the future. No matter how much our enemies reviled us and wished us to disappear, they could not take away the stories of our people's encounters with God, stories that were, like God Himself was for the Jewish people, "true, firm, established, and enduring."

So long as we embraced our collective memories found in the Bible and relived them in their full dramatic power each year, we were – and remain – an indestructible people. We may be persecuted and severely diminished in some generations, but like nature itself we blossom again and spring forward into an even greater version of ourselves than we were in the past.[1]

Over the millennia, Pharaoh and Haman, Antiochus and Hadrian, Chmielnicki,[2] and Hitler battered the Jewish people with their considerable power and resources in an attempt to obliterate us and our way of life. In the end, they were the ones who were obliterated while we rose from the ashes, dusted ourselves off, and proceeded to live another day. It was not because of any genetic superiority that we survived and learned to thrive; it was because we held on tight to our God, to our people's stories, and to our covenant and civilization to carry us, like a life raft, over the stormy waters of history. Our relationship with God, our sacred narrative, and our sacred holidays infused our people with the strength and meaning to overcome all challenges to our existence.

Over the past year, friends and colleagues have asked me, with some puzzlement, why I was writing a book on the Jewish holidays when the very survival of the Jewish people and the Jewish state seem currently at issue. My response has been, "That is precisely why I am writing this book now! It is those holidays, and the events that they relive, that give us the strength and fortitude to ride out the hurricane forces that are swirling around us." The Jewish holidays, rooting us deeply in the God of Israel, the eternal people of Israel, and the Land of Israel, fortify our resolve to carry on our sovereign existence and distinct way of life.

The holidays that reenact our rendezvous with God do not only anchor us as Jews, they liberate us and empower us to flourish as full human beings. Indeed, the holidays represent some of the most fundamental values that enable us to deal with the challenges of the human condition.

The Exodus from Egypt, commemorated on the first day of Passover, gave us the gift of freedom. Without freedom, human beings are no more than molecules of matter, subject to the physical laws of

---

1. Micah 7:8: "Do not rejoice over me, my enemy, for though I fell, I rose again."
2. The leader of the Cossack massacres against nearly seven hundred Polish Jewish communities in 1648–1649 CE. Hundreds of thousands of Jews perished in those two years.

entropy – here today and gone tomorrow. Our freedom to choose is what gives the human species our unique status and dignity on this planet and makes us true images of God. The political and existential freedom of the Exodus experience empowered the members of the Jewish people to choose to live in responsibility toward each other and toward God when they arrived at Mount Sinai.

The splitting of the sea, commemorated on the seventh day of Passover, freed the Jewish people from their deep-seated fears. So long as human beings feel themselves to be under imminent threat or danger, they cannot think about their long-term future and instead become overly focused, even obsessed, with their immediate survival. A person or nation under threat lives in a virtual nightmare. A secure person and nation can dream for the future.[3] The splitting of the sea and the demise of their enemies enabled the members of the Jewish people to witness God's power in its full glory and to give voice to their dreams.[4]

The provision of the manna, commemorated by the Omer and Shavuot, freed the Jewish people from the ravages of hunger. Human beings who are starving cannot develop themselves, their families, or their own cognitive abilities. In contrast, a people that is physically satiated can actualize its higher intellectual and spiritual faculties, thereby transcending the rigors of daily existence.[5] The members of the Jewish people began to trust the universe, and the benevolent force behind the universe, when they received God's sustenance in the desert.

The Sinai revelation, whose shofar blasts we remember on Rosh HaShana, gave us a set of moral laws, which organized our society around the twin pillars of empathy and justice. No human being and no civilization can exist long without the rule of a just and equitable legal system. The Torah bestowed upon the Jewish people such a system, along with a set of rituals, which infused our individual and collective lives with expressive drama and personal meaning. The giving of the Torah also

---

3. This is why the second half of the Song of the Sea envisions the planting of the people in God's land and on God's mountain. See also Joel 3:1.
4. "This is my God and I will glorify Him" (Ex. 15:2). The Song of the Sea not only praised God for destroying the Jewish people's enemies but put forward their vision of the future culminating in God's eternal kingship (Ex. 15:13–18).
5. Maimonides, *Guide for the Perplexed* III:27.

gave rise to an intellectually vigorous culture in which thinking, learning, and teaching were considered to be among the highest virtues.[6]

The forgiveness after the Golden Calf, commemorated by Yom Kippur, taught us that, contrary to ideologies of fatalism or determinism, human beings are capable of change and behavioral growth. It proved that accepting responsibility for our mistakes and genuinely repenting for our errors in judgment, rather than blaming others and wallowing in self-pity, was the way forward, and that forgiveness and acceptance of ourselves and others was a sign of strength.

Building a home for God in the desert and settling in "God's home," the Land of Israel, for which we celebrate Sukkot, taught us not only to live with God in our hearts and souls, but also to shape visible, tangible places where we could dwell with God and with each other in this real, physical world. A nation that does not have a national home cannot actualize its values and culture in the public square. Like the sacred time of Shabbat which was set aside at the beginning of our people's story so that God and human beings could dwell with one another in attentiveness and harmony, the sacred space that we reenact with our sukkot challenges each of us to fashion homes for our families, our communities, and our nation. In those, we can live once again with God and God can be proud, once again, to live with us.

Reliving our people's stories and internalizing the values of our holidays animates our lives as human beings every day of the year, all year long, giving each of us the possibility of experiencing, once again, the many instances of divine redemption. It also serves to inspire us to emulate God's redemptions by redeeming other human beings in our sphere of influence who are still enslaved, endangered, impoverished, undereducated, despondent, or homeless. By serving as role models and teachers of our people's stories, and agents of the values that emanate from those stories, we can play a small but important, catalytic role in redeeming the world.

In our founding year as a people, God rendezvoused with us. For every year since then, we have been rendezvousing with God through

---

6. In this spirit, see the fascinating volume by Maristella Botticini and Zvi Eckstein, *The Chosen Few: How Education Shaped Jewish History* (Princeton University Press, 2012).

the Jewish holidays, drawing life-sustaining meaning and inspiration from those encounters. So it has been since our dawn as a people. So can it be for us today in the midst of very challenging times. So will it be, God willing, for our children and all their descendants, in the emerging horizon of the future.

Index

A

Aaron, 17, 26, 54, 58, 116–7, 119–20, 125–32, 135, 140, 156, 173, 175–8, 193, 215, 243

Abel, 148, 151

Abraham, xxi, xxxi, 17, 20, 27–8, 30–1, 35, 49, 52, 67, 81–2, 97, 100, 106, 120, 135, 173, 196, 205, 248, 253

Adam, 70, 104, 148, 151, 181, 205, 213, 226, 230

afikoman, 16, 22–3

Akeda, xiii, 81–2, 106, 135

Alenu, 109

Amalek, 256–8

Amida, 39, 49, 79, 88, 90, 92–3, 109–11, 160, 177, 199, 225, 255–6, 258

anti-Semitism, 264

Arami oved avi, 28

Ark, xxxii, 34, 58, 94, 127, 130–1, 172, 178, 197, 204, 214–5, 217–8, 220, 222, 242, 244

Azazel, 130–1, 133–5, 159

B

Baal Peor, 132, 151–2

Bar Kokhba, 47

Beitza, 8–9

Boaz, 69–71, 195

C

Cain, 148, 151

Caleb, 147, 150

charity, 67, 71

Chernick, Michael, xxix

cherubs, xxxii, 34, 131, 172, 204, 214–5, 217–8, 220, 242

Christianity, 105–6, 157

Clouds of Glory, xxxii, 91, 167–9, 171, 180, 185, 196, 199, 221

Copper Sacrificial Altar, xxxii, 208–9

covenant, vii, xx, xxvi, xxx, 20, 25, 30, 33–5, 42, 52, 67, 85, 88–90, 92–4, 96, 99, 102–3, 105, 108, 110, 112, 118, 139, 144, 185, 213, 215, 218, 229, 232–3, 236–7, 243–4, 264, 266

cup of Elijah, 28–9

D

David, King, 106, 252

Dayenu, 10

Deborah, 82
Diaspora, 39, 48, 72, 103–4, 177, 187–90,
  192–3, 201, 264
din, 90, 217

E
Elijah, 26–9, 43
Elimelekh, 195
Ephraim, 106
Esther, 252, 257
eternal flame, xxxii, 215–6, 242, 245
ethics, xxv, xxix, 3, 29, 32, 66, 108, 194,
  245–6, 261
Eve, 148, 151, 181, 205, 226
exile, 20, 28, 75, 86, 103, 107, 148, 154, 184,
  188–9, 201, 253, 265
Exodus from Egypt, xix–xxi, xxiii–xxvii,
  xxix–xxx, xxxii, 1–4, 6–14, 16, 18–20,
  23–7, 29–38, 46, 48–9, 54–6, 58–60,
  65, 67, 74, 78–80, 83, 88–90, 93–5,
  108–9, 113, 117, 126, 132, 166, 168, 175,
  198, 205–7, 209, 215, 226–9, 232–5,
  244, 246, 248, 256, 266–7
Ezra, 86, 108, 112, 229, 235

F
Four Questions, 3, 6, 23, 49
Four Species, 49, 164, 175, 178–83, 185–6, 213
  citron (etrog), xiii, 164, 175, 179, 187
  palm (lulav), xiii, 164, 175, 178–9, 187
  myrtle, 164, 175, 179, 187
  willow, 164, 175, 179, 185–7

G
Garden of Eden, 15, 181, 207, 226, 230,
  237–8, 242
Golden Altar of Incense, xxxii, 211
Golden Calf, xx, xxii, xxiv, xxvi, xxxii,
  25–6, 79, 90, 95–6, 99–102, 114, 116–21,
  123–32, 135, 137, 146–7, 151–3, 156–7,
  159, 165–8, 175–6, 182–3, 212, 237, 268

Grace After Meals, 23, 73, 255–6
Groom of Genesis, 190
Groom of the Torah, 190–2

H
hakhnasat orḥim, 70, 196
Hadrian, Emperor, 135, 266
haftara, 63, 93, 115, 153, 214
Haggada, xiii, 1–4, 6–7, 10–2, 15, 18–9,
  23–8, 32, 34–6, 52, 94, 207, 210, 258
Hakafot, 177, 190, 192
Hakafat HaMizbe'aḥ, 190, 192–3
Hak'hel, 84, 190–3
ḥalla, 72, 94
Hallel, xiii, 19, 23–4, 28, 37, 43, 256, 261
ḥametz, 3–6, 21, 28
Haman, 252, 257, 266
Ḥanukka, xxviii, 213–4, 251–2, 254–6, 258
Hannah, 106
ḥaroset, 8–9, 15, 21–2, 51
Havdala, 243
ḥazeret, 8–9
ḥesed, see loving-kindness
hester panim, 257
High Priest, 34, 57, 121, 123–4, 128–30,
  134–5, 175–6, 184, 197, 208, 211,
  215–6
Hillel, 22
Holy of Holies, xxxii, 34, 127–31, 156, 172,
  176, 178, 197, 204, 208, 211, 214–5,
  217–22, 242, 244
Horeb, *see Sinai*
Hoshana Rabba, 164, 184–7

I
Isaac, xxxi, 20, 27, 52, 81, 120, 135, 173
Ishmael, 106

J
Jacob, xxxi, 13, 20, 27, 31, 37, 52, 120, 173
Jericho, 186–7

Jerusalem, xi, 10, 22, 28, 31, 43, 50, 64, 124, 157, 178, 184–8, 191, 199, 220, 228, 254, 261
Jonah, 115, 154–5
Joseph, 29, 131–5, 148, 151, 156, 159, 173
Joshua, 62–3, 118, 146–7, 150, 257
Jubilee years, 52, 63, 104

K
Kiddush, 11–2, 36, 79, 90, 93, 142–3, 177, 190, 193–4, 198, 225–8, 232, 243
kittel, 116, 122
Kol HaNe'arim, 192
Kol Nidrei, 115–6, 131–2, 140, 144–5, 150–1, 156–7, 183
Korah, 130

L
Laban, 37, 253
Land of Israel, 27–9, 59–60, 62, 69–70, 72–3, 86, 102, 117, 123–4, 138, 146–7, 152–4, 155, 157, 164, 180–2, 184–6, 188–9, 192, 195–6, 199, 206, 213–4, 235, 248, 252–4, 256–7, 266, 268
leḥem mishneh, 56, 61, 244
Lekha Dodi, 75, 109
Levites, xxxii, 10, 17, 130, 241, 244–5, 247
Lot, 30
loving-kindness, xvii, 33, 71–2, 139, 141–2, 148, 222

M
Maccabees, 214, 251–2, 254–6, 260
Malachi, 28
Malkhuyot, 88–9, 92, 110
manna, xx, xxiv, xxvi, xxxii, 40, 53–72, 74–5, 78, 94–5, 105, 113, 146, 168–9, 180, 210–1, 234–5, 239, 244, 267
maror, 8–9, 19, 21, 42, 51
martyrology, 134–5, 159

matza, 1, 3–6, 9, 17, 21–3, 28, 38, 41–2, 49, 52, 55–6, 59, 94, 244
melakha, 206, 229, 235
Menora, xxxii, 197, 204, 206, 210, 212–4, 218–9, 222, 242, 252, 255–6
Messiah, 38, 107
Midianites, 133–4, 152
mikve, 93
Miriam, 17, 248
Mishkan, xix–xxi, xxv, xxvii, xxxii, 6, 8, 14, 22, 25, 34, 48, 57, 64–5, 124–33, 146, 165–7, 169–78, 180, 182–3, 187–8,190, 193, 196–8, 203–21, 227, 229, 235, 237–45, 247, 253–4
Mordekhai, 252, 257
Moses, xix–xxi, xxiii, 6, 12–4, 17, 20, 22–8, 30, 37, 41–3, 45, 48, 52–6, 58–62, 64–5, 70, 73, 83–6, 88–9, 91, 96, 98–9, 102, 108, 110–1, 116–27, 129–31, 134, 137–44, 146–56, 164–6, 168–9, 172–4, 176–79, 181–2, 184–6, 189–91, 194, 196–7, 204, 206, 210–2, 215, 217, 219–21, 228–9, 232–3, 245, 248, 253, 255–7, 259
Mount Sinai, *see* Sinai
Musaf, 88–9, 91–2, 110–1, 115–6, 123–4, 134, 136, 159, 161, 190, 193, 199, 244

N
Nadav, 126, 129, 176–7
Naomi, 69–70
Nehemiah, 86
Ne'ila, 116, 144, 155–7
Nishmat, 24
Noah, 25, 91–2, 213

O
offerings, *see sacrifices and offerings*
Ohel Moed, xxiii, 204
Omer, xxii, xxiv, xxv–xxvi, xxxii, 45–51, 54–68, 70, 72–5, 78, 94, 97, 103, 105, 169, 184, 211, 234, 236, 244, 267

P

Passover, xii–xiii, xvi, xxii–xxvi, xxviii–
  xxix, xxxii, 1–15, 17, 21–,2, 24–9,
  36–9, 46–53, 56, 59, 62–4, 69, 78,
  93–5, 104, 113, 117, 156, 161, 163–4,
  168, 183, 188, 198–9, 207, 209–10, 216,
  233–4, 236, 243–4, 255, 258, 266–7
Pesukei DeZimra, 39
Pharaoh, xxx, 6, 15–6, 20, 22–4, 27, 34–5,
  37, 52, 266
phylacteries, *see Tefillin*
pidyon haben, 32
pidyon shevuyim, 29
Pinḥas, 152
Pitcher and Basin, xxxii, 209–10, 219–20,
  222, 243
post-modernity, 107, 200, 246, 248
Pour Out Your Wrath, 24, 26, 43, 210
priestly blessing, 11, 176, 194, 220–1, 243
priests, xxvii, 14, 17, 34, 60, 88, 91, 173–5,
  177–8, 184–6, 190, 192–3, 197–8,
  208–10, 212–3, 215–6, 220, 237–8,
  241–3, 245, 255
Promised Land, *see Land of Israel*

R

Rachel, 106
red heifer, 129
repentance, 98–9, 102, 114, 118, 125–6, 131,
  136, 143, 145, 151, 153–4, 157–61, 165,
  182–3
Rosh HaShana, xii–xiii, xxii, xxiv, xxvi,
  xxxii, 2–3, 61, 77–113, 121, 135–7,
  139–41, 143, 157, 185, 188, 215, 228,
  236–7, 242, 267
Ruth, 69–70, 195

S

Sabbatical years, 52
sacrifices and offerings, xix, 61, 137, 150,
  173–5, 79–80, 198, 200, 215–6

barley offering, 48, 61
first fruits offering, 58, 64, 105
ḥalla offering, 72
incense offering, xxxii, 126, 129–31,
  135, 156, 165, 176, 193, 211–12,
  219, 245
meal offering, 57
Musaf sacrifice, 89, 115, 123, 134, 136,
  159, 161, 190
Omer offering, xxii, 48, 51, 58–61,
  63, 66, 68
Paschal sacrifice, 8, 21–2, 35, 42
sin offering, 92, 129–31, 133, 175
wine libations, 243
Sanctuary, *see Mishkan*
Sarah, 133, 248
Seder, 3–29, 36–8, 41, 43, 207
Seliḥot, 115, 136–7, 140–1, 143–4, 160
seuda shel Mashiaḥ, 38
Shabbat, xxvii–xxix, 30, 32, 35–6, 45,
  49–50, 56–7, 61, 64–6, 68, 71–2,
  78–9, 84, 95, 97, 100–1, 109–10, 114,
  125, 140, 142, 161, 165, 185, 189, 192,
  196, 199, 211–4, 225–9, 231–47, 249,
  255, 265, 268
Shalom Aleikhem, 242
Shavuot, xii, xxii, xxiv–xxvi, xxxii, 32,
  45–75, 78, 95–8, 100–5, 113, 161,
  169, 184, 188, 211, 213, 234, 236,
  244, 267
Shema, xxix, 36, 39, 108–9, 188, 264
Shemini Atzeret, xxii, xxiv, xxvi, xxxii,
  163–201, 233, 237–8, 242–3, 254–5
shofar, xiii, 80–9, 91–3, 95, 98, 111, 156–7,
  185–6, 215, 267
Shofarot, 87–8, 91–2, 110
Show Table, xxxii, 57, 204, 210–11, 218–19,
  222
Simḥat Beit HaShoeva, 164, 184, 190,
  192–3
Simḥat Torah, 96, 163–201

Sinai, xx, xxii, xxxii, 27, 31, 47–9, 56, 74, 78, 82, 83–95, 97–8, 100–11, 139, 191–2, 236, 265, 267
slavery, xix, xxix–xxx, 2, 15, 29–31, 35, 38, 42, 48, 51–4, 58, 67, 113, 131–4, 159, 232–3, 240, 265
Solomon, King, 89, 178, 181, 188–9, 252, 254
Song of the Sea, xxix, 10–1, 24, 37, 39, 43, 219, 244, 253, 267
splitting of the sea, xx, xxiv, xxv, xxxii, 10, 14, 23–4, 36–8, 53–4, 74, 113, 168, 210, 219, 234, 243, 253, 255, 267
State of Israel, xii, 214, 259–61
Sukkot, xii–xiii, xxii, xxiv, xxvi–xxvii, xxxii, 33, 46, 48, 50, 78–80, 161, 163–201, 212–4, 217, 237, 242, 254, 256, 268
sukka, xiii, 164, 166–75, 178, 180–1, 183, 185, 196, 199, 214
synagogue, xi, xiv, 37, 64, 71, 87, 111, 116, 141, 175, 186, 192–3, 197–8, 214, 243, 244

T
Tabernacle, *see Mishkan*
Taḥanun, 160
tallit, 140, 150, 198
Tefillat Geshem, 164, 184–5
tefillin, xxix, 32–5, 198, 218
Temple service, xiii, 123, 134–5, 159, 211–2
Temple, xiii, 8–10, 22, 28, 31, 34, 47, 50, 51, 57, 59–60, 66, 73, 75, 101–3, 107, 109, 113, 123–4, 134–6, 150–1, 159, 178, 181, 184–94, 197–8, 200, 206, 210–2, 214, 220, 238, 241, 244–5, 247, 252, 253–6, 258, 261
Ten Commandments, xx, xxvi, xxxii, 27, 30, 35, 48, 56, 58, 88–92, 94, 96, 98–101, 107–10, 113–4, 116–8, 131,

138–9, 146–7, 165, 172, 214–5, 228, 232–3, 236
ten spies, 147–9
ten plagues, 13, 20, 52–3
tekia, 83–4, 87–8, 92, 185–6
terua, 80–4, 87–9, 92, 95–6, 98, 104, 185–6
teshuva, *see repentance*
thirteen attributes, 90, 115, 136–44, 148, 150, 152, 154–5, 157
tikkun, 74–5
Torah scrolls, 150, 177, 190, 201
Tree of Knowledge, 148
tzedaka, *see charity*

U
Ushpizin, 164, 173

W
wine, 11–4, 20, 23–4, 28, 38, 181, 193, 226–7, 243
Woman of Valor, 242

Y
Yael, 82
Yitro, 13
Yizkor, 177
Yom HaAtzma'ut, xii, xxviii, 258, 260–1
Yom HaShoa, xiii, xxviii, 258–60
Yom HaZikaron, xvii, xxviii, 90, 111, 258, 260
Yom Kippur, xii–xiii, xxii, xxiv, xxvi, xxxii, 3, 78, 87, 90, 92, 95–100, 102, 113–161, 163–4, 166–7, 175, 178, 183, 187–8, 195, 208, 211–2, 219, 237, 245–6, 268
Yom Yerushalayim, xii, xxviii, 29, 258, 261

Z
zero'a, 8–9
Zikhronot, 88–9, 92, 110–1

The fonts used in this book are from the Arno family

Maggid Books
The best of contemporary Jewish thought from
Koren Publishers Jerusalem Ltd.